Profitable Product Management

The Marketing Series is one of the most comprehensive collections of books in marketing and sales available from the UK today.

Published by Butterworth-Heinemann on behalf of the Chartered Institute of Marketing, the series is divided into three distinct groups: *Student* (fulfilling the needs of those taking the Institute's certificate and diploma qualifications); *Professional Development* (for those on formal or self-study vocational training programmes); and *Practitioner* (presented in a more informal, motivating and highly practical manner for the busy marketer).

Formed in 1911, the Chartered Institute of Marketing is now the largest professional marketing management body in Europe with over 24,000 members and 28,000 students located worldwide. Its primary objectives are focused on the development of awareness and understanding of marketing throughout UK industry and commerce and in the raising of standards of professionalism in the education, training and practice of this key business discipline.

D0802460

Books in the series

Below-the-line Promotion
John Wilmshurst

Creating Powerful Brands
Leslie de Chernatony and Malcolm H. B. McDonald

How to Sell a Service
Malcolm H. B. McDonald

International Marketing Digest
Edited by Malcolm H. B. McDonald and S. Tamer Cavusgil

Managing your Marketing Career
Andrew Crofts

Market Focus
Rick Brown

Market Research for Managers
Sunny Crouch

The Marketing Book
Edited by Michael Baker

The Marketing Dictionary
Edited by Norman A. Hart and John Stapleton

The Marketing Digest
Edited by Michael J. Thomas and Norman Waite

Marketing Led, Sales Driven
Keith Steward

Marketing Plans
Malcolm H. B. McDonald

Marketing to the Retail Trade
Geoffrey Randall

The Marketing of Services
D. W. Cowell

Marketing-led Strategic Change
Nigel Piercy

The Practice of Advertising
Edited by Norman Hart

The Practice of Public Relations
Edited by Wilfred Howard

The Principles and Practice of Export Marketing
E. P. Hibbert

Professional Services Marketing
Neil Morgan

Profitable Product Management
Richard A. Collier

Relationship Marketing
Martin Christopher, Adrian Payne and David Ballantyne

Retail Marketing Plans
Malcolm H. B. McDonald and Chris Tideman

Solving the Management Case
Angela Hatton, Paul Roberts and Mike Worsam

The Strategy of Distribution Management
Martin Christopher

Profitable Product Management

Richard A. Collier

Published on behalf of
the Chartered Institute of Marketing

BUTTERWORTH
HEINEMANN

Butterworth-Heinemann Ltd
Linacre House, Jordan Hill, Oxford OX2 8DP
A division of Reed Educational and Professional Publishing Ltd

ℛ A member of the Reed Elsevier plc group

OXFORD   BOSTON   JOHANNESBURG
MELBOURNE   NEW DELHI   SINGAPORE

First published 1995
Reprinted 1996

British Library Cataloguing in Publication Data
Collier, Richard A.
  Profitable Product Management –
  (Marketing Series)
  I. Title II. Series
  658.5

ISBN 0 7506 1888 4

Printed and bound in Great Britain by
Clays Ltd, St Ives plc

Contents

Managing problem products – Portfolio perspectives on range management – Handling rationalization exercises effectively – Minimizing the 'drag factor' of lower-performing lines – Late-life product actions markets – How these factors impact on branding and other product marketing issues – Implications for a branding approach and brand portfolios – Branding and advertising standardization or adaptation – Issues of standardizing strategy and other elements of the marketing mix – Organizational implications of operating regionally or globally

Preface

Profitable Product Management takes the earlier John Ward book of the same title into the company and market realities faced by product marketing in the 1990s.

It is primarily intended for individual managers performing the role in any product setting – consumer, industrial or service – and provides a comprehensive review of how to handle the total role more effectively and profitably.

For a more experienced practitioner, it offers the stimulus to freshen and update thinking, and further consolidate personal and professional skills.

For relatively new or aspiring product managers, it provides a total overview of what their role needs to cover, how this is changing, and practical guidelines on how to handle its many facets.

Although written for the 'practitioner', its up-to-date and comprehensive coverage of product marketing activities and issues could also be of value to many students of marketing, particularly those working through the CIM's qualification route, as the book overlaps syllabus requirements in several areas.

It could also contribute to the overall 'tool-kit' of many other managers or directors directly involved in product marketing issues, or tasked with improving overall product profit performance for their organizations.

The approach of the book is informative but practical, allowing you not only to gain knowledge and skills, but to be able to directly apply them. This is aided by many illustrations, examples and case histories from a range of businesses, and by the checklists and suggestions for further reading at the end of each chapter.

Starting with a review of the scope, roles and responsibilities of the job, the book goes on to cover the 'basics' of handling key information needs, understanding how your product's financial performance can be improved, and the need for clear goals and 'strategic intent' to guide your overall actions.

An extended chapter on developing strategy and positioning thinking is then followed by a series of chapters on key marketing mix and implementation issues: managing new and existing products, pricing, presentation and promotion, product support and channels.

Final summarizing chapters include: developing a sound product or brand plan, the issues of the increasing internationalization of markets and brands, and the likely future for product management.

Although designed to be read as a complete book, most chapters are largely free standing, which allows you to dip into topics of particular interest in any order that suits your own priorities.

Acknowledgements

The book largely follows the structure and content of the Profitable Product Management (Industrial Products and Services) course I have run since 1987 at the CIM College of Marketing, and I am therefore indebted to the many fellow course directors or guest lecturers whose ideas or examples may have been absorbed over the years.

I am particularly grateful for the ideas and advice of my colleague Dr David Shipley on both structure and content.

Specific thanks also need extending to Derek Beasley, Harold Shilling and Norman Waite of the CIM for their continuing help and encouragement, and to Simon Bellinger for the production of illustrations.

The authors or researchers whose ideas have been incorporated have received direct acknowledgement, but the many companies and individual managers whose collective experience has been distilled in the book cannot be. They are too numerous to mention. They may recognize cameos of themselves in places, but the thoughts and views expressed throughout remain my own responsibility.

1 The role and responsibilities of a product manager

How the role has developed – Key tasks, roles and responsibilities – Handling the responsibility/authority mismatch – Interfaces to be managed – How organizations measure their product managers.

HOW THE ROLE HAS DEVELOPED

It is useful if we start by reflecting on where your job is coming from – how it has developed historically and as a job – so you can put your own activities into a wider context.

The product manager role has developed mainly because, once successful businesses reach a certain size, they start to lose focus on the individual parts of their business.

Its development is a twentieth-century organizational response to the challenges of effectively developing profitable multi-product business, within changing markets, from a largely departmentally-structured company base.

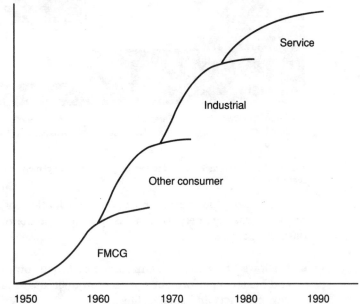

Figure 1.1 Broad adoption pattern of product management by business sector in the UK

Even though it was successfully in place by the late 1920s within pioneering companies such as Procter & Gamble and Libby, McNeil and Libby, the main adoption of the product manager system was from the 1950s in the USA and the 1960s onwards in the UK and other European countries. In most countries, product management was adopted first by fast-moving consumer goods (FMCG) companies, followed later by other consumer products and later still by industrial and service businesses. Figure 1.1 illustrates the approximate sequence of adoption in the UK and then Figure 1.2 provides more detail on the pattern of introduction of some of the later-adopting sectors.

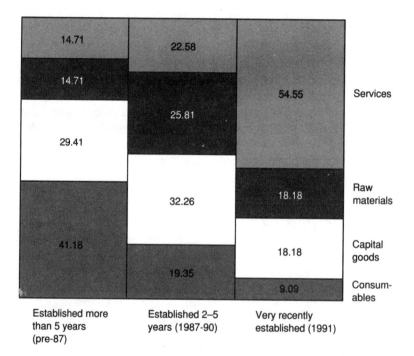

Figure 1.2 Pattern of introduction of product management within later-adopting sectors

The reason for the almost universal adoption of some form of product management is that, as a system, *it works*. And it works basically because:

● It allows single-minded entrepreneurial focus on the development and business performance of each product line or group, including new products and smaller lines.

- It provides a core of specialist expertise and information on the product and the changing requirements of its marketplace.
- It provides a market-centred and integrating influence across what would otherwise be an internally-focused, functionally organized company environment.
- And by giving promising executives high levels of early responsibility, together with strong functional links right across the company, it can produce a pool of 'rounded' business managers to secure a successful long-term future for the business.

Together, these features and advantages of the system offer the potential for significantly superior long-term performance to a company successfully adopting the system.

WHAT THE JOB INVOLVES

In essence, product management involves the company making an executive (i.e. you) partly or fully responsible for the development and business performance of a specific product, related group of products, or 'system' offering to a specific marketplace. Part of the role involves you acting as a **specialist**:

- The company's *expert* on the product and the requirements of its marketplace.
- The *planner* and *manager* of all marketing activities to support it.
- The dedicated *custodian* of its longer-term development and shorter-term business performance.
- And the recognized *champion* for the product within the company.

But the role also involves **generalist** skills, to *integrate* and *co-ordinate* a wide range of internal and external resources in the effective support of the product and its marketplace requirements.

Internally, this requires interfacing effectively with peer groups and more senior management across most departments and functions of the company.

Externally, your role is likely to involve close liaison with a wide range of agencies and outside specialists, together with trade contacts, key first-line customers or 'influencers'. In some businesses this could also extend to key suppliers, original equipment manufacturers (OEMs), system providers or alliance partners.

Stages of development

What has just been described is the fully developed product manager role, where you and your range of activities and responsibilities are not too dissimilar from that of a 'general manager' further up the organizational structure. But in your case, these are being applied at junior or middle-management level, with great intensity at a highly focused product or business area.

Some of the FMCG pioneers (such as Procter & Gamble) *introduced* their systems in this fully fledged form for their brand managers, as did many other later-adopting companies in consumer markets.

In other markets, the pattern has often been more of an 'evolutionary' process, involving transition through a series of stages of increasing involvement and responsibility. Typically, these can be summarized as follows:

Stage 1 – **Support Role**   You act as a product expert or facilitator, either working to support sales performance, or as a technical expert to support product use and development.

Stage 2 – **Coordinator**   You handle all the integrating functions associated with product management, but often without full organizational recognition or any direct business responsibility.

Stage 3 – **Product Champion**   You are fully recognized by your organization as being the person responsible for all aspects of product management, but without the 'line' authority to actually make it happen.

Stage 4 – **Mini-MD**   The classic FMCG brand manager role – a highly responsible line manager, fully profit-responsible for the product's performance and development, with directly controlled budgets and resources, and enjoying high levels of recognition and authority across the whole organization.

Table 1.1   Incidence of role type by sector

	Mini -MD	Product Champion	Coord- inator	Sales Support	Technical Support
		Overall role (%)			
Capital goods n = 22	22.73	63.64	9.09	4.55	–
Raw materials n = 15	53.33	26.67	13.33	6.67	–
Consumables n = 21	28.57	42.86	9.52	9.52	9.52
Services n = 18	22.22	50.00	22.22	–	5.56
All PMs n = 76	30.26	43.37	13.16	5.26	3.95

Source: CIM Survey of industrial product managers in UK companies (1991)

Using these perspectives, some consumer product managers are still in a Product Champion role and many others have slipped back into this as a number of FMCG multinationals have moved key decisions up their organizations. Contributing factors have been the sheer scale and the internationalization of many major brands, which has meant most major decisions being taken at general management or even corporate level.

Conversely, in the later-adopting industrial and service sectors, the process through the stages is still visibly and rapidly taking place. In fact, recent research by the CIM indicated that up to 30% of these product managers had reached Mini-MD stage, with a further 40%-plus acting as Product Champions. Table 1.1 gives more detail on specific progress by sector.

KEY TASKS, ROLES AND RESPONSIBILITIES

Having talked about the role generally, we now need to explore in more detail exactly what a product manager *does* and what *responsibilities* the job entails. This does tend to vary by business setting and also by level of responsibility.

Consumer product/brand managers

A 1993 study of more than 300 product managers in the USA by Quelch looked at this from two perspectives: job content and job processes.

Job content was divided into a number of basic areas, but showed that for the product managers themselves, three were relatively more important:

- Trade and consumer promotions
- Advertising
- Managing the product itself (including new products)

Each of the others represented around, or just over 10% of time:

- Forecasting and budgeting
- Research and analysis
- Developing strategy and marketing plans
- Training, recruiting, managing staff.

For more junior staff this pattern changed. For example, product assistants spent most of their time across just three of the more 'nitty-gritty' activities:

- Organizing promotions
- Research and analysis
- Forecasting and budgeting

Job process categories looked at how much time in the job was spent in communication, analysis and planning, or training and coaching.

● Meetings demanded most of communication time, with writing/revising memos and reports second and telephone contact third.
● Most time in analysis and planning was spent in reviewing others' work or in planning or prioritizing progress.

The study also showed these product managers spending around 70% of total time at their own desks or elsewhere at head office.

Industrial and service product managers

Recent CIM research on industrial and service product managers in the UK gives a more detailed and rather different picture. Basically, this studied the product managers' level of involvement, responsibility and authority within 21 job areas suggested by earlier research as being characteristic of the role. What emerged were three levels of involvement:

1 *Low or no involvement areas*

● Dealer selection or management
● Logistics (i.e. distribution, stock and supply decisions)
● Pricing/discounts to *specific* customers
● Field service and technical support

(But both these last two areas had minorities for whom these were important roles.)

2 *Important but secondary roles*

● Involvement in groups/committees handling general company issues (e.g. quality)
● Market research and analysis
● Sales strategy and direction
● Corporate or longer-term planning
● Setting performance targets/objectives
● Involvement in exhibitions
● Advertising, PR and promotions

(This last area also had a minority for whom it was an important role.)

These were all areas where the product managers were expected to get involved and at least make a contribution. They may, as with committee involvement, corporate planning and exhibitions, also be very time-consuming. But they were not where their *real* responsibility and authority lay.

3 *Primary or 'core' roles*

This third category really defines the key roles and responsibilities of these product managers, with a number of them also involving significant levels of authority for the managers concerned. In order of reported importance, these were:

● Managing, improving or modifying existing products
● Providing information/reports for management
● Strategy development/ marketing planning
● New product development (NPD)
● Pricing policy
● Monitoring product performance/satisfaction
● Monitoring sales/profit performance
● Forecasting/liaison with production
● Setting up/supervising trials and testing
● Advertising, PR and promotions (see above)
● Office/field sales training and support.

It is no surprise that **managing the product itself** is the dominant key role and, in fact, a number of other highly-ranked roles relate directly or more loosely to product-oriented issues (as with NPD, trials, training and performance/satisfaction monitoring).

The second group of key roles relate more to **managerial or strategic aspects of the job**. These include strategy development and planning, reports to management and sales/profit monitoring.

And finally, **pricing policy and promotional activities** stand out as the other key 'marketing mix' involvements, other than product itself.

This was the general picture revealed, but the study also highlighted some interesting differences in role, responsibility and authority between the different product manager role types.

First, Table 1.2 reveals the clear steps shown in terms of areas of high job involvement by role type. Product managers in support or coordinator roles appear to have very little scope in their jobs, particularly compared to the much broader-based activities of a product champion. But even they are not involved in some of the more 'line' -oriented activities of the Mini-MDs (marked with ** in the table).

Table 1.2 Areas of high job involvement by role type

	Mini-MD	Product Champion	Co-ordinator/support role
Market research/analysis			★
Setting performance targets/objectives	★★		
Strategy development and marketing planning	★	★	
New product development	★	★	
Managing/improving/modifying existing products	★	★	★
Pricing policy/terms of trade	★	★	
Pricing/discounts to specific customers	★★		
Advertising, PR and sales promotion	★★		
Exhibitions			
Sales strategy/direction			
Office/field sales support and training	★	★	
Setting up/supervising trials and market testing	★	★	★
Monitoring sales &/or profit performance	★	★	
Monitoring product performance and customer satisfaction	★	★	
Dealer selection/management			
Forecasting/liaison with production or purchasing	★	★	
Distribution/stock/supply decisions			
Field service/technical support/trouble-shooting	★★		
Corporate planning/long-range business or technological forecasting	★★		
Involvement in groups/committees handling general company issues (e.g. quality)	★★		
Providing information/reports for general or corporate managers	★	★	★

Source: CIM Survey of industrial product managers in UK companies (1991)

Table 1.3   Percentage of broad role types with responsibility *and* authority in key responsibility areas

	Mini -MDs (n=23)	Product Champions (n=36)	Others (n=17)	All PMs (n=76)
Management of existing products	47.83	50.00	29.41	44.74
Strategy development and marketing planning	39.13	33.33	17.65	31.58
NPD	39.13	44.44*	17.65	36.84
Pricing policy	73.91**	25.00	17.65	38.16
Monitoring sales/profit performance	73.91**	33.33	11.76	40.79
Mean score	54.78	37.22	18.82	38.42

Source: CIM Survey of industrial product managers in UK companies (1991)

Secondly, Table 1.3 illustrates how different role types also enjoy markedly different levels of authority in the five key areas illustrated. Other than Product Champions showing a slightly, but not significantly, higher rating than the Mini-MDs in the management of new and existing products, the pattern is quite clear, with 'steps' in authority between each level of role.

Of particular note is the commanding level of authority among Mini-MDs in the key 'line' areas of pricing and sales/profit performance, with Product Champions also having significantly more authority than less developed roles in NPD.

However, if these figures are turned around, they show that for more than half of these product managers, authority does not keep pace with responsibility in most key areas. This is an in-built problem for almost all product managers, which we need to explore more fully in the next section.

HANDLING THE RESPONSIBILITY/AUTHORITY MISMATCH

This is a problem very familiar to anyone working in product management and has existed as long as the role. The basic issues are two-fold.

First, there is a **vertical dimension**. The whole idea of product management is to push responsibility for running the product down the line to middle or even relatively junior management. But how far does this delegation go? Does the decision-making or sign-off authority go with it? And what specific areas of responsibility does this apply to?

The second dimension arises because product managers also have to operate **horizontally** across many other functions, often dealing with considerably senior or more experienced colleagues in these departments.

In both cases, this may cause conflict with the established power or authority structure of the business; particularly so if your product manager role is fairly new to the organization.

How much power or authority is really delegated?

If the Clewett and Stasch research (1975) and the views of many recent writers are to be believed the answer to this question is, unfortunately, 'very little'.

Particularly in larger FMCG companies, with many layers of involved management above the product manager (commonly Group Product Manager, Marketing Manager, Marketing Director), and general or corporate management also seeking a say on major issues, many areas of activity for the product manager stop at the 'recommend' level. Here, bureaucracy can easily take over, with the so-called 'manager' of the product ending up producing an endless stream of papers, proposals or reports to go 'up the line' or into an established committee system.

In smaller, flatter and more dynamic organizations the need for approval does not go away, but far more of it becomes *informal*, often just requiring a brief verbal update for your immediate boss. Here, only annual plans, major changes or significant investment decisions would need to go to higher levels for approval. Even in this more favourable environment, this is a long way from the 'mini-general manager' concept we talked about earlier. True entrepreneurs make their own decisions and succeed or fail by them (but they also risk much more than their job!).

Consumer market product managers are often young (early to mid-20s), very bright but still relatively inexperienced, and are often only expected to stay in a particular job for one or two years.

Given these realities, and the commercial importance of the brands they are managing, it is not totally unreasonable for the companies that employ them to put some limits on their authority.

Outside this heartland of brand management, the CIM research and a number of recent writers suggest that the later-adopting industrial and service organizations are often delegating higher levels of authority, particularly to their more senior product managers, the Mini-MDs.

This could be happening for a number of reasons:

● They are generally older and more experienced.

- They may have held a fairly senior sales or technical position before moving over and can transfer established credibility to their new role
- Their products or services may be highly technical or specialized and, lacking detailed knowledge themselves, management may be more inclined to delegate
- Or it may simply be because the position is relatively new and, unlike most consumer companies, there are no previous generations of product managers up the hierarchy who want to keep some involvement in their 'babies' and in the excitement of day-to-day management.

How can you win more authority?

If you work in the strait-jacket of a bureaucratic organization you have less scope for genuine initiative or authority, but even here successful performance helps. Writers going back to the 1960s (when most brand managers almost certainly had more authority) recognized this.

The US National Industrial Conference Board (1965) talked about much of the product manager's *real* authority 'flowing from above' through *implied authority*, or from simply proving a point by track record. On these issues they say:

> If a product manager can convince his superiors that he has the right program, he has a lot of authority. If he can't, he has no authority.

> Ultimately, it is broad management support that serves as the product manager's ace in the hole, enabling him to function effectively without having clear authority in all situations.

Others suggest a kind of 'case law' develops via your track record. If good decisions and product actions are seen to be taken, then you develop much more *'informal authority'*.

These points apply particularly in terms of your immediate boss, whom you should be continuously seeking to convince that you can handle more and more of the job with only informal supervision.

In terms of higher management, you tread a more dangerous line. Many of this group will be battle-hardened veterans who will need a lot of convincing before they take anything or anybody on trust. Generally, they will not respond favourably to clever ideas from anyone who has not yet 'proved themselves'.

They need to be kept informed of your successes as they occur, so you gradually win over their confidence and respect, but only in more significant matters. You need to avoid 'showering them with confetti' or your *real* achievements will not stand out.

Marketing planning or major proposal presentations are an excellent vehicle for you to build credibility, and should be handled with the utmost professionalism.

In many companies there are also variously-called 'skip meetings', where you have an opportunity to meet more senior managers in an informal setting. Prepare well for these also, as they are not so 'informal' as they seem, and offer another opportunity for you to create the right kind of impression, and build trust.

Your authority across other functions

Outside your own department, your power and authority are likely to be more circumspect and protocol-ridden. You are operating in other peoples' 'fiefdoms' and they may not be slow to remind you of this – often by actions rather than words, by stressing the need to conform to various systems they operate. (Finance are often masters of this particular technique).

Managers in other departments may also be sensitive to the apparent 'power' of marketing generally in the organization, so you need to think carefully about how you handle, and build, relationships of trust.

An early study by Gemmill and Wilemon (1972) suggested most product managers attempted to use four forms of power or influence over departmental colleagues:

1 *Reward Power* – where you are able to gain their compliance because of a perception that you can directly or indirectly dispense rewards or favours.
2 *Punishment Power* – the opposite. You are perceived capable of directly or indirectly dispensing punishments for non-compliance.
3 *Expert Power* – you gain support because you are seen as the 'expert' and your business or technical judgement is respected.
4 *Referent Power* – your views or requests are listened to and followed because people identify with you, have friendship ties with you, or respect your position.

The original research was re-run as part of the CIM study and came out with very similar results (see Figure 1.3).

Basically, this showed that both Reward and Punishment power had only limited use (mainly by Mini-MDs and some Product Champions). Over half the product managers *never* used them. Expert Power was seen as particularly useful in less-developed roles, where there is probably a greater need for 'proving yourself'. Product Champions scored highest on Referent Power (though still second to Expert Power). This might suggest they still need to put more

Source of power/influence	Extent to which this can be used in your experience			
	Not used at all	Limited use	Some use but cannot overplay	Generally more useful
Reward Power	50.00	32.89	15.79	1.32
Punishment Power	61.84	26.32	10.53	1.32
Expert Power	-	9.21	23.68	67.11
Referent Power	1.32	6.58	44.74	47.37

Figure 1.3 Use of sources of power or influence by industrial and service product managers

emphasis on personal relationships than their Mini-MD colleagues who have more real, or implied, line authority.

INTERFACES TO BE MANAGED

One thing your job does not normally lack is variety! In fact, your range of contacts as a product manager is probably the most extensive of any middle manager in your organization. And your success in the job demands high levels of contact, direction and motivation to be applied behind the product – both internally and externally.

Some writers list up to 30 possible interfaces to manage, but the main ones are summarized in Figure 1.4.

The relative importance of these interfaces for you will vary from industry to industry. In consumer goods, you would normally expect

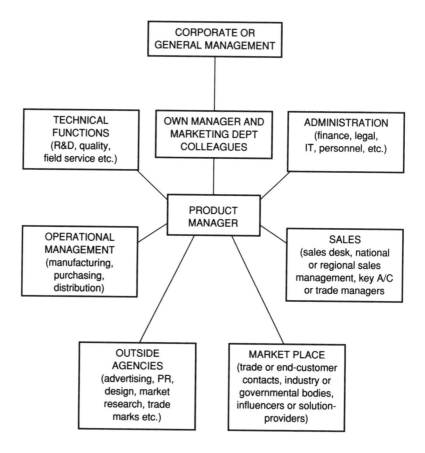

Figure 1.4 Interfaces of a product manager

to spend quite a lot of time with your advertising agency, whereas many industrial products will require the main contacts to be technical or market-based. They can even vary from company to company within an industry, depending on your company's size, management style and consequent structure and organization. But most of this large network of contacts remains common for all product managers, with only the balance or priority changing.

Links within your own department

Much of your contact with your immediate boss (and his boss or bosses) will revolve around developing and gaining approval for your plan, then implementing it and monitoring achievement. You may also need his approval or sign-off for various decisions, actions or areas of spending. This gives an on-going framework of communication which may become more intense and time-consuming at various times. For example: when finalizing the plan or related budgets, monthly reviews, or major changes in price or advertising.

In many companies you may also have to link effectively with product manager colleagues in related product fields, or where you have common customers, trade channels, or where some other form of information-sharing or coordination is required.

Larger companies may have functional specialists providing marketing services across the product manager teams, such as marketing research, sales promotion or a separate advertising department. You also need to dovetail effectively with these in-house specialists, and ensure your own products' priorities are being attended to.

In most companies, all these relationships are fairly harmonious. They are 'within the family'. But occasional problems may flare up and these should be promptly sorted out face-to-face with the individual concerned or – if they can't be – by the next level up acting as a 'referee'.

Links with technical functions

Unless you are from a technical background yourself, there is a risk of a 'culture gap' intruding here, particularly with internally based **R&D** people. Just a few of the different perspectives and job approaches you need to be aware of are:

Technical view	*Marketing view*
Very specialist and highly focused in approach	Take a wider view and tend to be more 'creative' and flexible
More excited by break-through products and those with 'technical merit'	Also have to ensure necessary but relatively minor incremental improvements pushed through and that *market* perceptions and *perceived benefits* are built in
Are often looking for product excellence in *technical* terms	Want products which are highly *marketable, but 'on time' rather than 'Rolls-Royces' and late.*
Work in a dedicated way within 'office hours', which also means taking proper lunch break, tea breaks etc.	Work longer than 'official hours' to cope with new problems and issues arising constantly. Take breaks when and if able to.
Prefer systems and certainties	Thrive on uncertainty and being able to 'bend' or circumvent restricting systems to 'get things done'

This theme is picked up again in Chapter 4 when we look at your role in the new product development process.

Outside of R&D links, there may be specialist technical functions such as **packaging** or **quality** where you have to work effectively with the experts, lay down specifications, or handle problems or potential improvements.

In some companies there may also be a **field service** function supporting your product, who can provide you with an excellent first-line feedback channel in terms of any developing problems or opportunities at customer level.

Links with operational management

More progressive companies in recent years have set up an all-embracing *materials management* function, which simplifies your liaison on operational issues. In most organizations, though, you may still need to deal with a number of separate operational functions, all with their own functional priorities.

Here, the main contact will tend to be with **production** or **factory management** or with a specialist **product planning** section. As with your technical links, this is an environment and culture where efficiency, technical merit and certainty are highly prized, and you may be seen as a prime agent for upsetting this equilibrium and 'causing them problems'.

For example, unless informed (or proved) otherwise, your annual planning requirements for the product will tend to be treated as 'gospel', and many resource levels and supply arrangements planned accordingly. Remember, if your sales are significantly down on forecast, operatives may have to be laid off or sacked, or difficult negotiations with suppliers may be needed.

Other areas where you need to exercise great care in your decisions or dealings are:

- Letting production know as far in advance as possible about likely seasonal patterns, or specific deals, promotions or major orders, so these can be smoothly planned in.
- Letting them know in sufficient time, and consulting them effectively, about any product or packaging design or specification changes coming through.
- Being flexible about the balance between holding low stocks and having efficient (i.e. reasonably long, uninterrupted) production runs.

In some companies there may be bought-in products within your range, or you may need to liaise separately with **purchasing** on required volumes or the sourcing of key raw materials, components or packaging to go into production. You may also need to conform to purchasing procedures in areas of your own spending, such as obtaining alternative quotes, or using suppliers with 'approved' status.

Finally, you may need to liaise with **warehouse managers** on stock or with **distribution** on special delivery requirements. Both may also want a say in any packaging decisions or changes you make (e.g. different outer shapes or sizes may affect pallet fit or count).

Links with outside agencies

In most companies, you as an individual product manager would not have discretion over choice of **advertising agency**. But your relationship with the agency for all significantly branded products (particularly in FMCG) is likely to involve more of your time than most of your other interfaces. A day a week, i.e. around 20% of time, is not uncommon.

Managers where the brand cannot justify significant support, or where 'house branding' or no branding is involved, will tend to have a much lower-key relationship, meeting monthly or even less frequently, as the work requires it.

In all cases, though, spending through the advertising agency is likely to be a substantial part of your budget, so we will look in more detail at how you can optimize this relationship in Chapter 6.

A larger agency (or some of the more generalist agencies industrial companies tend to use), may also supply you with – or at least offer – a range of further marketing services, such as MR, PR or literature design and production. Or you may need to source these, and other similar services, separately via existing company arrangements or by selecting suppliers yourself. This could extend to quite a large share of time again.

Outside these most common links, you may have dealings with product name or new product design specialists, pack designers, point of sale specialists or (where this is not handled in-house) with trade mark specialists.

In industrial marketing generally, all links with such outside agencies and suppliers are likely to be less extensive, more intermittent and generally lower-key.

Links with the marketplace

It is argued by many writers that these tend to be more extensive and time-consuming for product managers in industrial markets. In many cases this is clearly true. And where the product manager is also the technical or applications expert, this is almost inevitable.

A good example of this situation is in replacement joints (hips, knees etc.). Here, the product managers for all the companies concerned spend considerable time 'in-theatre' with orthopaedic surgeons and their teams – partly in a 'training' role where the product or the surgeon are new, but also generally 'advising' on new and improved procedures for conducting the operations themselves.

Many industrial markets are also more complex, involving multilevel relationships with intermediaries, system-providers or professional advisers, as well as multi-industry customer bodies. All of these require that the product manager has at least an understanding of key requirements and relationships, even if this does not involve regular contact.

In other markets such as defence industries or telecommunications, **governmental links** may need to be maintained by the product manager alongside, or in support of, sales or technical colleagues.

In consumer markets, you as the product manager will almost certainly be involved in regular contact with, and presentations to major trade partners, or retail or wholesale groups where relationships are being developed.

Where trade marketing specialists or key account functions are a major force within the company, a significant amount of your time may need to be committed to meeting the special product or promotional requirements for key customers rather than the general market.

In *all* markets, there may be some contact directly or indirectly with **end-customers,** with a need to provide help, advice or to deal with specific complaints or problems. This may just be a matter of handling an occasional letter effectively, or perhaps providing back-up as required to the salesdesk or customer care function.

But for many industrial product managers, where central contact points may not have the specialist knowledge required, this can represent a significant share of time. Many product managers of software programs or specialist systems spend a major share of time – on-line or on the telephone – in providing this.

Links with sales

The **salesdesk** was mentioned in the previous section, as was the need to directly support sales activities on major business. What now needs adding are the wide range of links you may need to maintain with the salesforce itself.

Many of these will be at **sales management** level. Whether you have a single salesforce or one which is split by industry, application, trade sector or in geographical regions, the basic issues are the same.

You are basically fighting a 'hearts and minds' battle for a proper share of sales attention for your product. You also need to ensure that development priorities, time-scales and specific activities are in conformity with your plan and are being executed effectively.

Sales management can be useful contributors to your under-standing of product and pricing requirements – they have a lot of first-hand experience of what will work. Their views on some promotional activities may not always be too objective, but you would be well advised to seek their views on specific promotional deals, appropriate point of sale actions and the relative attractiveness of customer and salesforce incentives.

Finally, the sales performance of your product needs tracking from as many perspectives as possible. Your understanding of successes and failures, or general variations in performance, can be much enhanced by talking directly with the sales managers concerned, rather than just reviewing the 'dry figures'.

You may also have some less frequent contact with the **salesforce** itself. This may involve making presentations at sales conferences or launch meetings, but your attendance at regular sales meetings can also be valuable for the two-way communication, understanding and support you can develop.

You may also find it useful to spend some time on **field visits** with individual salespeople for the even more direct feedback this provides. In some companies, brighter or more motivated salespeople can be an extremely valuable extension of marketing out into the field. This may involve their participation in brainstorming sessions on potential developments, or simply providing information or feedback, for example on key competitors' pricing or field activities.

Links with administrative functions

Your main channel here is almost invariably with **Finance,** and a very vexed relationship this can be if you have the misfortune to work for a financially driven organization, or even one where the 'bean-counters' still retain substantial powers of veto or challenge in areas of spending or the assessment of results.

These types of environments do tend to breed the archetypal 'negative' and 'audit' mentality that can be so time-consuming and demotivating to a product manager trying to *build* the business, rather than just be constantly checking it. And they overshadow the tremen-dous aid that a positive, commercially minded accountant can bring to helping you shape your thinking, or making good decisions, in so many areas of managing your product.

Whatever the 'nature of the beast' you have to face off against in Finance, the most common areas of contact are likely to be in:

- Developing product **costings** and reviewing the impact of forced cost changes, or changes you wish to push though yourself (e.g. a pack change).
- **Setting or changing prices**, or introducing new pricing or discount schemes. (An extreme of this is in some car manufacturers, where Finance actually set overall model prices, rather than the marketing people.)
- **Evaluating forecasts** and developing **budgets**, particularly as part of the one-year or longer-term planning process.
- **Monitoring sales, spending and profit performance**, alongside any tracking you are doing.
- In some companies, tracking your product's **stock and debtor levels**. Debtors will only apply if you have a free-standing customer base, where you may also be drawn into liaison on credit limits, 'stops' on late or slow payers, or decisions on bad debts.
- **Investment appraisal**, for example in reviewing new product proposals, or requests for higher spending or new assets.
- Last (but not least !), getting your **expenses** paid.

Outside of Finance, there may need to be intermittent contact with other administrative functions such as **Personnel** in organizing training events, or the **Company Secretariat** or **Legal** department in areas such as trade marks or major contracts.

Finally, in many 'lean' companies without individual or departmental secretaries, you may have to exercise your persuasive skills to the full with **secretarial services** personnel to get your typing done!

Links with corporate or general management

The main points about your dealings with general management have already been made. But in many larger companies it does not stop there.

Many multinationals operate corporate or **international product managers**. These may just be a 'staff' function you need to liaise with, but in other cases they may have considerable power over areas such as product, pricing or brand policy and you have to listen a bit more closely.

In many European multinationals, such as CIBA–Geigy or Philips, the central product managers control all R&D activities and range decisions, so as a national market product manager you really have to ensure your voice is heard, in terms of ensuring your own national market's requirements.

Likewise, both European and (particularly) US multinationals can be very strict on branding detail, design (e.g. the blue Ford oval) and advertising. Even in these areas, though, if your ideas, arguments or proposals are strong enough you can often win them over, just as happened with the UK-developed Levi 501 advertisements.

HOW ORGANIZATIONS MEASURE THEIR PRODUCT MANAGERS

To progress in product management, you not only have to do your job well but this has to be *recognized* by your manager and the rest of the organization. This has a potentially negative side, as well as being a major opportunity.

First, by being in such a highly 'visible' position, you are likely to be under constant appraisal by senior management. In recently established product manager systems where 'instant results' may be unrealistically expected, this can be a particular problem.

But even when the system is well established, there can be a lot of pressure in some organizations to deliver results in the *short term* – sometimes at the expense of the more strategic aspects of your role and long-term position-building for your product.

Some of the most common **traps you need to avoid** in this context are covered in more detail in later chapters. They include:

- Cutting costs or investment in vital areas such as perceived value, marketing research, R&D or promotional support (Chapter 2).
- Compromising on your targeting or positioning to seek to attract a wider business base; or allowing your competitive advantage to weaken (Chapter 3).
- Going too far down the 'brand extension' path and weakening your core business in the process (Chapter 5).
- Spending too much of your advertising budget tactically (Chapter 6).
- Pushing price up too high, so you improve short-term profits, but damage share position or perceptions of value in the process (Chapter 7).
- Putting too much emphasis on price-cutting channels which may provide volume but can also damage your image (Chapter 9).

Even your managers may be unaware of some of these traps or may be seduced by their short-term benefits when 'the heat is on'. But any of them can severely damage your product's long-term health, unless managed extremely carefully.

You need to know about them. But even more important, you need to be able to make an alternative case and argue it convincingly and successfully – without making enemies in the process.

There are product managers around who are happy to keep a low profile and 'go with the flow' in terms of kow-towing to conventional company wisdom and bean-counter pressures. They will probably be happy remaining as mediocre product managers (or maybe mediocre group product managers – eventually). But if you are serious about attaining general management in your career, then you have to think and behave with a general management perspective as early as possible. And that demands a high level of strategic awareness and the courage to 'fight your corner' and win when it really matters. Handled well, this really marks you out for higher things.

However, getting off the soapbox and back to your own reality, the type of organization you work for will clearly have some bearing on how you are expected to operate in your role and how you are measured.

The measurements used

Handscombe (1989) outlines the way product manager appraisal is normally conducted by immediate management (Figure 1.5) and the style of product manager this tends to develop.

Laissez-faire	Qualitative evaluation	Quantitative evaluation
● No formal system	● Input related	● Output/input related
● *Ad hoc* short memory decisions	● Personal criteria only	● Personal and shared criteria
● Favouritism	● Subjective assessment scales	● Challenging objectives
● Bias		● Quantified assessment scales
● Inequity	● Soft interpretation of results	● Tough interpretation of results
	● Boss evaluation discussed with subordinate	● Self-evaluation discussed with boss
● Tends to develop 'administration' style of product manager	● Tends to develop 'management' style product manager	● Tends to develop 'leadership' style product manager

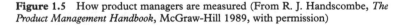

Observed trend

Figure 1.5 How product managers are measured (From R. J. Handscombe, *The Product Management Handbook*, McGraw-Hill 1989, with permission)

If you are really confident of your ability and want your responsibility to grow, you should be constantly trying to push the basis of your measurement **to the right**. In terms of the 'outputs' being measured also, you should ensure this reflects your true current responsibility, but be seeking to move **down** this particular scale (see Fig. 1.6).

Measurement used	Examples
Qualitative or non-financial objectives	● Achievement of job-related tasks ● Improvements in product awareness or ● Market share performance
'Input' measures	● Quality of forecasting and planning ● Management of spending budgets
'Output' measures	**Sales-related** ● Volume or unit sales ● Value sales **Profit-related** ● Gross profit or contribution ● Contribution after sales and marketing costs under your control ● Net profit or contribution ● ROA or ROCE

Figure 1.6 *Range of measurement for product managers*

Many writers have argued that measurement of individual product managers should not go beyond **gross profit** or your **contribution to profit after controllable costs**. This is probably the **optimal measurement** for Product Champions and even many Mini-MDs, as beyond this you are often being held accountable for costs or activities you do not control.

However, this has not stopped some organizations taking the measurement right down to **net profit** or even **return on assets** or **return on capital employed** (ROA/ROCE). If you are in this situation of full profit responsibility, the most obvious problem you need to be aware of concerns:

● **Allocations of general costs or overheads** being applied to your product. Are they realistic, and do they fairly reflect the resources required to support your product

If your measurement is down to ROA or ROCE, this also involves issues of effective asset management, such as:

● Are you fully involved in all significant investment decisions that affect your **fixed assets**?
● On **current assets**, do you have sufficient control of **stock and debtor policy** as it affects your product and are you fully involved in on-going key decisions in these areas?

Whether you are profit-responsible or not, many of your decisions will have significant implications for the profit performance of your product. Most of these are covered in the next chapter, but also re-emerge later, particularly in Chapter 7 when we look at certain key aspects of pricing.

CHAPTER CHECKLIST

Some questions to ask yourself on your role.

1 Where does your **current role** fit into the four stages of development of product managers? (Tick where you think you fit.)

Support	Coordinator	Product	Mini-MD
Role		Champion	

2 How is your overall role **changing** and in which direction is it moving? Where does this suggest you will be in one or two years' time?

3 Consider the research findings on **specific aspects of role** then think about the extent to which your own involvement and responsibility fit in with the general pattern.

   Can you see any useful ways in which your detailed role or responsibilities could be **enhanced**, to add further responsibility or job satisfaction?

4 How well does the overall pattern of **interfaces** we described fit your own contact network? Are there any notable exceptions to this general pattern, or further interfaces you recognize you need to cover for full effectiveness?

5 Estimate roughly what **share of time** you currently spend with each interface. Is this 'about right', or does it suggest you need to re-evaluate priorities or manage your time better?

6 How does your organization **measure** you and your performance? Is this changing, or does it need to change?

7 Identify at least **three ways** you can enhance the way your performance is measured by your immediate manager or more senior management.

Further reading

Clewett, R.M. and Stasch, S.F. (1975) The shifting role of the product manager, Jan/Feb, *Harvard Business Review*.

Cosse, T.J. and Swan, J.E. (1983) Strategic marketing planning by product managers : room for improvement, Summer, *Journal of Marketing*.

Gemmill, G.R. and Wilemon, D.L. (1972), The product manager as an influence agent, January, *Journal of Marketing*.

Handscombe, R.S. (1989), *The Product Management Handbook*, McGraw-Hill, (Ch. 1).

Luck, D.J. (1969) Interfaces of a Product Manager, **33**, October, *Journal of Marketing*.

Mazur, L. (1986), Branded as Yesterday's Heroes, *Marketing*, 24 July.

National Industrial Conference Board (1965) *The Product Manager System – Experiences in Marketing Management No. 8*, The Conference Board, New York

Quelch J.A., Farris, P.W. and Olver, J. (1993), The Product Management Audit : Design and Survey Findings, *Journal of Product and Brand Management*

2 Getting the basics right

Managing your workload – Your information needs as a product manager – Product and company information you should have at your fingertips – Understanding the financial performance of your product and how this can be improved – External information you need on the product in its marketplace – Using MR as an effective tool in this process – The need for clear and directional goals: a 'strategic intent' for your product.

As we saw in reviewing your interface profile, your job is a fairly complex and multifaceted one. A lot of your time needs to be spent on paperwork or in meetings, and you are constantly responding to requests for information, situations requiring decisions, or resolving problems.

Unless you are very careful, you can end up on a 'hamster wheel' of being busy, and lose sight of the basics of what you were trying to do, and what you really should be concentrating on. Remember the alligators and swamp joke? (When you are surrounded by alligators, it is easy to forget that your original intention was to clear the swamp.) You can also drift into being tactical rather than strategic, efficient rather than effective, and making too many 'seat of the pants' decisions because of the pressures on you.

A good **marketing plan** for your product can provide overall shape and priority to your actions and decisions, and we will look at how this can help in Chapter 10. But even the best plan cannot anticipate and cover *everything* that is likely to 'hit' you.

Good **time management** and prioritizing the constant 'pile on your desk' can also help, and we will look briefly at this next.

But the main 'basics' I want to cover in this chapter are:

- Looking at your **information needs** – what you need to be finding out, updating and reviewing, to be both efficient and effective in your job. We will also look at how marketing research can help in this process, and how it can best be used.
- Making sure you understand the financial aspects of any proposals or decisions for your product – how you can effect improvements in performance – in short, how you can manage your product more **profitably**.

- Also stressing the vital importance of you thinking and operating strategically and purposefully in all you do – setting goals and objectives which lay down your **'strategic intent'** for the product.

MANAGING YOUR WORKLOAD

Product management is one of those jobs where there never seem to be enough hours in the day, and the paper arrives on your desk faster than you can clear the previous pile.

If *you* are in this situation, you would be well advised to read something specifically on time management. But these are some basic tips you may want to think about:

- Put a *value* on your time. Ask yourself: 'What is this activity going to contribute to my product's performance or profitability – so how much time does it justify investing?'
- Avoid unnecessary meetings, or parts of meetings which don't concern you. Don't meet unless something important needs progressing, discussing or deciding. Always have an agenda even if there is only one item on it. Set finish as well as start times for meetings, and stick to them unless it is vital to continue.
- Try to reduce or simplify non-essential paperwork or computer reports coming in to you. Take yourself off circulation lists where it is stuff you never read anyway.
- Simplify and shorten your outgoing paperwork. Try to use one-page format wherever possible. Hand write your comments or answers on incoming memos when this is all that is required. Use fax or E-mail rather than letters.
- Unless your job requires you to be constantly accessible to customers and colleagues, try to minimize telephone interruptions. 'Educate' the company people most likely to contact you to ring at certain times, say early morning or late afternoon. Use the switch-board or a secretary as an intercept to catch messages, then – apart from emergencies – do your ringing back in concentrated bursts.
- Particularly if you work in an openplan office, carve out some 'quality time' each week. Take half a day at home, book a meeting room, or use a spare office, to allow concentrated effort on the really important things.
- Involve your immediate boss in what you are trying to do and seek his or her support. One particularly valuable area of support is for them to field or filter the flow of requests for information from the executive floor – maybe even taking some of the load on answering this where no further briefing from you is required.

And you can help yourself simply by checking and challenging the importance and urgency of what you are dealing with, using Fig.2.1.

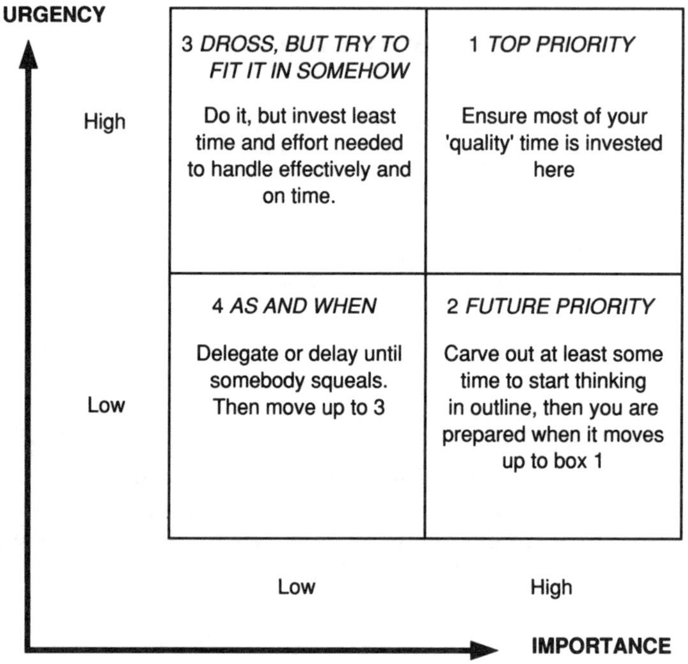

URGENCY

High	3 *DROSS, BUT TRY TO FIT IT IN SOMEHOW* Do it, but invest least time and effort needed to handle effectively and on time.	1 *TOP PRIORITY* Ensure most of your 'quality' time is invested here
Low	4 *AS AND WHEN* Delegate or delay until somebody squeals. Then move up to 3	2 *FUTURE PRIORITY* Carve out at least some time to start thinking in outline, then you are prepared when it moves up to box 1
	Low	High

IMPORTANCE

Figure 2.1   Urgency/importance matrix.

YOUR INFORMATION NEEDS AS A PRODUCT MANAGER

Your role puts you at the interface of the company and the market for your product, and you need quality input from both sides.

- To be **effective** as a product manager, you must have access to a flow of key external data. This will help you shape your strategy thinking and give focus to any tactical actions which may be required. Without it, you are 'flying blind'.
- To be **efficient** in 'making things happen', you also need to be actively 'plugged into' key internally generated information flows, systems and communication channels.

Figure 2.2 summarizes the main details of these two sides, and later sections look in more detail at both your internal and external requirements. But first, let us think a little bit more about 'efficiency' and 'effectiveness' in your role.

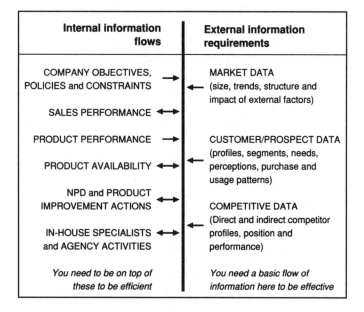

Figure 2.2   Your information needs as a product manager

Efficiency and effectiveness

Efficiency is all about *'doing things right'* – about maximizing outputs from inputs, smooth running and things happening when and how they should.

> *An engine which gives higher power output or lower fuel consumption is efficient.*

> *Japanese and Swiss railways are efficient.*

You are considered efficient if, for example:

- You handle all the necessary detail to launch a product on time,
- You are accurate in your sales forecasts or manage to run your product on lower back-up stocks,
- You quite simply do things when various company systems require them – like submitting monthly reports, for example.

In fact, most aspects of your efficiency require an *internal focus*, or you meeting internal priorities. This may keep the company happy, but it does not necessarily sell any more product or even generate any more profit. Though clearly some of these actions will help.

Effectiveness is different. It means ensuring you are '*doing the right things*'. It demands an *external focus* and covers activities such as:

- Ensuring your new product is being launched at the right time to capitalize on latent demand. That it is based on a platform of careful research and analysis to ensure it will be a 'winner' with its target audience.
- Applying your limited resources selectively, where you will achieve the greatest return,
- Consistently making the right choices between 'winner' and 'loser' options in your competitive actions.

> Renault were effective with the Espace, which now holds around 60% of the fast-growing European 'people-carrier' car segment.

> Cannon were effective in the photocopier market by avoiding a 'can't win' direct fight with Xerox, and concentrating on lower-cost machines for small businesses and home offices, marketed through new channels.

You are considered effective if your new product sells extremely well; if you significantly improve the position or performance of an existing product, or achieve budget. In fact, most measures of effectiveness applied to you will be related directly to your overall **business performance** and the **soundness of your strategy**.

However, in spite of the fact that your efficiency only *might* affect your results, and your effectiveness *certainly will*, many companies put the emphasis on monitoring and recognizing efficiency rather than effectiveness.

Check your job description and think about what is covered in your job appraisal. You will probably find efficiency measures predominate by three or four to one.

But *you* need to know that in the changing market for your product, efficiency alone is not enough. How many highly efficient manufacturers of buggy-whips or vinyl LP records are still in business? They simply got left behind.

> Think about the problems Kodak face when their 100-year old base, and legendary efficiency, in chemically-based film and processing come under attack from a host of Japanese majors moving this market towards electronics technology to produce photographic images.

But the 'good news' is that providing you are basically *effective* in your marketing, you will *survive*.

Land-Rover are not the most efficient producer of 4x4 vehicles, but their marketing – particularly with Discovery – has been most effective, allowing them to produce the only worthwhile profits in the pre-BMW Rover Group.

Philips cannot live with the efficiency of Sony in compact disc and in most markets have the minor share. But the concept, timing and benefits package of compact disc were very effective, and a 20-30% market share still earns good profits for the company that invented the product.

The 'ideal' is clearly to be *both* efficient *and* effective. With this combination, you will *thrive* as a business and as a product manager.

The big message is that you need *both* sides of Figure 2.2 to achieve this in your job. As it says at the bottom, you need to be on top of the key internal information flows to be efficient, and have at least a minimum flow of key external data to remain effective.

PRODUCT AND COMPANY INFORMATION YOU SHOULD HAVE AT YOUR FINGERTIPS

As product manager, you are the **'intelligence centre'** for your product within the company, with a major tracking and coordinating role to fulfil yourself. Plus, a wide range of other people will rely on you for information, direction and decisions on your product.

As the arrows in Figure 2.2 suggested, some of these information flows tend to be more one-way, bringing information *in* for you to assess and act on. Others are two-way, and require you also to feed relevant information or decisions *out* to the individuals and functions supporting your product in the rest of the company or in agencies.

To be able to fulfil both these types of activity efficiently, and be *seen* as efficient by your organization and management, you need to be regularly and systematically reviewing information, progress and performance in at least the following key areas:

Information area	Checks for you to make
Company objectives, policies, constraints	● Am I fully aware of all those that affect my product? Do I have copies of all relevant documentation? ● Is what I am doing with the product fully in line with these overriding 'internal givens'? ● If not, have I got good answers ready as to why my product should be treated as an exception?

Sales performance	● Am I actively reviewing all aspects of my product's current sales performance?
	● Am I doing this in sufficient item, segment and geographical detail to allow corrective action or improvement opportunities to be clearly identified?
	● Am I putting this into perspective by also looking at versus-budget, year-to-date position and year-on-year performance?
	● Can I effectively explain any differences?
Product performance	● Am I fully 'up to speed' with all relevant technical aspects of my product and its use?
	● Am I receiving active feedback from sales, service and technical colleagues on product performance and acceptability?
	● Does this include identifying development potential *and* any areas of dissatisfaction?
	● Does this also extend to reviewing opportunities to improve product costs by improved design, or more cost-effective materials, components or packaging?
Financial performance	● Am I receiving detailed and regular breakdowns on my product's profit and loss (P&L) performance?
	● Am I tracking and investigating all budgeted (and non-budgeted) factors affecting this?
	● Is my product costing and margin information up to date?
	● Do I have full information on discount or promotional arrangements affecting my product?
	● Am I tracking all items of my spending budget, including any variations from plan?
Production, stock and supply information	● Am I accurately forecasting demand for my product, and updating this systematically as new information comes in?
	● Are production and purchasing meeting my forecast requirements? Are any bottle-necks developing, or are there any future supply constraints I should be anticipating?

- Have I plugged all promotional and key account activities into my forecast, and made adjustments for any known competitive actions?
- Is stocking in line with agreed policy and level of service? Are any problems developing in shipping or delivery service?

NPD and product improvement programmes

- Am I providing leadership, clear direction and full briefings and specifications to all programmes?
- Are priorities clear and all projects being actively monitored and managed to plan?

In-house specialists and agency activities

- The same points as for NPD, but here it concerns MR projects, design, advertising or promotional activities, which need active monitoring and management. In some cases this will also involve assessing and reviewing incoming information.

Use these points and questions as a checklist, to ensure that you *are* remaining totally efficient. You may need to change or add one or two to make them specifically relevant to your own situation.

Above all, ensure you are *keeping good records* of key information, either on computer or via a **product book**. This makes life much easier for you, and is far more impressive to colleagues or bosses than scrabbling through a pile of separate files.

UNDERSTANDING THE FINANCIAL PERFORMANCE OF YOUR PRODUCT AND HOW THIS CAN BE IMPROVED

Amongst all the internal data you have to deal with, financial information is often the least well understood. Many product managers only have a superficial knowledge of what the numbers they are looking at actually *mean*, and the range of options available to improve their product's financial performance.

If 'the cap fits', this section should be of some help to get over these barriers. If you are already fully financially-literate, it may be useful as a reminder (or just skip to the next section).

We are going to look at a number of financial perspectives, but the best starting point is almost certainly the profit and loss (P&L) or profitability statement, which many companies now break down to product group (or individual product or brand) level.

Tracking P&L performance

The P&L basically records your **trading performance** and is normally laid out under the following headings.

Net sales

This records your sales during this trading period (month or 4 weeks) and year-to-date. Back-up analysis often includes a comparison with last year and budget, showing any changes or variances.

It may also give a more detailed breakdown from gross to net sales value showing, for example, the level of discounts, credits or returns **netted off** for that period.

Remember, the sales figure is net of these adjustments and of any sales tax (eg. VAT). It is not just the sum of all the invoices for that month.

To track your performance against budget you need to know how any adjustments are affecting your product(s).

> *For example, there may have been a number of heavily discounted orders going through, so your volume looks OK but achieved sales value falls short.*

You also need to use any breakdowns available to further analyse this, for example by region, pack size or channel, so you can identify where the 'unders' and 'overs' are occurring within your overall sales.

Cost of goods sold (sometimes called cost of sales)

This section records the production or supply costs for the product you have sold.

If you manufacture yourselves, this will include the direct costs which have gone into the product (e.g. materials, packaging and labour). Many companies also include an element of manufacturing overhead here also.

If you are a service business (e.g. a fast-food chain), this may simply cover costs of ingredients and packaging, as the labour element is largely a 'fixed cost'.

Where product is 'bought in', then this will cover cost of acquisition, including any incoming freight and duty.

Again, you need to track these costs monthly, to pick up any major changes or unplanned variances occurring. In some cases, these may be very significant in their profit impact, as with changes in exchange rates on imported items.

Gross profit

Gross profit is what is left after these direct costs but before any overheads.

This needs tracking very closely as a value figure but also as a percentage on sales – your **gross margin.**

Slippage of margin may be telling you that you are operating with the wrong product or customer mix, compared to plan, or that some key element of product cost needs attention.

Overheads

Companies record costs outside the product itself in different ways, but this section of the P&L will basically capture product support costs (many of which you may have budgetary control over) and allocations to your product.

So there may be a number of cost lines you need to track particularly carefully because of their budgetary significance (e.g. advertising), and others you keep a 'watching brief' on for any variances.

Net profit (or loss)

This is what is left after *all* relevant costs have been deducted. Hopefully, this will be a positive figure. But if you are managing a start-up product, this may run at a recorded loss for a period. You may also show losses some months if your business is highly seasonal.

Increasingly, this is the line product managers are being measured on. Just as with your gross profit, you need to track it in value and as a percentage on sales – **net margin** or as some US companies describe it, your return on sales (ROS).

In tracking your product's net profit performance, *any* of the above areas may be contributing to overall variances. Sometimes, it may be just one or two big items influencing the figure. These are generally easier to understand or explain. But more often, quite significant overall differences can result from a combination of a series of relatively small variances anywhere throughout the P&L, all acting together on the final result.

How you can improve your P&L performance

There are some *general rules* here which we need to get out of the way first.

> *Rule 1 The 'higher up' the P&L you are making improvements, the bigger the 'multiplier effect' on your net profit.*

For example, a 1% increase in average achieved prices will normally give a better profit improvement than a 5% (or even a 10% or 20%) reduction in an area of support costs. This is simply because you are working with 'bigger numbers'.

So, if we take an example, 1% on a £1million sales product can put an extra £10 000 on to gross and net profit. But a 5% saving on a £50 000 promotional budget only offers £2500 (and maybe less in reality because underspending may mean we fall short on sales).

> *Rule 2   Value improvements will normally be more 'enriching' in profit terms than just generating extra volume.*

Volume gains can be useful, even essential in a fast-growing business, to hold or improve share. But in more mature businesses, all too commonly they can dilute gross margin (e.g. through higher discounts or special deals), or hit net profits because they need high levels of support costs (e.g. extra sales incentives).

Conversely, most **value** improvements (e.g. better control of discounts or more cost-effective packaging), will not only provide better profits, but will also enhance the *rate* of profit achieved at gross and net level.

> *Rule 3   The best overall profit improvement programme will normally be one which effects small but achievable gains in a number of areas.*

This is basically the formula that most successful Japanese businesses apply in a *consistent* way to their products, with the wider team all contributing to this process ... and it works.

Now we need to look in more detail at some of the general types of improvement you can think of using.

Improving profits via your sales mix and performance

The formula here is made up of three elements:

Net sales = Volume x Value – Adjustments
　　　　　　(No. of　　(Ave. net　　(Credits, returns,
　　　　　　units)　　selling price)　cancelled orders, etc.)

Each element may offer some scope and you need to think through what the main possibilities are for your type of business.

1 **Volume**

Can we improve *overall* volume performance for example by:

● Targeting a wider customer body or additional channels?
● Increasing usage rate or customer share of spending?
● Improving product appeal without passing this on in price?

Can we improve volume *selectively*, for example by:

- Concentrating on 'levelling up' weaker regions, segments, channels or pack sizes?
- Introducing new variants or sizes to better meet specific identified needs?
- Targeting the business of a particularly vulnerable competitor?

Many of these volume-oriented actions may require some additional investment, or attract additional costs, so the 'net benefit' needs looking at very carefully.

2 Value

- Can we improve 'achieved price' by better management of discounts or by a change in customer or channel mix? (i.e. put more emphasis on less highly discounted business)?
- Could we manage the product mix better, putting more sales and marketing emphasis behind higher-margin parts of the range?
- Do we have opportunities to bundle more added value into our offering (via product, branding or service enhancements) which would allow more of a premium to be charged?

Handled well, all these types of action can help improve the rate of gross margin achieved. As before, though, there may be some incremental costs which need netting out to measure the true benefit.

3 Adjustments

- Can we manage these down to lower levels by changes in policy, improved efficiency or quality, or just by better salesforce disciplines? (Many of these adjustments arise because we have been selling the wrong products or the wrong quantities – sometimes to the wrong customers).

Improving product costs

For products or services with high **fixed costs**, extra volume may help, by spreading these more thinly over a wider base and reducing **average costs**. In most cases, though, the main opportunities lie in:

1 Reducing key costs of present products

- Are you making full use of innovation, new materials or technology or value engineering in the product itself?
- Are any 'bought-in' elements being sourced most cost-effectively?
- Is there any scope for cost reduction (without damaging perceived value) in your packaging method or materials?

2 **Reducing range**
● Are you pushing costs up with unnecessary complexity and inefficient production (e.g. too many short runs)?

Better management of sales and marketing costs

There may be a limited amount of scope to **cut out some 'fat'** in certain areas of spending, for example attendance at duplicated or 'dubious' exhibitions, or peripheral media spending in yearbooks or directories.

But where sales/marketing costs are already being managed fairly tightly, the main emphasis needs to be on ensuring and improving **productivity from spending** rather than simple cost-cutting.

Some areas you may have control or influence over are:

● Better planning and targeting of sales effort, including better prequalification of prospects in new business areas.
● Better sales across the range, or of tag-on items such as service agreements. Where your sales costs are largely fixed, any improvements can give a very rich profit benefit and are usually worth supporting with some kind of incentive programme.
● Better returns from advertising and promotional activities via better targeting and feedback on what is really working for you.

Tracking your return on assets

Some product managers are already measured in this way, and it is likely to become much more common in the future.

What return on assets (ROA) measures is not just your profit on sales (as in the P&L), but also how efficiently you are using the assets supporting your product.

$$\text{Return on assets} = \frac{\text{Net profit}}{\text{Assets}}$$

$$= \frac{\text{Net profit}}{\text{Sales}} \quad \text{X} \quad \frac{\text{Sales}}{\text{Assets}}$$

So it is made up of two elements:

1 All the things we have just been looking at which can help improve your net profit margin (the net profit over sales element) and
2 You can also look at ways of improving your **asset turnover** (i.e. the productivity you are getting from your assets – the Sales over Assets element).

If we concentrate on this second element, then clearly if you can *increase your sales without proportionately increasing the assets needed to support them,* this will have a beneficial effect.

However, growth by itself does tend to push up the working capital needed to support your product (through extra stocks and debtors). High growth may also mean you need more capacity, i.e. fixed assets.

So growth alone will not by itself always help give improvement. And whether you are enjoying growth or not, you also need to look carefully at the assets you are employing.

In practice, you may have little scope as a product manager to influence the fixed assets behind your product (e.g. premises, vehicles, plant and machinery). So the main emphasis tends to be on the *better management of current assets,* or working capital, your product is tying up. For example:

- Is there scope for running on lower overall finished goods stocks, or can 'stock mix' be better managed?
- Can you reduce or simplify raw material or packaging stocks supporting your product? ('Just-in-time' delivery clearly helps here).
- Can terms of trade or efficiency of collections be tightened up, to reduce the level of trade debtors you have to carry?

Improving profit from a fixed resource

A final perspective on profit performance which can be relevant both for manufacturing or customer-facing service businesses, is to track your performance in relation to some **'limiting factor'** on your operation.

Some manufacturing industries, e.g. papermaking, have fixed machine capacity and find it useful to measure **profit per machine hour** very closely. Here you are required as a product manager to manage your product and customer mix to optimize the figures achieved. In a restaurant or other food-dispense business, you may need to track **profit per cover** or customer, as a way of improving. Here, for example, if you can boost sales of high margin dessert items, this can be very beneficial.

Many retail service businesses have fixed floor or shelf space, and need to track **profit per square metre**, or per metre of shelf. Here the equation also needs to take into account stock turnover, to see how many times per month or per year that profit is being made:

$$\frac{\text{Profit}}{\text{Metre of shelf}} \quad X \quad \text{Stock turnover}$$

So whether you are in this type of business yourself (or marketing to them), you have to take the full equation into account. Just talking simple margin on sales is not sufficient:

● Many 'speciality' lines can score by offering significantly higher margins, to offset their lower stockturn.
● Products near the 'commodity' end of the scale rely largely on the heavy stockturn they offer.
● And one of the big benefits of well-branded products is that they can offer both: good margins through their premium prices and high stockturn because they are well-supported 'preferred choice' products.

EXTERNAL INFORMATION YOU NEED ON THE PRODUCT IN ITS MARKETPLACE

As we discussed earlier, your *external* information needs and the way you use this information can be *even more important* than the internal flows you are receiving. The right external information allows you to 'navigate' your product effectively through difficult waters and safely reach your destination. It helps you to avoid the shoals and icebergs along the way.

There are major differences in the amount and quality of external information between markets.

● Many FMCG and pharmaceutical markets are extremely well-covered by external information in all major markets.
● Products requiring licensing (e.g. cars or commercial vehicles), also tend to be well-documented. In the UK this probably reaches its extreme, with daily market shares being available – broken down by model class and area.
● Many industrial or less well-developed consumer markets face a different situation. Whatever governmental or trade body information is available may be incomplete or inappropriate (e.g. sanitary ware is recorded in *weight*!). There may be no MR agencies providing regular product category or industry reviews. In any case research budgets may be very limited, so much of the information has to be collected by the company itself, or by cooperative efforts with competitors or trade partners.

Case history: collecting external information in a 'difficult' market

A good example of how one company has overcome these difficulties is in **marine paints.** These are bought and used in three main ways:

- When new ships are built.
- When ships come into dry dock for refits or hull maintenance.
- At sea, where the superstructure needs almost continuous routine maintenance-painting by the crew.

New shipbuilding is now highly concentrated, with over 70% of larger-capacity freight vessels (tankers, container-ships etc. – the largest segment) being made in Japan and Korea by very secretive major conglomerates.

Naval and smaller vessels (e.g. fishing boats and small freighters) are more widely built, but again ferries (another major segment), are highly concentrated, with the Baltic countries being particularly significant.

Maintenance and dry dock activities have a different geographical pattern. Again Japan and Korea are important, but other locations such as Singapore, Brazil and South Africa, are also significant.

For **routine maintenance painting**, paint may be bought from chandlers at ports anywhere around the world, wherever the vessel is sailing.

Tracking world sales in sufficient product detail (type of paint, quantities and colours), and with enough competitive data to provide reasonably accurate market size and share information, is a formidable task. But one UK company – which also happens to be world market leader – successfully does this.

They do it by making systematic information-gathering a major priority for their sales people, technical back-up staff, and agents around the world. This is supplemented by close contact with the owners and managers of major fleets, who supply advance information on their plans for vessels, and other back-up sources such as Lloyds Register information.

All this information is fed into a central computer *ahead of* building and refit projects to give a very accurate picture of potential. The information is then reconfirmed from various sources as the work is done.

Finally, the third segment, routine mainentance at sea, is covered on an 80:20 basis, by tracking a sample of the most important ports.

As well as tracking business flows (market size, trends and shares) and potential, the system also includes a flow of 'softer' data – on why certain paints were chosen, why a certain supplier or channel was preferred, and so on. All this information is segregated and fed through to the relevant product managers, to allow highly directional planning and action for the specialist sales teams and agents.

Altogether, this provides the company with a formidable marketing weapon – probably far more significant to their continued success than their availability of world-class technology and products. They have a view of the world market that no competitor can match, which allows them not only to optimize their sales efforts but also be very proactive in their overall marketing strategy, new product development, and directed support activities.

The basic external information you need

Whatever your own industry of product situation, the basic message is that, to fulfil your external role effectively, you must ensure you have fairly complete answers to at least the following basic questions:

1 How is the **market** for my product changing?
  ● What is happening to overall *market size* (units, value, remaining potential)?
  ● Can I explain any *trends* that are taking place? (external influences, derived demand effects, lifecycle influences, etc.).
  ● Do I know what is happening *structurally* to the market for my product (by product segment, region, channel etc.)?

2 How are **customers** and their needs changing?
  ● Do I have a clear view of who is 'in the market' for my product or service, or who could be? Do I have a relevant database, or at least some basic information on customer profiles and relevant segmentation, to help the *targeting* of my activities?
  ● Do I understand different channel, industry or end-customer *segments' needs and requirements*? Have I carefully analysed how these can be 'matched' most effectively? And how they are changing?
  ● Do I understand in sufficient detail how these targeted customers *perceive, buy and use* my product? What keeps them loyal? What would persuade them to change in my favour?

3 Do I know what is happening **competitively**?
  ● Do I have good profile information on key *direct and indirect competition* (their market share, image and acceptability, all aspects of their offering and ways of operating, and their strategic intention)?
  ● Have I identified which of these competitors are 'winners' or 'losers', strong or vulnerable, and why? i.e. am I able to also *target* my competitive actions?

Armed with this overall understanding, you can start reviewing basic aspects of your own strategy, positioning and performance, and identifying how they can be improved.

At a practical level, you also need to keep updated summaries of key external data accessible and together, as we recommended for your internal product data. If you are not already doing this, think about a convenient way to hold this on your PC or in your Product Book.

USING MR AS AN EFFECTIVE TOOL IN THIS PROCESS

Depending on your budget, different forms of marketing research (MR) can be useful for a wide range of **information or guidance needs** you may have.

They will never give absolute *certainty* to what you are doing, but:

- Some will be an aid to understanding
- Some are useful for monitoring position or progress
- Some will help develop your plans and strategic thinking
- Some will provide direction on specific decisions or tactical actions.

Common roles of MR

Among the most common roles of MR in this process are:

Role	Approach used
To monitor changes in your market and more general trading environment	Market/segment size and trends External factor analysis
To help shape strategy.	The above, plus: Market share analysis Segmentation studies Competitor analysis Trade developments and performance
To give a better understanding of customer needs, wants, behaviour.	Customer attitude and value surveys Image studies Purchase and usage patterns via panels or surveys
To check on the desirability and effectiveness of proposed marketing changes.	Product and pack testing Advertising and branding research Pricing studies

- To help minimize   New product screening
  the risk of new   Test marketing
  investments
- To provide feedback   Trade studies/attitude surveys
  on the needs and
  satisfactions of trade
  channels

Continuous or on-going research

Many forms of MR information are only really useful when they are available to you continuously, or at least on a regular periodic basis. For example:

To know that you were stocked by 22% of outlets in an important secondary trade channel at one point in time, is only of limited use. You need to know if this is improving, stable or worsening. Then you can plan your required actions accordingly.

Some of the most common tools or sources of this type of continuous data are:

1 **Company data**
   - Various forms of pre-sales or sales data, broken down in detail.
   - Feedback on customer satisfaction, or complaints.

2 **Published data or subscription services**
   - Government, industry or trade body statistics
   - Cuttings services or databases (e.g. the CIM's Infomark service)
   - Market reports or updates (as produced by EIU, Mintel etc.)
   - Retail audits (e.g. Nielsen)
   - Panels covering consumer purchase and usage, or readership/viewing patterns

3 **Syndicated or multi-client studies**
   - A number of agencies allow you to 'buy in' to market-specific or more general (omnibus) surveys by including questions you would otherwise have to mount your own survey to ask. This offers major savings and allows you to afford to track some key data on a more regular basis.

Other research needs require more *specific guidance* on a problem, opportunity or proposed marketing change. Figure 2.3 illustrates how any such study should be approached, and the following comments offer some practical hints on how each stage can best be handled.

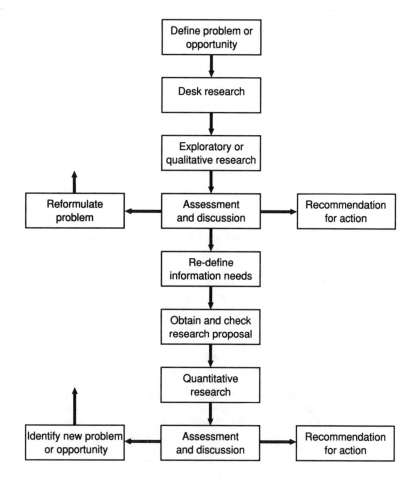

Figure 2.3 The research approach to use

The right approach to mounting a specific MR study

1 Properly identify and define the issue

One of the most common mistakes made by product managers is to go rushing into detail before they have got the 'basics' straight. It may be fun drafting out questionnaires, but you are probably wasting your time. It is best left to professionals. You wouldn't go to your advertising agency and tell them what they should be producing (I hope not!), so why do it here?

To put the study in context, try asking yourself:
- What *exactly* is the marketing issue you are addressing?
- How does it relate to other things you are trying to do?
- Exactly *what* is it you need to know, and *from whom*?

Then ask:
- What are you going to *do* with the information when you have got it? Do any real choices exist?
- How *important* or critical is the issue? What level of research investment does this justify?
- What *timescale* do you have available? Does this *allow* enough time for a full survey?

Whoever is going to do parts of the research, this gets you off on a professional footing – with a sound briefing document.

2 Use 'desk research' whenever possible

Before going into expensive forms of original external research, thoroughly check what is already available – inside and outside the company. It is usually surprising how much useful information is available from published sources or databases (see the example of sources of competitive information in Figure 2.4), or can be derived from internal data with a little thought or analysis.

	Public	Trade/ Professionals	Government	Investors
What competitors say about themselves	• Advertising • Promotional materials • Press releases • Speeches • Books • Articles • Personnel changes • Want ads	• Manuals • Technical papers • Licences • Patents • Courses • Seminars	• Security and exchange reports • Testimony • Lawsuits • Anti-trust	• Annual meetings • Annual reports • Prospectuses • Stock/bond issues
What others say about them	• Books • Articles • Case studies • Consultants • Newspapers • Reporters • Environmental groups • Unions • Who's Who • Recruiting	• Suppliers/ vendors • Trade press • Industry study • Customers • Sub-contractors	• Lawsuits • Anti-trust • State/federal agencies • National plans • Governmental programmes	• Security analyst reports • Industry studies • Credit reports

Figure 2.4 Sources of competitor information

If you are part of a larger group or multinational, see if anything relevant has been done at corporate level or in other markets. It may not give you all you need, but could save time, provide guidance, or allow you to save cost by avoiding unnecessary repetition.

> *A UK glass company fell into this particular trap. The product manager concerned commissioned a major study into changing perceptions and usage in a fast-growing sector. It 'blew' most of his annual budget. Shortly afterwards, he discovered Corporate Marketing had just completed a virtually identical study, but neither he nor they had thought of picking the phone up to discuss their work!*

3 Check whether qualitative or exploratory research may be more suitable

Sometimes it is more valuable to have a greater *depth* of information from a few key individuals, than a little from a large number. This particularly applies when you want to explore how customers *really think or perceive* something.

This **qualitative** approach can be handled using individual 'depth interviews', but more commonly would involve group discussions (often called 'focus groups'). Both tend to use a more free-flowing format than a normal questionnaire-based interview, and are clearly best handled by a professional or agency.

In other situations, **exploratory** research can be conducted by yourself. This may cover discussions with informed opinion in customer, trade or even academic or research environments; with colleagues in parallel markets; feedback from sales or other customer-contact staff; or simply by observation. Much Japanese research is of this type.

Then see what you have been able to put together. Sometimes, enough information is available for the issues to have been clarified and a decision taken. In other cases, what emerges is that the issue is a very different one to your original thoughts on it, and your brief or emphasis needs re-thinking.

A third outcome may be that some clear indications are emerging, but you (or your management) would like the confidence of some 'bigger numbers' before taking the final decision. You need to go into **quantitative** research, with a full survey.

4 Quantitative research – handling a survey

The first need is for you to check that your original brief still holds good, then take your thinking a little further. For example:

● Is there a particular form in which you now realize the information would be more useful?

- Do some areas now need more precision in their answers?
- Do you need to re-think your target group (sample), e.g. do you need to consider boosting the sample of key sub-groups?

All these details and many more can be sorted out for you by the agency or professional actually doing the survey for you. They will be fully covered in their **research proposal**.

This is an important stage and you must make sure you allow time to fully check the draft questionnaire and other detail this involves, as any changes you make later will significantly increase costs.

If you are happy to go ahead, think about running a **pilot survey** with, say, 10% of your sample first. This may add a little to cost, but gives you a final check that the questionnaire is fully understood, and is likely to actually provide you with the information you need.

In terms of the survey itself, you basically have three choices in terms of *how* the information is collected:

- **By post**, where the questionnaire is mailed out with a covering letter and reply-paid envelope. This is relatively quick and cheap, but there may be concerns about both the level of response you will achieve and the quality of information it will yield. In any case, you would be well advised to keep the questions short and simple, and questionnaire layout clear and inviting, as this approach does require *self-completion* by the respondent. Think about whether any gift or payment would help motivation here.
- **By telephone**, which is also relatively quick and cheap, but again best kept short and simple for best results. There may be limits on when certain people are contactable on the telephone, or on what they are prepared to discuss in this way. In some markets – notably France – this approach has been 'spoiled' by telesales companies posing as researchers.
- **By personal contact**, where an interviewer goes through the interview face-to-face with the respondent. In consumer markets this may be on the street, at the respondent's home, or in some other convenient contact point (hotel or town hall, for example). Off-street interviews are generally more productive and also allow opportunities for showing material (packs or ads), or for testing, touching or tasting the product. In industrial markets, interviews will largely be confined to the workplace.

Personal interviewing usually allows the fullest and most reliable research information, but can take more time and involve more expense. Unless trained staff are used, there can also be some questionmarks over its complete reliability, so think twice about just doing it 'on the cheap' using your own salespeople.

5   Producing and presenting the report

After fieldwork, the information needs checking, analysing and interpreting, to allow a final report to be drawn up.

Some product managers try to cut costs by taking on some, or all, of this stage themselves. But remember, this can occupy disproportionate amounts of your scarce time, and *bias* can creep in at this stage just as easily as in an interview.

Where an agency has been involved throughout, it is usually better to ask them to make a **verbal presentation** of findings and conclusions, so these can be fully discussed by everyone involved in the decision. With the alternative approach of just sending out copies, there is a big risk the findings will not receive full attention and the decision may be delayed.

Handling the information you are receiving

There are many points you need to think about here, but two deserve special mention.

The first concerns the **validity and credibility** of the data being offered to you. A few researchers (but particularly your advertising agency or your own managers) may be putting more emphasis on some points or differences than they merit.

Always bear in mind the sample size used and the consequent error band around findings. A 5% difference may look important, but is it **significant**? Can you base a major decision on it?

The second point is a reminder of the absolute need for you to retain your **objectivity** when reviewing research findings. It is a very human trait to apply 'selective perception'. In this case, this means listening to the bits of research you agree with and discounting those you don't.

THE NEED FOR CLEAR AND DIRECTIONAL GOALS: A 'STRATEGIC INTENT' FOR YOUR PRODUCT

In many larger organizations, various levels of company planning will have laid down key goals and objectives for your product area. These may be presented to you – without your involvement or discussion as a *fait accompli* – as something you *must* achieve and the overall way you must operate with your product.

Similarly, in most FMCG multinationals and other companies with powerful brands, *overall brand strategy* and related goals may be set well above your level, and you will simply be tasked with their achievement in your defined market.

In both cases, the *WHAT* is laid down and even the *HOW* of its achievement may be strictly constrained by overall company or brand policy, or by *international* strategic requirements.

With major brands this is very understandable. You may be only a 'temporary custodian' of a brand with considerable heritage to protect. Brands like this exist as a valuable entity – much bigger, more important and probably more lasting that any particular form of the product itself.

> *For example, Coke has long outgrown its distinctive bottle shape, and Dunhill has little to do with smoking accessories any more.*

But it is vital that every product under a major brand umbrella supports and strengthens overall brand perceptions and values – or helps the brand move in a direction the company wants or needs it to go.

As product or brand manager, you may be just a 'bit player' in this grand design, or strategic intent, for the brand as a whole. This may place some definite limits on your actions or decisions while you are in charge. But at least it is *clear* where you are going, and how you should be operating.

In many other companies – particularly those where branding is not so significant, or the product/market scope of the business is more diverse, there may be *no overall framework of thinking for your product area*, other than financial requirements. You may, in fact, be expected to develop this for yourself, particularly within a conglomerate type of business, where no one at more senior level really *understands* your part of the business.

If you are in this position, the main point to bear in mind is that *you need more than just a set of short-term objectives and strategies*. With only these, you may just be 'oscillating around a point' and not really making overall progress. *You need a clear, far-sighted view of where you would like to take the product – the 'end-game' position you want to attain over at least a three- to five-year time frame.*

This may be a **market share** or **positional ambition:**

> 'To achieve 20% market share by 1999'
> 'To move from No.4 to a challenging No.2 position within three years'.

It may be to achieve a **watershed financial result**:

> 'To achieve product sales of £10 million by year 4 after launch'
> 'To double profit on sales to 10% within 5 years'.

Or, if you read Hamel and Prahalad's article on 'strategic intent', you will find they believe a **competitively focused aim** can be one of the most powerful:

> 'To beat Xerox' (Cannon).

With your overriding aim set, all the rest of your thinking and actions have a *context*:

● It can bring much more *direction and focus* to what you need to do over the short to medium term.
● It absolutely forces you to think and act more *strategically*.
● Above all, it gives you a *destination*, towards which all your annual plans and strategies can be seen as 'milestones'.

Handled well, it can fire and bind together both your management and your functional colleagues with a tangible '*big idea*' that you are all working towards achieving.

Without some form of strategic intent, you are just 'going through the motions' to please someone else, and the annual planning cycle has as much excitement and motivation as daily commuting. Having this type of powerful 'magnet' to attract you and pull you on is every bit as basic to your success as having – and effectively using – the right information on your product.

Even when your goals are clear, though, you may still need to be highly flexible and creative in aspects of your strategy for achieving them. So we will move on now to look in some detail at the 'building blocks' of your strategy thinking in the next chapter.

CHAPTER CHECKLIST

Some questions to ask yourself on whether you are getting the basics right

1 Are you managing your time and priorities as effectively as you could? The answer is almost certainly 'no', so think about:
   (a) Are there any things among the suggestions made (or other things) you should be doing to address this?
   (b) Are there some particularly time-demanding contacts you need to be more assertive with?
   (c) Are you really distinguishing between importance and urgency in your prioritizing?
   (d) Are you making the best use of your boss in this process?
2 Are you both efficient *and* effective in your job? Rate yourself out of 10 on each, then set yourself a target for improvement over the next year, and spell out how you will achieve it.
3 Are you fully 'plugged in' to all the internal information flows, systems and communication channels you need to be? Use the points provided (plus any others specific to your own situation), as a checklist of *where* you need to improve. Then think about *how* you are going to do it.

4 Do you have the key financial information you need to allow you to manage your product *profitably*? Do you have a regularly updated 'gameplan' on how you can best achieve this?

5 Do you have all the key external information you need? Check where the major gaps are, then plan realistically how you can fill some of the more important ones.

6 Are you using MR as effectively as you can in this process? Specifically think about:
   (a) are you using MR *widely* enough? (Use the list of common roles of MR as a checklist). And is the *balance* right between tactical and strategic uses?
   (b) Are you making full use of the continuous research available to you? Are you committing enough time to fully analyse and *digest* it?
   (c) Can you see ways in which your approach to specific studies could be improved?
   (d) Are you challenging and checking the *validity* of research findings being presented to you? Are you reviewing these findings *objectively*?

7 Do you have *clear and directional strategic goals for your product*? (Either an overall brand strategy, or a specific set of longer-term goals for your product you have discussed and agreed with your management.) If not, make sure this is handled as a priority before the next planning cycle comes round.

Further reading

Crouch, S. (1993) *Marketing Research for Managers*, Butterworth-Heinemann

Hamel, G. and Prahalad, C.K. (1989) Strategic intent. *Harvard Business Review,* May–June

Handscombe, R. (1989) *The Product Management Handbook*, McGraw-Hill, pp. 51-5

Harrison, T. (1989) *The Product Manager's Handbook*, Kogan Page, chapter 11

Murdock. A. and Scutt, C. (1993), *Personal Effectiveness*, Butterworth-Heinemann

Ward J. (1984) *Profitable Product Management*, Heinemann, pp. 10-14

Ward, K. (1989) *Financial Aspects of Marketing*, Heinemann

3 Getting your strategy thinking right

Ensuring your strategy thinking is complete – Approaches to generating all relevant options to consolidate or develop your product's business base – Using segmentation-targeting-positioning thinking to deliver a 'winning' offering – Developing competitive advantage and effective competitor strategy for your product – Reviewing your strategy options.

You cannot develop effective strategy for your product in a vacuum, or by taking an 'ivory tower' view of your business. Strategy thinking must be based on your sound market knowledge and the realism and understanding which analysis of this provides you with. Your strategy must also work *tactically* – on the ground – and with the resources you have available.

Many companies use some form of **SWOT analysis** as a tool here, to reveal the best combinations of company and product capability against market opportunity (see Figure 3.1).

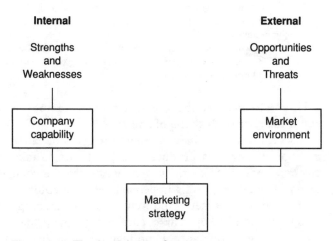

Figure 3.1 The determinants of strategy

When reviewing your range of strategy options, remember:

● A strategy which is built on a '*good fit*' between these two factors will normally have a better-than-average chance of success.

- A strategy based on making major *changes in your image or capabilities* to take advantage of a changing market is feasible, but usually higher risk.
- However, a strategy based on *changing the market* to fit your capabilities or strategic requirements is the highest risk and the most likely to fail.

Aspects of your strategy will always be slow to change. For example, major changes in channel strategy. But markets can be even slower to change, particularly when you are seeking changes in habits, attitudes or perceptions.

ENSURING YOUR STRATEGY THINKING IS COMPLETE

> *Strategy thinking must be **purposeful**. It is your overall 'game-plan' to achieve both your short-term objectives and longer-term goals for the product. It is the **consistent direction** which all your actions must support.*

Many product managers mistakenly believe that a few key points on overall strategic direction are all that is needed here, and the rest is down to taking a strategic overview of marketing mix actions.

Statements like this are quite common in product or brand plans:

> Our traditional segments are becoming crowded and highly competitive. Our overall strategy is therefore to take the brand up-market to less competitive areas.
> This will be supported by pack and design improvements and reinforced by a new ad campaign, firmly linking our brand with upper-market lifestyle associations.

Hmm! Remember the points we made in the previous section about the risks of this type of strategy?

Also, is this really *a fully-developed strategy?* For example, there is no mention of how this product manager hopes to take their existing customer base with them (*they* may not like the changes!). Or how they will win over existing upper-market competitors' customers (the pushed-up mid-market brand may be totally unacceptable to them). And what about the up-market competitors, many of whom may have great 'heritage', snob appeal and high customer loyalty to work with. Are they going to simply roll over and *give* the business to us? Only in the land of make-believe. Joshua may have defeated the 'softies' of Jericho by blowing his own trumpets, but there are not too many cases of this happening in the tough marketing battlegrounds of the 1990s.

The point being made here is that to develop a *winning* overall strategy, you must clearly and fully define:

- *Your strategy for developing the business*
  A series of actions or steps you plan to take to both defend what you have, and improve your overall position and share.
- *Your strategy for taking customers with you*
  Clearly defining any changes to the segments you are targeting, how you will effectively position or reposition your product or service, and the benefits on which you will base your 'winning appeal'.
- *Your strategy for beating competition*
  Well-thought-out plans in terms of how you will position against competition, again including specific targeting, and what actions, strengths or competitive advantages you will use to win the competitive fight that you face.

The best strategies have thought all these elements through. There are overlaps between them in that each defines different aspects of your overall *positioning* in the business. And in the most successful strategies they will gel into a single 'winning thrust' or coherent set of winning actions.

But to get there, you have to have 'covered all the angles'. So we will keep them disaggregated, to look at each of the thinking processes involved in more detail.

So where do we start? Basically, by a full review of all the options you have available to consolidate or further develop your product's business base.

APPROACHES TO GENERATING ALL RELEVANT OPTIONS TO CONSOLIDATE OR DEVELOP YOUR PRODUCT'S BUSINESS BASE

Successful companies use a number of frameworks to structure their thinking in this key area. We will look at two ways to do this which are effective and relatively straightforward to use.

Approach 1 – The Ansoff Matrix

Igor Ansoff's four-box way of looking at your options (Figure 3.2) has been around a long time, but remains one of the most powerful tools you can use.

Product Market	Present product	New product
Present customers	Market penetration	Product development
New customers	Market development	Diversification

Figure 3.2 The Ansoff Matrix

The thinking process is this:

> 1 *If I basically 'stay where I am', what opportunities do I have to consolidate or further penetrate the existing market for my product? (Market penetration)*

This is the territory of the well-trodden paths of packaging re-design exercises, increased trade and end-customer promotional activities, on-pack offers etc., etc.

When you still have realistic opportunities to improve share, this is a good 'box' to commit a significant amount of your effort to. And in competitive markets, the downside is that – if you don't – competition will use these types of activity to take share from you.

However, if you believe you may be 'peaking out' at your existing share levels, you need to defend here, but concentrate your main development effort in one (or more) of the other 'boxes'.

> 2 *Can I build on my strengths in product, image or technology, by extending or strengthening my market coverage? (Market development).*

This may involve relatively minor re-merchandising actions such as offering larger or smaller pack sizes to appeal to different segments.

A common route has been for FMCG companies to extend into foodservice (catering) business, for example with portion packs.

Different perspectives which might come into play here are:

● *Extending to new end-customer segments*
As BMW are doing with the 'compact' version of the 3-Series, which takes them into volume mainstream segments.
● *Moving into new industries/applications or into new channels*
An example of the former has been the development of carbon fibre into an increasingly wide base of industrial use; and the latter, the move of Harrods and other prestige retailers into airport duty-free shopping areas.

● *Encouraging new uses for the same basic product*
Carbon fibre again, or Cadbury's moves to promote Bournville chocolate in cooking applications.
● *Expanding geographically*
Through your national market, like Sainsbury's move north in the UK; international, as with Halford's expansion into Northern Europe; or fully global, like Laura Ashley, Bodyshop or IKEA.

> 3 *Can I build on my strengths with existing end-customer groups or trade channels, to broaden or upgrade my product offering? (The product development route)*

This may be relatively minor, as with reformulations, innovative packaging, or other types of simple product improvement. In FMCG, again this is a frequently used option, with recent examples being laundry product liquids and concentrates, cheaper refill packs etc.

It can also involve a broadening of product offer, as with a daily newspaper like the *Independent* also offering a Sunday paper, or a cable TV company promoting new channels or telephone services. Gillette have followed this route with Oral B (from toothbrushes to a full oral hygiene range), and Reckitt & Colman with Dettol (Dettox, Dettol Fresh, Deep Fresh Bathgel etc.).

In more high-tech markets, the Japanese route has often been to pour a stream of innovative new products into an existing market (as with portable audio or fax machines).

A more aggressive alternative is deliberately to use new technology to obsolete the previous-generation product, as Motorola are seeking to do (to Intel) with their new generation of Power-PC chips.

> 4 *Do I have opportunities to move further, by introducing new products to new markets? (Diversification)*

This is the route Apple took, first with the Apple II, then again with the Macintosh – both with some considerable success.

It was also the approach of Cannon with their range of new-technology small photocopiers aimed at small business and home users. In this case, this involved a third 'new' – the opening up of office supply and high street outlets as a new channel.

But for every success there are many more failures, caused by companies (and their product managers) venturing into uncharted territory, or areas of business where company experience and resources are not appropriate or sufficient to ensure success.

One of the big problems is that some of these moves may not be recognized as diversifications – just fairly straightforward market extensions which *also* happen to involve a new product, or form of product.

> *John Deere's move into 100HP+ bulldozers with the JD750 was a classic example of this. The technology of the product was new to the market and based on a hydrostatic drive (so the operator could change gear or direction automatically, without disengaging power). Fortunately, the new technology worked. But Deere were sunk in their attempt by other problems, mainly the inability of their small dealers to handle large-contractor business and their demands for 'instant' spares provision.*

All these four main options are expanded further in Figure 3.3, which offers a fuller 'menu', in terms of how it can be done.

Product / Market	No technological change	Improved product technology	New product technology
No market change	Refreshment	Reformulation	Replacement
Strengthened market	Re-merchandising	Improved product	Product line extension
New market	New use	Market extension	Diversification

Figure 3.3   Expanded Ansoff options

One final point on Ansoff needs making. There is generally a close link between the sequence of these options (1–4) and the **risk** each of them entails. You may want to argue over the relative risk of market or product developments but, without question, diversification of any type involves significantly higher risk than the other options. The risk profile also goes into a steeper gradient, the further into each box you go (i.e. the further away from your existing business base and expertise).

So, a market development like Halfords into the Netherlands (same products, similar market, low competition) is significantly lower risk than when the market *is* new, different and highly competitive (as with BT's move into the USA).

At the other extreme, the risk is clearly at its highest when contemplating market extensions which involve major cultural, social and economic differences, in markets such as Eastern Europe or the People's Republic of China.

Approach 2 – the Three Circles

This is a similar approach, which again makes you think step-by-step through your options in a systematic way. Which you use is a matter of personal preference.

Strategy 1 – hold/increase existing market share

As with Ansoff, this starts with your present product/market base, or 'served market' (see Figure 3.4).

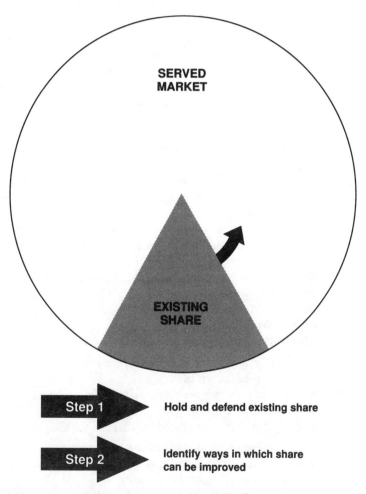

Figure 3.4   Strategy 1 – increase existing market share

By definition, this is the part of the business where you are operating at present – where you have product, customer, sales and distribution coverage.

This first stage requires you to think through the full range of options available to help consolidate or improve share. This is best done as a two-part exercise.

Step 1 is to fully examine how you can best **hold** your existing business.

An appropriate analogy is of a bucket. You are trying to get the level of liquid up (your share), and this is much easier to achieve if you can minimize losses from leakage (lost business)

In higher-value, infrequent purchase items like cars, it is critical to try to preserve your 'owner body', for two main reasons. First, it is extremely costly to win over competitors' customers. And secondly, a significant element of overall manufacturer and dealer profit is generated by parts and service business on cars less than 3 years old. If you miss the repeat car sales, you suffer a 'triple-whammy' effect (lost profit on vehicle, parts and service).

To put this in perspective, mainstream manufacturers like Ford or GM normally achieve 70%+ retention rates. Mercedes achieve well over 80%. But Fiat and Seat only achieve around a quarter of this rate in the UK.

Think about it. If you are the product manager for the Tipo or Ibiza, you have to *replace four-fifths of your customers* every buying cycle – just to stand still !

This is the reason why the car manufacturers are putting so much effort into 'customer care' programmes. A happy customer is much more likely to keep coming back (70% more likely, one major manufacturer has proved). It also helps to explain the popularity of roll-over financing deals like Ford's 'Options', or the recent introduction of GM and Ford credit card schemes which offer discounts on car purchase.

Also in this category of actions are:

- The offering of Air Miles or stamp collection schemes.
- Newspaper 'bingo cards'.
- Hotel and airline 'frequent user' benefit schemes.
- No claims bonus on your motor insurance.
- Sets of free items in breakfast cereals for kids to collect.

All are proven devices for helping to improve your 'loyalty factor'.

Step 2 is to identify ways in which share can be **improved** (still within your existing business base).

Clearly, some of the schemes mentioned above can also partially have this affect. (Many parents will have been pestered to buy a particular product which is not a normal choice because their kids want a plastic monster or some piece of character merchandise.) But in most cases, this will involve you identifying some way of '*levelling up*' weaker areas of your product's performance.

So questions to ask are:

- Do you have geographical areas that are performing below average?
- Are there certain pack sizes with lower distribution or sales?
- Are there channels where you could improve penetration?
- Are there specific customer segments, or individual major customers, where you could target improvements in share?

Your effectiveness in getting results from this kind of action will be improved if you can specifically target 'softer' (i.e. more fickle or persuadable) customer groups, and 'softer' (i.e. weaker-loyalty or more vulnerable) competitors, for your gains.

Strategy 2 – move into new areas

This requires you to identify areas of business (additional customer groups, products, channels) which you could expand into from your present base (Figure 3.5). It is called 'available market' because it is not potential – the business already exists – but you do not have a presence. It is all currently held by competition.

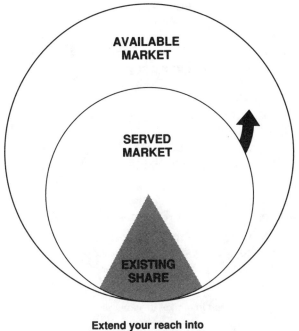

Extend your reach into competitive territory

Figure 3.5 Strategy 2 – move into new areas

The key is to be selective. There will be parts of this available business which are neither attractive nor accessible. These need to be filtered out.

What you are really looking for are areas with the best combination of *high appeal* (growth, profit potential, or weak existing products or competitors) and the possibility of an *edge* in your own competitive capability.

It was this type of scenario which probably prompted Unilever to move the Persil brand into dishwasher detergents. Or Wiggins Teape to develop a new base of profitable business for Conqueror paper in quick-print and other high street outlets.

In fact, much of the brand extension of the late-1980s and 1990s has been this type of strategy – moving strong brands out of their 'heartland' territory into adjacent or related business areas.

We will come back to this later when we look at customer strategy.

Strategy 3 – develop the potential market

Where large parts of available market are unappealing or strongly defended, it is often better to concentrate instead on identifying areas of *latent demand* which have not been effectively addressed so far (Figure 3.6).

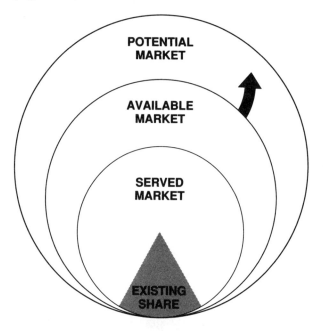

Lead in market development

**Be quick to recognize and act
on market shifts**

Figure 3.6 Strategy 3 – develop the potential market

This gives you the opportunity to *lead in market development* and build a position in these prospects' minds as their 'choice' product before competition arrives. Done extremely well, it can give you almost a 'generic' status, as happened with Sony's Walkman, or Sun Microsystems in work-stations.

Clearly, there is considerable risk in putting all (or too much of) your effort only in this strategy. It is not for the fainthearted. Good research is essential, as is correct timing. But above all it requires real entrepreneurial flair – you have to be quick to recognize *and act on* market shifts before others see the opportunity.

USING SEGMENTATION-TARGETING-POSITIONING THINKING TO DELIVER A 'WINNING' OFFERING

Your plans and actions for the product must have a strong customer focus. *Markets don't buy anything, customers do*, so you need to take your thinking right down to customer level to plan for detailed execution of your gameplan.

Markets where customer needs, buying patterns and usage are totally homogeneous are as rare as unicorns. So most successful customer strategy thinking requires the skillful application of a segmentation-targeting-positioning approach.

Segmentation	A thoughtful analysis of how the whole market can be broken down into sub-markets, each with their own sets of characteristics and needs, each offering different business or potential levels.
Targeting	Where you make decisions about which segments to concentrate your marketing effort on. Then consider what is required to exactly tailor your offering to target segments' needs.
Positioning	The process of adjusting and presenting your offering in such a way that it becomes the most attractive choice for your target customers.

Segmentation

The most useful forms of segmentation require you to go beyond the 'obvious' ways of breaking your market down. For example:

Bags of flour are bought and used predominantly by older age, lower social class women. They are a commodity product. The buyers are largely brand-loyal or price-shoppers. If you look only at demographics or purchase/usage patterns, you are likely to be fighting to hold share in the same key segments with all your major competitors ... not a very productive or profitable way to handle your business. Particularly if you are a lower-share player or new entrant.

What you need is some further way of breaking the business down which allows you to avoid the commodity straitjacket and build a premium or niche position. This may be with, for example, more health-conscious customers, or younger housewives who want to include some 'real food' (i.e. cooked and not processed) in their family's diet.

This is not intended to dismiss simpler forms of segmentation. 'Factual' ways of breaking your business down do provide a useful starting point for most products. For any kind of business, these usually include:

- **Geographic factors**
  Different regions or countries may have widely different requirements, or offer different levels of potential.
- **Demographic factors**
  Age, sex, class and size of household in consumer markets have their rough equivalents in business markets with factors such as size of company, industry type or SIC code, type of ownership etc.
- **Purchase and usage factors**
  Who buys, how regularly, in what quantities and where/how do they buy are all common factors. As are: who uses, how much, how often, for what applications, etc.

To make your segmentation more directional, these often need overlaying with other less tangible factors that may be applicable for your type of business, such as:

- Basic values, attitudes and predisposition towards suppliers or brands
- Personality factors or psychographics (mainly lifestyles)
- Basic buying motives – both overt and covert, and
- The relative influence of peer or reference groups, outside suppliers, or 'experts'.

Targeting

Segmentation is just an analysis stage, allowing you to understand the way the market for your product is – or could be – broken down.

The process of *targeting* goes beyond this, and involves decisions on *where and how to concentrate your marketing effort*, so you avoid a wasteful and ineffective 'scattergun' approach.

In most markets, various groups of customers will have different levels of importance in terms of the present share of business they represent. But they may offer a quite different pattern in terms of their development potential (See Figure 3.7).

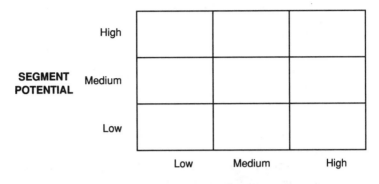

SEGMENT SHARE

Figure 3.7   Present share and future potential relationships

You need to plot where various customer segments for your product fit on this grid and what they offer you as options. Then superimpose your own pattern of business and see what this is telling you.

> *Maybe you are trapped with customer groups who are important now but offer very low further potential (like the previous flour example). You are trapped in the bottom-right corner and need to find a way of tapping into some further growth potential.*

The myth of targeting major buying groups

One of the many myths of marketing is that you should always target the major buyers and users of your product, as they offer a bigger 'target' for gains. In practice, these are often the toughest groups to win over, as they tend to be either 'price-buyers' (and therefore offer no stability of business) or they are highly loyal to their present brand or supplier (and therefore not available, or at best very difficult to win over).

Many successful strategies have avoided this trap by targeting high potential segments, and bringing them through to become a major share of overall business – as loyalists to the brand that initially won them over. Pepsi is a classic of this approach, with their consistent targeting of younger-age cola drinkers.

Some further considerations in targeting

In selecting or re-evaluating your key target groups, there are other considerations you need to be aware of.

First, you have to be *capable of offering a 'match'* to a target segment's needs. And be able to do this competitively. In some cases, you may not have the necessary customer awareness, image, resources or 'capability to operate', needed for success. These segments are effectively 'out of play' unless you are able to make major changes.

Secondly, your *existing position and goals* are likely to be major target selection factors. If you are already a 'leader', you will probably aim to be dominant in existing major segments, be strong in chosen secondary segments, and be targeting some further growth opportunities. With a lower share, you may be better to seek to dominate a secondary target group, or be first in identifying and developing major new potential.

Thirdly, you also need to be thinking about the *longer-term strategy implications* of your targeting decisions. There are several factors to consider here.

Some business may be *mutually exclusive*. If you target one group this may make you unacceptable to another. This particularly applies to fashion or 'lifestyle' products. For example, in one household the three males might all wear different trainers:

> Dad – Reebok (because he thinks they are still British)
> Son 1 (19) – Nike (because they are 'cool')
> Son 2 (12) – Puma (because he would not be seen dead
> in trainers his dad or 'ancient' brother wear)

Other business may be of *strategic importance for the future*, hence banks targeting students for the future profit they offer when they get their high-earning jobs as product managers (or equivalent professional careers), after graduating.

A further common scenario is the need to *sequence* your targeting from a narrow to a wider base over time, as you take the product through its life-cycle and related adoption curve. A classic of this was Flora margarine, moving from a health product for people with heart problems to its present position as 'a healthy spread for all the family'.

Fourthly, for certain products, your targeting thinking may need to be *multi-level* or *multi-point within the customer*. For example:

- With a new high-quality paper for promotional mailings, targets may need to include:
    Design houses and advertising agencies
    Direct mail companies
    Clients with different requirements (multi-segment)

- Many business products face off against a complex decision-making unit (DMU) within companies in certain segments. If this applies to your product, it means you have to:

    Identify your best *point of entry* into those companies (the so-called 'gatekeeper' you need to convince to start the process off).

    Understand the customer's total *buying process*, so you effectively cover all the stages and main players involved

    Identify the *key relevant benefits* you need to stress with each part of the DMU (buyers, users, influencers, senior decision-makers etc.) to win the whole customer over.

Positioning the product effectively

Positioning is not an area of strategy thinking confined only to larger advertising agencies or fast-moving consumer goods. *All* products and services need to be positioned effectively – it is fundamental to ensuring that your overall strategy works *at customer level*.

Let's get back to basics and think about what positioning involves. To be understood by customers, and also become a 'winning choice' for them, any product or service must clearly communicate the following messages:

- This is the kind of product or service I am. I belong in *this* (new or existing) category.
- This is whom and what I am intended for.
- These are the reasons (not too many !) why I am exactly the *right* choice for you and my intended purpose.
- And these are the *key* reasons why I am a *better* choice than anything else you may have been using or considering.

This process involves three key stages.

First, you must decide where in **category** terms you want the product to sit – where you want customers to see it belonging. Sometimes there may be a choice, which relates directly to where it is displayed at the point of sale and what it is seen as competing against. In other cases, you may want to consider positioning it as belonging to a *new* category, as Toshiba did with their lap-top computers. This can effectively make you the *only* choice, or at least give you a major advantage if you create this position first.

Then, secondly, you need to go through the process illustrated in Figure 3.8, where you think through the best combination of customer 'fit' and competitive edge to emphasize, which will put your product in a 'winning' position.

On the customer side, it is vital you go beyond the superficial list of 'customers wants'. You have to think about whether there are any

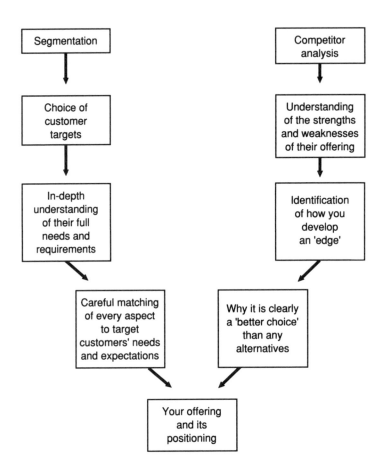

Figure 3.8 The process of positioning

important latent desires or needs that are not being currently fulfilled – any 'surprise and delight factors' you could major on. Or any emotional appeal or deeper psychological satisfaction which could be firmly linked to your product in an exclusive way.

On the competitive side, the area where you concentrate to gain your 'edge' must be recognized as important by customers and your superiority must be easy to appreciate and difficult to imitate.

Figure 3.8 shows this as two separate processes, but often there will be heavy overlaps and interplay between the two. In any case, what you are looking for as an end result is a powerful argument or **proposition** for your product which combines within it the two strands of:

● This is why I am **right for you**
   and
● This is why I am **the right** (i.e. a better) **choice**.

Thirdly and finally, you need to decide how this message can best be **communicated**, through your advertising, supporting literature and sales messages.

While some companies will involve their agencies throughout this process, their key role is clearly at stage 3 – to convey your positioning message to the target customers in a creative and compelling way.

Although your product's positioning will be explained or supported by various forms of marketing communications, it is *not* just an 'advertising exercise'. Clear thinking on positioning is fundamental to the whole product concept, and needs to be reflected in every part of your offering. It is really *central to your role as a product manager*.

The need for simplicity

The simpler and more sharply defined your product's positioning, the easier all aspects of the product's marketing will be to execute.

If the product is trying to be too many things, or to appeal to too many disparate sets of needs, there is a big risk of it falling down the holes in the middle. It may confuse customers or intermediaries, not have a strong enough appeal to any particular target group, and fail to be fully competitive.

Remember, customers have little space in their minds to collect or hold information on any product category. They are not usually interested in detailed or unfamiliar cases being made to them. They want 'easy choices'.

There are some real barriers to overcome here, but this will be greatly helped if you follow some simple rules.

Rules for successful positioning

1 *Good positionings get over a **simple** message*

They do not try to get over a complete or complex 'sales pitch', but concentrate on a key attribute or association which will really hit home with the target group. For example:

Apple Mac = friendly and easy to use

IBM = safe choice

This can be limiting, though, as very strong positioning associations can make it difficult to extend a brand or house name into other applications. It may even make it unacceptable to other target segments. For example:

Flymo = *hover* mowers

Wolf = *professional* (i.e. heavy duty and expensive) tools.

2 *The positioning does not have to be completely 'factual', but it must be*
   credible
Many successful consumer positionings incorporate aspirational elements or strong emotional associations which, whether factual or not, add considerably to their appeal. For example:

Marlboro = freedom, rugged independence

Bacardi = millionaire lifestyle.

3 *Good positionings stress **benefits** rather than features*
The important thing here is to find a way to communicate this in a graphic, emotional or otherwise memorable way. For example:

Fairy Liquid lasts longer (tables of dishes)

Andrex is longer and stronger (puppy).

4 ***Consistency** plays a large part in longer-term success*
When a powerful positioning is reinforced consistently over an extended period of time by effective communication, distinctive packaging (or some other recognition-triggering device), successful brands can assume almost a 'generic' status. They become the standard by which other offerings are judged at a rational level, and they enjoy subliminal advantages in routine choice situations.

This is a fantastic advantage to enjoy, but it can be severely undermined by too much minor tinkering or change to packaging or advertising message.

Bert Lance's axiom: 'If it ain't broke, don't fix it!' is an excellent piece of advice to all product managers, but one which is frequently ignored – especially in FMCG areas, where pack changes or new advertising strategies often seem to be a 'macho' symbol of 'making your mark'.

DEVELOPING COMPETITIVE ADVANTAGE AND EFFECTIVE COMPETITOR STRATEGY FOR YOUR PRODUCT

Competitor analysis

It is not enough to think only about how to win and hold your chosen customers. You also have to think about winning the battle with your competitors.

The first stage in winning this competitive battle is always to **know your enemy,** and in terms of key 'facing' competition, this requires you to:

● *Know the strength of their position*

An important measure is their current *market share* and how this is changing. Are they winning or losing? Are they performing at different levels in different segments, regions etc.

Look behind this, though. Are they developing a strong image or trade position which will pay off later in higher share? Are they concentrating efforts in key niches which offer high development potential, or the base for a future position?

● *Know the strength of their offering*

Analyse *all* aspects of your competitors' offering, not just product and price. How satisfied are their customers or dealers? This further perspective can be useful in arriving at a more objective measure of strengths and weaknesses than just relying on simple point-by-point comparisons.

● *Know the strength of their resources*

You should know the size and quality of their salesforce and dealer base; their capacity and efficiency of production; their speed and effectiveness in product development; strength in key areas of technology; and the financial resources behind their operation.

● *Understand their objectives and strategy*

Try to discern their 'strategic intent' and be able to predict likely actions or reactions. This gives you an opportunity to avoid being trapped in endless 'catch-up', 'can't win' or 'lose-lose' situations, and a better chance of developing a winning position for yourself.

> *You cannot make the right decisions on your strategy and competitive actions without fully understanding your key competitors' position, strengths and weaknesses, strategy and resources. If you have gaps in your knowledge, make assumptions, and constantly check their validity as 'hard' or 'soft' information becomes available.*

Taking a wider view of competition

Competition may be wider than the direct 'facing' competition you know well. It can come from four other directions, as illustrated in Figure 3.9.

For example, over the longer-term, rising bargaining power and the intensive use of 'own-labels' has proved a major threat to many branded-product companies in areas of FMCG and consumer electronics. In some cases, *more* of a threat than that posed by other brands.

Figure 3.9   Identifying wider competitive threats

Similarly, in industries like photography, is the real threat to Kodak going to come from Fuji, Agfa-Gevaert and Konica? Or is it from companies with the ability to switch the basis of the product from silver-based chemical processing to digital electronics?

If you are not scanning widely enough for potential threats, you can miss the need for change and lose all or part of your market, as happened to many typewriter manufacturers with the advent of PC-based word processing.

Separate fax machines and telephone handsets could face a similar fate, as PCs and workstations continue to add to their communication capabilities.

Gaining competitive advantage

Michael Porter (1985) argues there are three main strategic options to gain competitive advantage for your product: cost leadership, differentiation and focus. We will look at each of these and see how they can be used.

Strategy 1 – cost leadership

How it works: Using higher volumes or other cost efficiencies to make you the lowest-cost operator. You can then operate profitably at price levels competitors cannot match, or enjoy significantly higher margins.

When to use it: In a price-dominated market, or to attack a cost-heavy leader. Many major brands also enjoy this advantage, but do not use it overtly in their pricing. For them, it is more analogous to the 'nuclear deterrent'; it is enough that their competitors know they have got it and *will* use it if attacked.

Options exist to win on cost at any stage of product life. Some lower-cost winners, like Honda small motorcycles or Bic razors, have opened up a whole new category. Other companies, such as Amstrad, have generally waited until a mass market has developed before launching their low-cost entrant.

In mature markets it has been used very successfully, as with MFI or IKEA in furniture, or Federal Express in small parcels delivery.

Even in late-life there may be options, if some residual volume remains, to take over with a simple lower-cost offering, as has happened in black and white TVs and small portable audio.

Strategy 2 – differentiation

How it works: You build a position of uniqueness or major difference based on a set of benefits or satisfactions which customers value, and believe they can only fully obtain from your product.

When to use it: In the mainstream segments of most markets when you have sufficient share, visibility and resources to support it. Or in niche markets, in combination with focus, when you don't.

You must avoid the 'better product' trap. Many product managers just keep adding product features but are not effectively differentiating. It only *works* when customers recognize and value the extra features *and* they can not be easily copied by competitors.

It is rather like the thinking we described in the positioning section. You have to *really understand* what will make your offering stand out.

It may be in some aspect of product, but could equally be via service superiority (as with Radio Rentals in rental TVs) or in an unmatchable delivery promise (Domino Pizzas), or simply in a key aspect of customer care (Singapore Airlines).

The key is to find a benefit (or set of benefits) that customers will put a high value on, and to make it *yours*. This then becomes the 'reason for choice' rather than just buying on price.

This clearly has to work on the company side as well as with customers – the 'economics' of your being different or special have to pay off in extra profit or share terms.

Strategy 3 – focus

How it works: You become more specialist, to more closely meet the needs of only part of the market, i.e. a good 'niche player'. You may limit geographically, or just aim to appeal to certain tightly defined customer groups, or be a 'product specialist' rather than offering a full line.

When to use it: When you are new to a market, or hold a lower share, i.e. when it is difficult to match the costs or achieve the visibility of the major players.

The key is to achieve the *right* basis of focus so that you can effectively defend against larger generalists, but still have enough scope for growth and profitability.

There are some good examples of 'how to do it' in the travel business. Here, it is very difficult to cope with the cost advantages of a major like Thomson Holidays. There are also a number of further major players with high visibility. So you set out to make a particular type of holiday *yours*, like Kuoni in exotic long-haul; or you focus only on one customer segment, like Saga Holidays and the over-60s. You become the *specialist*, and that is the reason for customers choosing you.

In this area of competitive advantage, there is *no competitive strength in a policy of 'equality', or a strategy of following the leader.* You have to have some advantage or you are stuck in the 'dead ground' in the middle (see Figure 3.10), and likely to remain just a weak 'follower'.

Japanese companies normally seek to achieve *multiple competitive*

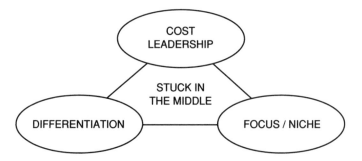

Figure 3.10 Routes to developing competitive advantage

advantage for their products, and often seek to do this in unconventional ways. Kenichi Ohmae covers this thinking particularly well in his book *The Mind of the Strategist* (1983).

Military analogies in competitive strategy

Many writers have drawn analogies between successful military strategy and good competitor strategy in marketing. One best-selling example of this is the Ries & Trout book *Marketing Warfare* (1986), based on the thinking of the nineteenth-century Prussian general, von Clausewitz.

Though some European military theorists, notably Liddell Hart and Lanchester, have been high sellers in Japan, it is normally Asian military thinkers who are claimed to have the greatest influence on Japanese competitive strategy. Among these, two stand out.

Miyamoto Musashi wrote in the seventeenth century on how to avoid ever being beaten in combat. In his book *The Five Rings* his basic ideas were to stress single-mindedness (nowadays this emerges as 'strategic intent'); to know the enemy's mindset but give him no idea of yours; to always try to take the initiative so he is unprepared; and to 'injure the corners' first, i.e. attack in less obvious places and weaken the enemy's overall strength.

An even greater influence probably stems from **Sun Tzu**, the Chinese general who in the fourth century BC wrote the classic *Art of War*. He stressed the importance of 'picking your battleground' based on superior knowledge of the terrain, so you are always fighting on favoured ground, or you can lure and trap the enemy due to his ignorance.

The major thrust of his advice is the avoidance of direct confrontation unless you have overwhelming superiority, but rather to seek opportunities for flanking attacks, pincer movements, or actions to weaken the opponent's ability or willingness to fight.

To Sun Tzu, the *worst kind of strategy* is to attack the enemy in his 'walled cities', where he is most strongly defended, and any ultimate victory for the attacker is likely to be ruinous in cost and losses. (Many European and US product managers would do well to reflect on this advice, and avoid head-on battles in competitors' strongest business areas. There are always 'other ways to skin the cat'.)

Direct, frontal attacks in which both enemies use all their available resources are, in fact, seldom launched by Japanese companies. If frontal attacks are used, they are normally on a narrow front, and employ overwhelming force against a point of weakness.

They prefer encirclement attacks (OEM contracts for key parts or components, for example), and flanking attacks which attack the competitor where he is weakest in terms of product, segments or geographical coverage.

A by-pass attack basically leaves the competitor 'stunned', and is often made possible by switching to entirely new technologies, or changing established 'rules of the game'.

Figure 3.11 shows the full spectrum of strategic options, which also include guerrilla warfare tactics such as hostile takeovers, well-timed and ruinous price battles, or the hiring of key people (or whole teams of top managers or researchers) away from competitors.

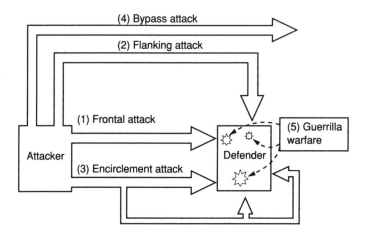

Figure 3.11 Military approaches which can be used in your competitor strategy

REVIEWING YOUR STRATEGY OPTIONS

As we said at the start of this chapter, many aspects of your strategy thinking for the product are interwoven. Breaking the separate strands down can help understanding and ensure you put the necessary detail into your thinking. But when your strategy 'hits the market' it should be *seamless* – all parts totally integrated to give a total winning effect.

We have covered a lot of detail in terms of the options you may be able to take. But this does *not* necessarily mean that 'doing a lot of things' is good. In fact, often the reverse, because this may dissipate your effort and resources, and not achieve the overall results you seek.

Normally, you need to concentrate all your effort on the few actions that will really count. You need to keep this as simple as possible and concentrate on *effectiveness* rather than effort. So you will need to fine down all the strategy options available for your product to the essential core that will really pay off. You cannot do everything, so you will probably have some tough choices to make.

We will look at two perspectives which may help in this process.

Re-using Ansoff

The Ansoff Matrix is quite a good tool to use again at this stage of the strategy development process. What you need to do is to look at the *balance* of your strategy thrust. One way of doing this is to simply allocate your main strategy initiatives into the box they belong in. Then see what they represent as a *percentage of your total growth requirement*.

Often this reveals a pattern you did not realize, or intend:

● Perhaps you are looking for 80% of your development from Box 1, when you already have high shares in your core business and should really be looking to broaden your base.
● Alternatively, you may discover a very high proportion of your development is from new products to new markets (diversification), and is higher risk than you want, or need, to take until other, safer, options are used up.

Looking at your strategy options in terms of risk and return

Many risks are *implicit* in a course of action and you need to recognize when this is the case.

Where there are a number of risk factors, do not forget these are *multiplicative* in their impact, not additive. If there are too many, your risk will go 'off the scale'.

And look at your options in terms of '*downside risk*', i.e. what is the worst case if certain key elements, or everything, goes against you.

You also need to look at the relative return of different options. Not just in terms of 'extra sales' or 'extra share' they offer, but also in terms of what it will *cost* you to achieve them, i.e. the *profit benefit* they offer over the short and longer term.

When you have done this, see where your options fit on the grid in Figure 3.12.

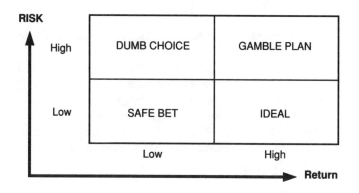

Figure 3.12 Risk/return matrix

Often you will find that a favoured course of action is, in fact, more of a 'gamble' than you realized. Some options will also be revealed as 'dumb options', and should almost certainly be discarded.

Don't forget, though, that *the right course of action also has an* **internal** *or company dimension.* Some organizations are quite prepared to accept a certain element of 'gamble' within their strategy. Many other, more conservative, companies will deliberately avoid anything in this box, and may even prefer to concentrate on the 'safe bet' options, rather than commit to the investment that 'ideal' strategies would entail.

CHAPTER CHECKLIST

Some checks to make on your strategy thinking

1 Is the strategy thinking for your product **complete**? Does it cover your overall defend/develop game-plan; how you will execute this at customer level; and how you will make it work competitively? Does this reveal any gaps in overall thinking you need to fill?
2 If you don't already use an approach like the Ansoff Matrix or the 'Three Circles', use one of them as a check on the completeness of your development option thinking.
3 Rate your present performance (1-10) in each of the areas of customer strategy thinking we outlined:

- Segmentation ☐

- Targeting ☐

- Positioning ☐

Now consider in detail how the weaker areas can be improved.

4 How complete is your current competitor information and analysis? Identify a few key ways this could be strengthened.
5 Identify the competitive advantages you do – or could – enjoy with your product. Plan how you could strengthen and improve them.
6 Pull out your present product marketing plan and apply the two checks suggested in 'Reviewing Your Strategy Options'. What is this telling you?

Further reading

Boston Consulting Group (1993), Discovering how to Maximise Customer Share, *Marketing Business* (September)
Clavell, J. (1983) *Sun Tzu – The Art of War*, Dell Publishing.

Levitt, T. (1980), Marketing success through differentiation – of anything. Jan/Feb, *Harvard Business Review*

Ohmae, K. (1983) *The Mind of the Strategist*, Penguin

Ohmae, K. (1988) Getting back to strategy, Nov/Dec, *Harvard Business Review*

Porter, M.E. (1985) *Competitive Advantage*, Collier Macmillan

Ries, A. and Trout, J. (1986) *Positioning: The Battle For Your Mind*, McGraw-Hill

Ries, A. and Trout, J. (1986), *Marketing Warfare*, McGraw-Hill

Ries, A. and Trout, J. (1993) *The 22 Immutable Laws of Marketing*, Harper Collins

4 Developing new products

The overall process – Techniques for generating a strong flow of new product ideas – Ways of checking and screening the concepts that emerge – Business analysis – Handling the product through development and testing – Planning and managing a successful launch

Not all product managers are totally responsible for this area. Some larger companies separate out the functions of managing new and existing products.

Where this applies, *totally* new products or brands are the responsibility of a separate manager or section, as happened on a large scale in General Motors with the 'Saturn' project to develop and produce a totally new car concept along 'Japanese' lines. The main body of product managers in this scenario are then left with the role of bringing through new versions of existing products, or widening the existing range.

In many multinationals, major new product projects are handled regionally or at corporate level, with national product managers expected to make an input on requirements, and to handle launch and business development in their own market.

These two circumstances, though highly visible, are nevertheless in a minority. Most product managers *are* responsible – at least in part – for this important area themselves. So it is right that we look at this area in some detail, as a separate chapter within this book.

If you are responsible for all the areas listed in the Contents to this chapter, read on. If only parts apply to you, 'cherry-pick' the sections which are most relevant .

THE OVERALL PROCESS

Figure 4.1 summarizes the normal stages involved, in taking a new product concept right through to successful commercialization. This may vary in detail in your company. For example, many British companies do not have a *formal* screening stage. Other, more sophisticated companies operate a more complex system than is shown in outline here. But the *principles* of handling this whole process successfully remain largely the same:

Stage 1 is described as '**exploration**'. It covers the first essential step of ensuring that the 'channels are open' for a strong input of ideas, on new product needs or possible product improvements.

It also involves you (and your technical or agency team) putting some 'shape' on them, in terms of better defining what is *really* needed.

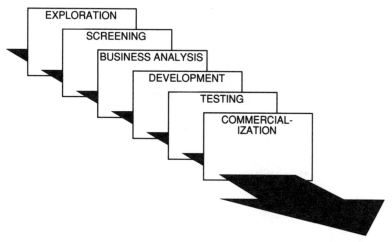

Figure 4.1   Stages in the new product development (NPD) process

Stage 2 is some form of **screening**. This requires you to objectively assess the idea in terms of its 'fit' with company and market requirements. It should also be a key stage for you to identify the potential 'winners' and 'losers'.

Stage 3 often involves more formality. It requires you to build a business case for the product, often requiring a fairly high-level signoff before you can proceed.

We have called it **business analysis**, but often it requires more than this. It is your first-stage marketing plan and, though it may need updating, will often provide the key parameters for how the product will ultimately be marketed, and how it is expected to perform.

Stage 4 assumes a company 'go ahead' decision, and requires you to manage the overall **development** of the product to final (or near final) form.

Stage 5 may partly run parallel to stage 4, or may follow on. Here, you are **testing** not just whether the product will *really* work in its intended environment, but often putting final shape on how it will be marketed (for example, with pack or ad testing).

Stage 6 involves all the planning and run-up decisions and actions to launch, the launch itself, and your post-launch care for the product until it is properly established, i.e., everything needed for successful **commercialization** of the product.

In your normal job environment, the first stage is an on-going activity, as is the management of development and testing. Launches tend to be *main events* which, while time-consuming and demanding, are also very satisfying when they are successful.

But research (especially a major US study by Booz, Allen and Hamilton Inc.), shows that stages 2 and 3 are often the critical ones, in ensuring not just a successful, but also a *profitable* flow of new products for your business.

The importance of the early stages

The reason is simple. *Most new product development programmes are very 'back-end-loaded' in terms of cost and investment.*

So if you are not to heavily *dilute* your effectiveness in successful new products reaching the marketplace, you must be ruthless in weeding out losers and weaker concepts *as early as possible*.

> The Booz, Allen study showed the 'successful' companies, on average, progressed only around 10% of their original new product ideas through into expensive development. Only 20% of ideas successfully passed screening and, of these, around half were rejected at business analysis stage.

This means the screening stage, in particular, is a key one in your overall success.

This is nowhere more true than when the 'table-stakes' of necessary R&D cost are at their highest, in areas such as pharmaceuticals. Successful companies in this business, like Glaxo, are reputed to have fall-out rates from concept to a successful product on the market of the order of 1000 to one, with most of this occurring at screening.

Types of new product

The relative importance and duration of each stage *will* vary with the *type* of new product being developed (see Figure 4.2).

Some companies recognize this by having a different process (and sometimes even separate R&D teams), for handling tactical changes and major new developments.

In most companies, probably including your own, the major new products tend to 'grab the headlines' both internally and externally.

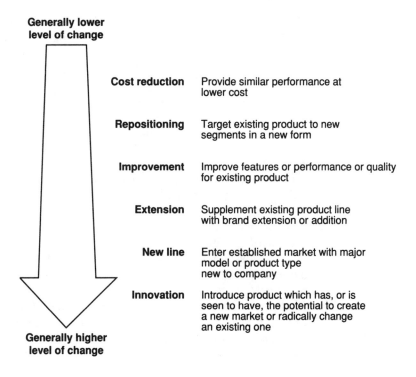

Figure 4.2   Types of new product

But this is not where the main effort, and resources, tend to be invested. In most British and many US companies, the main R&D activities (sometimes as much as 80–90% of R&D time) tend to be concentrated within the first four categories. They are largely *company or asset-driven developments* (see Figure 4.3).

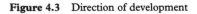

Figure 4.3   Direction of development

The big 'virtues' they seem to offer are that time-to-market is fairly quick, risks are low, and investment requirements are limited, so returns (at least in the short term) can seem very attractive. Also, because of the low perceived cost and risk, a fairly high failure rate can be tolerated in this process and still show a 'net gain'.

The *real* risks and costs are not always so apparent, but you need to consider if they apply to you and your company. They are:

● *You may not be getting the best overall results from your limited R&D resource* by choking them up in a welter of relatively minor, tactical, projects. As highly trained and 'goal-driven' people, this is very likely to affect their motivation and commitment. In the extreme, it may even result in your best technical people leaving.
● You have to think about the *marketplace results of your actions.* Whether, in fact, you may just be *confusing customers* by too much minor change or variety. Or significantly *diluting your positioning and branding* by over-extending. (Read Ries and Trout if you need convincing!)
● You may *lose ground competitively* to companies more prepared or committed to invest in genuine innovation. (Some Japanese companies also get heavily into product proliferation, but almost always still commit a higher share of resources to innovatory new products).
● Finally, and probably most important, you *risk losing contact with* what should be the main driving-force of your new product activities : picking up and creatively responding to *changing customer needs*.

The 'bottom-line' of this section is that you have to accept a certain level of risk and pioneering in your new product activities, to have a better chance of remaining successful in the long term. Otherwise you may just be refining the recipe, and dividing into ever-smaller slices, *yesterday's* cakes.

TECHNIQUES FOR GENERATING A STRONG FLOW OF NEW PRODUCT IDEAS

Idea generation is considerably helped if you have enough people – and the *right* people – involved in the process.

As product manager, you may be expected to be the main source of these ideas. But nobody, however bright or well-tuned to their market, can be expected to have a *monopoly* of good ideas. So you are best to make this a 'team' effort, with you acting as the 'lightning conductor' or synthesizer of all the ideas this generates.

Who can be involved?

This will clearly depend on the type of business you are in, but any of the following *could* be useful as part of your total network:

<table>
<tr><td rowspan="1">Potential
contributors </td><td>
● R&D, production, engineering, design
● Purchasing and key suppliers
● Salesforce, trade partners, end-customers
● MR, advertising, new product or design agencies
</td></tr>
</table>

The most obvious channel for you to keep open is the third one listed above. Ideas may come from well-motivated individual salespeople, or by you attending sales meetings, and making this a special agenda item.

Informed people in the 'trade' are often good conduits for required improvements or new opportunities, and can be helpful in the process.

In many industrial businesses, the impetus may come from leading companies directly, some of whom will be major users and very knowledgeable about your product. Sometimes, smaller and more innovative customers can fulfil this role also.

Where part of your range is 'bought in', you can share in key suppliers' developments. Or seek to incorporate other suppliers' new raw materials, components or packaging approaches which will enhance your own manufactured products.

An often neglected area is to encourage your own technical or operations people to make some creative input into the process. This may throw up new lines of thought, or allow the incorporation of highly 'practical' improvements in design or usage, with related customer benefits. They are also well-placed to input on possible cost savings.

Finally, in many consumer goods areas, a major channel is via a range of agency inputs, whether this be holding exploratory focus groups, or commissioning new concept development projects. There are also a number of well-proven techniques to help the process of idea generation.

Techniques to generate new product ideas

Among the most common, and generally most useful are:

<table>
<tr><td>Techniques </td><td>
Segmentation studies, gap analysis and trend projections
Competitive analysis
Pointer and parallel markets
Brainstorming
</td></tr>
</table>

Segmentation studies

The basic process of segmentation is to find a way of breaking down the key parameters of your market, so you can see what is common and what is different.

Having segmentation data available, and using it creatively, can be a powerful tool in identifying unfulfilled needs or 'gaps' in the markets or your own offering. It can also be useful in pointing out possible 'connections' between customer needs and ways of fulfilling them.

A practical way of looking at this is suggested by Figure 4.4, and this is often useful raw material for a brainstorming session – especially when the axes are extended by asking 'what *could* we offer?' and 'what *could* be wanted?' or 'where *are* possible new applications?'

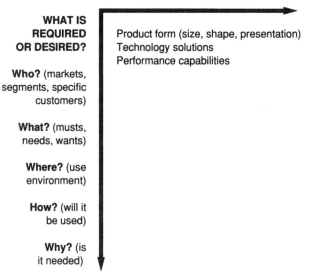

WHAT CAN WE OFFER?

WHAT IS REQUIRED OR DESIRED?

Product form (size, shape, presentation)
Technology solutions
Performance capabilities

Who? (markets, segments, specific customers)

What? (musts, needs, wants)

Where? (use environment)

How? (will it be used)

Why? (is it needed)

Figure 4.4   Segmentation to reveal product opportunities

In some markets further relevant questions could be 'what could we *combine?*' or 'What could be *separated out*, to meet more specialist needs?'

In many larger companies, the possible connections may be wider, and you need to look at *company capabilities* which could find a home in your product area, or within new integrated solutions.

An example of this occurred in the US chemical company I worked for:

> *The company had developed a new technology for safely and effectively cleaning aluminium in a kitchen environment. However, in another division - transport – the whole industry had problems cleaning aluminium-sided vehicles. Each division was self-sufficient, with its own sales, marketing and R&D resources. Nobody talked to each other.*
>
> *It wasn't until a brainstorming session was held looking at wider capabilities, that the connection was seen, and the new technology incorporated into a market-winning product for the transport division.*

The process here is *using analysis to identify possibilities and then carefully researching and assessing the ideas that emerge.*

But the process can also work in reverse. Doing things this way, you *start with research into underlying trends and see where this could lead you within your product area.*

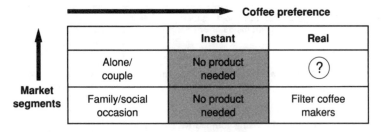

Figure 4.5   Underlying trends in the coffee market

A classic example of this is illustrated in Figure 4.5. Research in the early 1980s revealed two major trends in coffee-making:

1 An increasing minority of coffee drinkers wanting to move from 'instant' to better quality 'real' coffee.
2 Demographic changes, leading to a significantly greater number of coffee drinking occasions requiring only one or two cups.

Existing filter coffee-makers did not offer a satisfactory solution. They were designed to make 6-12 cups, for larger family or social situations. So there was an emerging need chasing a solution.

The solution, in fact, came in two forms. One was the move across to the domestic market of the Rombouts type of 'filter on the cup' system. The other was a scaled down coffee-making machine for one or two cups – notably the Philips Duo.

This market is now in second-phase development, as customer tastes and expectations continue to rise in the late-1980s and early-1990s, and the need now is for a *variety* of forms of 'real' coffee.

As well as stimulating multi-coffee versions of the Duo-type machines, this has also encouraged a number of major German and Italian manufacturers to offer scaled-down versions of cafe/restaurant type coffee machines for the home. It has also stimulated the coffee manufacturers to launch a series of 'authentic' premium brands (including espresso and cappuccino) in instant form.

Competitive analysis

Figure 4.6 shows some of the questions or 'angles' you could investigate. This will vary in its usefulness, depending on the level of openness or security-consciousness in your business. But it should not be ignored. At the very least, it will highlight any key gaps in your range, which may need filling to maintain market credibility or completeness of offering.

1 **What are competitors offering?**	Does this reveal 'gaps' or weaknesses in our range which need to be filled?
2 **How are they adapting their products to different needs or segments?**	Are they using product variants to develop new price/quality levels, new product-use applications, or new user group sub-segments?
3 **What are competitors developing?**	Which of their ideas should we be investigating or seeking to cover on our own offering?

Figure 4.6 Using competitive analysis

Analysing other markets

Another way of casting your thinking wider is to look outside your own product field or market, as a source of ideas or inspiration.

For example, if you operate only in one national market, there may be ideas from other markets you could consider or learn from. In most businesses, there tend to be one, or a small number of, **pointer markets** which tend to be at the 'leading edge' in your product field. For example:

Scandinavia:	furniture design
Italy:	coffee
USA:	fast food developments and personalized banking
Japan:	consumer electronics

You can also look 'horizontally', i.e. across other related industries or businesses with something in common with your own product area.

This may be, for example:

● The same or similar customers
● Areas of related need
● Products with similar applications or use environments.

These so-called **parallel markets** can also be a useful stimulus for your thinking, as some of the developments in them can potentially spill over into your own product area.

Brainstorming

Any of the approaches suggested so far can provide good raw material for a brainstorming session involving yourself and your colleagues. This can generate a strong flow of less conventional or creative ideas, some of which can be assessed and later developed into practical new product concepts.

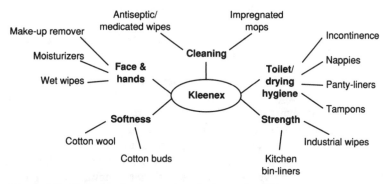

Figure 4.7 Brainstorming to reveal product opportunities

You may just want to involve company people, but many companies also extend brainstorming input to include outside 'experts', or even trade partners or customers as part of the process.

In fact, a number of consumer goods companies use this technique very powerfully as a way of generating new lines of potential development for an existing brand (see example in Figure 4.7).

WAYS OF CHECKING AND SCREENING THE CONCEPTS THAT EMERGE

Most companies find the main problem is not in generating ideas, but in successfully checking and screening them, and then developing the ideas into successful products. In consumer markets, emerging ideas are commonly checked by running **concept tests**, normally in a focus group format. In industrial markets formal concept testing is rare, but there is normally a degree of informal testing or sounding out with 'friends' in the industry.

Screening comes into play when the concept has been firmed up and you are basically trying to *prioritize* or *filter* what is coming through.

At the very least, concepts should be screened in terms of their 'company fit' and resource requirements, with key questions such as:

1 *Is the product in line with company strategy?*
  Does it take us in a direction we want to go?
  Does it build on proven strengths or overcome recognized weaknesses?
2 *Is it in line with company objectives?*
  Will it yield minimum required levels of sales, growth, profit or return on investment?
  Will it meet desired image objectives?
3 *Is it compatible with company resources?*
  Can we handle it in terms of financing and technology requirements, production or logistics facilities, sales and administrative resources? If not, can they be resourced at reasonable cost?

Other screening approaches take a wider view and attempt to assess a range of company and external issues. Often this will involve applying a 'weighting factor' to reflect the relative importance of different groups of issues (e.g. finance issues 10%, access to market 20% etc.), and then applying some form of 'rating' system, to assess this proposed product against a predetermined standard in each area.

One well-known confectionery manufacturer, for example, has organized its weighting and rating scales to give a possible maximum score of 100. The 'hurdle' they use is that any new concept has to achieve a score of 75+, to go automatically through to the next stage. Between 65 and 75 it goes back for review and the product manager has a second chance to make a revised proposal. Below 65 and the idea is rejected.

Other companies use a modified form of portfolio analysis, where they rate the new product on two scales of:

● **Market attractiveness** of your proposed product/market
● Your own **relative business strength** versus identified competition in serving this market.

This gives a positioning for the particular product idea on the grid illustrated in Figure 4.8, and a clear indication of what the decision should be.

RELATIVE STRENGTH	MARKET ATTRACTIVENESS		
	High	**Average**	**Low**
High	Go for it! Top priority	Maybe – Capitalize on strength	Probably not worth the effort
Average	Maybe – but build strength first	Hard work to make a go of it	Not worth the hassle
Low	No – unless you can acquire strength	Not worth the cost of building strength	Definitely not! Leave well alone

Figure 4.8 A 'portfolio' approach to screening. (With acknowledgements to Dr David Shipley, Graham Hooley and John Saunders.)

From the USA, the **Schrello Screen** (Figure 4.9) has some useful ideas, which you may be able to build into your own screening approach.

1. Is it real?

Is the market real?
- Size – potential?
- Growth?
- Segmentation?
- Barriers to acceptance?
- Geographic location?
- Who are the end-users?
- Are they **willing** to pay?
- Are needs being satisfied by other products?
- Duration (movement, will it last)?
- Why haven't others done it?
- What is the likely life cycle?

Is the product real?
- Does it have a function/work?
- Who would use it?
- What value-added value?
- Can it be manufactured by us?
- Do we have the technology?
- Are materials available?
- Will it deliver the promises?
- Have you made one?
- Has it been tested?

Figure 4.9 The Schrello Screen

Figure 4.9 continued

2. **Can we win?**

Can our product be competitive?
- Is it unique?
- How long will it stay unique?
- Is competition established?
- Relative cost?
- Relative quality?
- Will our offering be competitive?

Can our company be competitive?
- Can opposition react?
- Can we dominate?
- What marketing communication needs?
- Are we currently competitive?
- Can we distribute?

---

3. **Is it worth doing?**

Will it be profitable?
- Adequate ROI?
- Adequate payback?
- Sales forecasts – trends?
- What prices?
- Sources of financing – internal – external – risk capital?
- Size of investment?

Does it satisfy company needs?
- Uses existing plant?
- Does the president like it?
- Fits existing product portfolio?
- Is it legal?
- Government standards?
- Do we have the expertise?
- Will it consolidate market share?
- Is it a growth opportunity?
- Can it be licensed/patented?
- Cannibalization?
- Impact on existing channels?
- Will it do anything for external image?

BUSINESS ANALYSIS (and first-stage marketing plan)

Some form of business case would normally need to be built by you for the new product, and in many companies this happens at an early stage. It may be conducted as part of a more demanding screening process (as with Schrello), or as a separate stage after this.

What this will normally focus on is an **outline strategy** for the product, and a check on the likely **financial performance** it offers.

The strategy element needs to put the product in context (basically, 'this is why we need it' and ' this is what it will do for us'). It should also cover basic lines of strategy thinking, as we discussed in the previous chapter.

The numbers may vary, but basically include:

● Market and segment projections to show market size, trends, and our position in share terms with and without the product.
● Sales projections for our product in volume and value terms (including any pricing assumptions).
● Cost assumptions for the product itself and any additional support costs involved.
● Profit projections, as P&L-type gross and net profitability, or in terms of additional contribution generated.

In more sophisticated organizations, or where the investment is more substantial, the financial case may also need to include:

● Risk factors involved (sensitivity analysis) and the overall downside risk.
● Cashflow implications (cash required to develop the product and build its market position, the ultimate cash yield it offers, and the timing of cashflows).
● Investment appraisal, in terms of the payback period and rate of return the product offers.

HANDLING THE PRODUCT THROUGH DEVELOPMENT AND TESTING

Development can be one of the most frustrating stages in the whole NPD process, and product managers are frequently critical of the time their technical colleagues seem to take to 'deliver the goods'. However, research has shown that the most frequent causes of delay are 'organizational' or are brought about by marketing people themselves.

For example, many companies impose time-consuming administrative requirements on their top technologists, or demand a rapid turn-round on urgent short-term technical problems or tactical product improvements. Both are usually at the expense of more important strategic projects.

As a product manager, ask yourself whether you are guilty yourself of 'short-termism', or any other of the following very common problems:

- Overloading the system with more projects than it can handle (this slows everything down).
- Not effectively communicating the priority or required timescale of projects up front, or frequently changing them when the products are in development (the first will mean everything will probably be given *equal* priority, and the second will guarantee extended development cycles).
- Failing to provide a full specification at the start of the project, or coming back with a stream of changes and additions (you have not done your homework properly and again the result will be greatly extended cycles).
- Failing to maintain effective and *formal* reviews on progress; relying too much on assumptions that things *are* happening, or on informal day-to-day contact and 'chases'. (This way, you can *guarantee* you are probably in for some nasty surprises).

Testing

Some industries have extended external testing requirements imposed on them, as with defence equipment or human and animal health products. Others have some external testing or certification as part of the process (e.g. electrical safety).

In all cases, though, some form of 'real life' testing is advisable before the product is finalized and launched. There may be unforeseen problems in real-life use. *A new high-productivity floor polisher was tested by Electrolux in the laboratory on a 3 metre square surface where a standard-length flex was no problem. In real life, in large hotel foyers or very long hospital corridors, an extra-length flex was clearly essential to enjoy the productivity benefits.*

Some consumer companies conduct rigorous product testing prior to launch. This may be **holistic**, where the total offering is checked with a sample of typical customers. Ford and other car manufacturers now do this as a matter of course, and many FMCG companies conduct 'home placement' tests to assess reactions.

Or it may be **atomistic**, where each separate element is carefully checked individually by research (pack tests, ad tests etc.).

With most industrial companies, testing tends to be smaller-scale and confined to putting the product out 'on trial' for a period.

Whatever type of business you are in, the testing stage is the *right* time to iron any final 'bugs' out of the product, and ensure it is fully understood and really works in its intended environment. Once any problems like these actually reach the market it is too late (you are unnecessarily risking failure or at least an unfavourable initial reaction), and they will almost always be more expensive to sort out.

PLANNING AND MANAGING A SUCCESSFUL LAUNCH

Prior to launch

Many final decisions (e.g. on pricing) may be left quite late in the pre-launch countdown, but others require careful pre-planning and the building in of sufficient lead-time to handle key stages or activities.

In the case of some advertising or promotional materials in particular, your lead-times may be quite extended, with photography, namechecks and media bookings being common examples. Normally your agency will advise you in these areas and help with the planning.

But similar lead-time issues also apply in the company itself, and here you are normally 'on your own'.

Production normally require extended lead-times for trial runs or final production, and this may be stretched further back in sourcing and ordering key components or packaging.

You are also likely to have to trigger some administrative actions, such as allocating product codes or loading product or pricing details into relevant systems. Training is also an issue that needs planning well in advance.

Launch forecasts

As product manager, you will normally be expected to provide *launch forecasts* for the new line, for sales, operational and financial purposes.

With a simple change, improvement or extension product, this basically involves judging the level of incremental sales this will generate. This is largely a matter of 'informed guesswork' and not too difficult. If you are launching a new line into an area of market you have not operated in before, it gets more difficult. And a totally new product for the market is more difficult still.

Normally some form of the basic **Parfitt-Collins Model** can give a helpful base to build your figures on. The formula is $S = prb$. This says that your ultimate *share* (S) will depend on three elements:

p = our product's ultimate penetration rate (the % of all
    buyers who *try* our brand)

r = our product's ultimate repeat purchase rate (the %
    of triallists who *repeat buy*)

b = the ultimate *buying rate* our product achieves (how
    often it is bought in relation to competitive products)

When the product is totally new, it is basically the $p \times r$ part of the formula which applies. If you want to get really clever you can build a model which looks at how this is likely to vary by segment. When competition also enters, then the b element needs adding in.

The launch itself

The launch itself may involve you in detailed planning – for in-company events such as a launch conference, or for key customer, press or dealer launch meetings. Venue bookings and launch presentation materials can often involve extended lead-times and need planning well in advance.

Depending on circumstances, you may need to consider different forms of launch. The main options are:

- **Test marketing** Where you seek to replicate the whole market on a smaller scale, and carefully test out the product or key parts of the marketing programme prior to committing to full launch.
- **Rolling launch** Where supply constraints or other issues require you to roll out stage by stage through your intended market.
- **Full launch** Full-scale commercialization in 'one hit' across the whole market.

Post-launch follow-up

Just as good planning and attention to detail are essential prior to launch, it is equally important that you put the right monitoring and follow-up in place *post-launch*. As well as tracking sales performance and the rate of trialling and repeat-buying, this may also involve you in:

- Follow-up activities with the salesforce or key customers to maintain momentum.
- Ensuring priority field technical support to deal with any early problems.
- Carefully monitoring the product supply position.

CHAPTER CHECKLIST

Some checks to make on new product development

1 Is your NPD process *complete*, in that it covers *all* the stages described in 'The Overall Process' section above? Specifically, do you have rigorous enough screening?

2   What is the current *mix* of your tactical and more strategic activities in NPD? How much of the impetus is from the company and how much from the marketplace? Do either of these need reviewing?

3   Are you *actively* using the full range of contributors who could play a part in idea generation? Are there any groups or individuals in particular that you ought to make part of your 'network'?

4   Are there any of the *techniques* we described which could be useful? Think about how you could adapt them to your business.

5   Think about whether any of the *screening processes* described (or parts of them) could be useful to you?

6   Can you see ways of improving the *business case* you could make for your new products?

7   How many of the problems you encounter in *development* are (at least partly) down to you? What are you going to do about it?

8   Are you building in sufficient *market testing* prior to launch? Can you see ways in which this could be improved?

9   Are there any particular parts of handling *launches* you could improve? Jot down a 'must do next time' list.

10 How good are your *launch forecasts*? Can you see any ways these could possibly be improved?

Further reading

Gilbert, X. and Strebel, P. (1989) From innovation to outpacing. Summer, *Business Quarterly*

Handscombe, R.S. (1989) *The Product Management Handbook*, McGraw-Hill, Ch. 3

Kotler, P. (1988) *Marketing Management – Analysis, Planning, Implementation and Control*, Prentice-Hall, ch. 14

Ries, A. and Trout, J. (1993) *The 22 Immutable Laws of Marketing*, Harper Collins, ch. 12

Souder W.E. (1981) Disharmony between R&D and marketing, *Industrial Marketing Management* , February

Wheelwright, S.C. and Sasser W.E. Jr (1989) The new product development map, *Harvard Business Review*, May/June

5 Managing existing products and ranges

Life cycle perspectives – Range management through the life cycle – Coping with change – Developing penetration – Managing problem products – Portfolio perspectives on range management – Handling rationalization exercises effectively – Minimizing the 'drag factor' of lower-performing lines – Late-life product actions

We looked in the last chapter at the issues of successfully developing and launching *new* or additional products. Now we need to turn to how we can most effectively manage our *existing* products or brands. The product life cycle is a good place to start.

LIFE CYCLE PERSPECTIVES

Though some people look at life cycles as 'marketing theory', there are a number of key aspects of this concept that we ignore at our peril. Three are particularly important.

1 At individual **product** level, we have to focus on different issues and priorities at different times in the cycle. We have to cope with various change factors along the way, and manage the product effectively right through to end of life.
2 At **range** level, the key issue is achieving balance and optimal range performance. This involves having products at different cycle stages to ensure overall balance in volume, growth, profitability and cashflow. It may also take you into rationalization or overall performance improvement exercises.
3 At **product category** level, stage in life cycle (not just of our product but of all products of this type) has a major bearing on how much effort or resource we are prepared, or it is sensible, to commit.

All these issues, but particularly (2) and (3), can be helped by maintaining the right strategic overview of what we are doing with our products, and 'portfolio' perspectives can be a useful tool in this process.

RANGE MANAGEMENT THROUGH THE LIFECYCLE

One important perspective is that – through life – your **strategic focus** needs to change in the way you manage your products. In Figure 5.1 this means basically a gradual move from left to right through the life cycle. Figure 5.2 goes on to look at this in more detail.

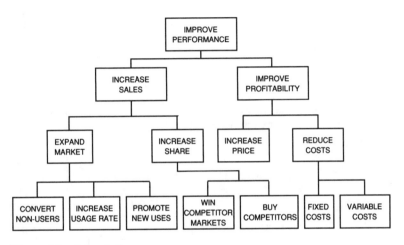

Figure 5.1   Strategic focus

New products

So for most *new* products or services, most of your marketing actions are geared to maximizing growth opportunities, establishing share and achieving **volume.**

Starting with a highly focused entry, with clear 'early change' or 'early adopt' targets, the key task is to ensure these target customers know about the product, trial it and come on board as buyers.

At this stage, product is normally a simple offering, designed to exactly match initial target segments' requirements. Price is often relatively high, and distribution concentrated in more specialist outlets.

Growth and early maturity

From this bridgehead, your next phase is usually to continue the conversion process with initial target groups, but – at the same time – also planning how the base of business can be broadened in a phased way through additional segments or channels.

GROWTH	EARLY MATURITY	LATE MATURITY/ DECLINE
Expand market	Maximize share	Improve productivity
Convert non-users	Reduce price in real terms, to attract more price-sensitive buyers and re-buys	Offer 'value for money' through cost reduction programmes and special value options (while mass market remains)
Develop new segments	Improve / re-launch product	
Maximize exposure in distribution channels	Make additions to product line	Later, perhaps increase prices as product is refocused and repositioned on narrower segments
Improve quality, add some new features	Motivate channels to maximize volume throughput	Change focus of advertising, with more emphasis on 'reminder' function
Focus advertising on developing awareness and encouraging trial	Focus advertising on new features and brand loyalty	Rationalize range and reduce variety

Figure 5.2 Typical action focus at different life cycle stages

This may require some new forms of the product to be added, together with some improvement actions to maintain product interest.

Price (and perceived value) may need some realignment across your now extended range, particularly by offering 'entry-level' options to bring in more price-sensitive groups.

Establishing repeat patterns can also be crucial, with sales, advertising and promotional actions all geared to maximize loyalty.

Maturity and late-life

From maturity stage onwards, there may still be some late-changers to pull in, or additional usage you can encourage, but growth will be largely confined to conquesting from competition.

Unfortunately, you will not be the only product manager following these priorities at this stage, and commonly profits will be squeezed from two directions, from:

- *Downward pressure on price,* because:
  (a) the product category has become more 'commodity' in nature: customers do not recognize added value or are not prepared to fully pay for it;
  (b) all competitors chasing available volume and share encourage this by developing a 'discount' mentality.
- *Increased support costs,* required to defend your existing base and look for some limited growth.

It is vital that you change your focus early enough from volume to **value** issues within this process.

If you are to maintain a reasonable margin platform with reducing prices, you *must* address your cost base and economics of operating early enough to keep some initiative. You must be planning for this and try to avoid decisions and actions which will have the effect of loading up your costs. Holding volumes and reducing costs are the key priorities.

In some capital-intensive markets, late-life can be very cash-rich, as earlier investments are fully recovered. So marginal cost pricing can be adopted, to keep this attractive volume going as long as possible.

In other markets, overall volume may fall away, but your older lines may continue to enjoy some residual business which is not too price-sensitive, so you can reposition them in niches.

In all cases, you must at some point face up to rationalization issues, and trim back or simplify your offering.

COPING WITH CHANGE

Many of the changes through life cycle are fairly predictable, even though their timing may be uncertain. But other changes are also likely to affect your product, which are sometimes much more difficult to influence or predict.

Some of these may be forced by the marketplace or external factors; others may result from internal changes (see the examples in Table 5.1).

Good market scanning and internal communications can often anticipate these 'forced' changes, so you can take early steps to review your options. This at least allows you to avoid being totally reactive and always 'on your back foot'.

One of the difficulties of these types of change, however, is that they are not always predictable, and you can find yourself very much in 'tactical mode', and risk losing sight of what is *strategically* important for your product.

Some changes will be very short-term in their impact – they are just 'blips' or temporarily 'fashionable'. You need to be careful that these are discerned, and separated out from any more significant underlying or irreversible changes or trends. Strategy should be a *long-term game*, not a series of unconnected tactical manoeuvres.

Table 5.1   Examples of external change factors

Factors	*Examples*
Changes in external environment	General economic environment, disposable incomes, interest rates, exchange rates. Regulations or taxation policy
Changes in customer base, needs or aspirations	Shift to more small households; ageing population (consumer markets); growth of small company/home office (business markets) Rising expectations (generally) Changing lifestyles or work practices
Competitive changes	New products or new features; price actions; new positioning or promotional actions; new channels or level of product support, such as improved warranty
Company changes	Launch of a major line which may overlap/ threaten substitution in some segments Change in policy, e.g. profit versus share Changes in resources or facilities

DEVELOPING PENETRATION

Regardless of your product's strategic position, company requirements may demand improved penetration – improved sales or share – even in a mature or temporarily difficult business environment.

There are quite a number of strategies which you can consider using. Sometimes major changes are required. In other cases, relatively small adjustments or realignments can significantly improve your performance.

Some of the most common approaches are contained within the following checklist. Normally, you would review them in the order listed (i.e. start with the easiest and quickest in effect first).

Sales improvement options

1 You can look at ways of *modifying or improving your product offering*, by

- changing the quality, features, performance, design or appearance of the product;
- adjusting the price or offering better value;
- improving merchandising, advertising or promotional support.

These strategies work by improving your product's relative appeal and thereby *increasing your share of the existing customer base*.

2 You can modify your *marketing approach*, by

- promoting more frequent use;
- developing new uses;
- finding new users;
- repositioning the product to give it a wider appeal.

These strategies rely on making *changes to the 'shape', habits or perceptions of the customer base* for the product. This can be more difficult, and certainly take more time to achieve, but may offer some scope if option (1) possibilities have been used up or are not appropriate.

3 On a wider front, you may sometimes need to look beyond simple product enhancement or purchase/usage stimulation, and find ways of developing *more radical and longer-lasting improvements in performance*. This may involve you in examining areas such as:

- **Supply chain efficiency**

  The cost-efficiency and competitiveness of your purchasing and production.

  Production flexibility to handle urgent business.

  Stocking efficiency and delivery performance.

- **Channel strategy**

  The appropriateness and quality of your present channels in meeting all available potential.

  Their product knowledge, commitment and motivation towards the product.

  Whether new channels need developing or channel emphasis needs changing.

● **Sales force support**

Are all parts of the salesforce really *selling* the product?

Are there benefits in performance to be gained by better product training, targeting and incentives, or by better management direction, discipline or support?

● **Company systems and support**

Are there 'information blocks' which are damaging performance? For example, can customers and salesforce obtain key information on prices or availability quickly and easily? (Are we 'missing' available business?)

Are all company support functions fully aware, and supportive of, key customer requirements in this product area? (Are we driving customers and prospects away?)

Is the product being effectively supported in use through the help-desk or field technical back-up? (Are we losing customers we shouldn't?)

Are we competitive in the warranty, parts and service elements of our offering? (Could this be affecting business retention or our image and acceptability?)

The 'bottom-line' on this section is that there are a wide range of actions which could figure in our plans for improving penetration. Some of them affect our ability to win over new business, but many help ensure we keep what we already have.

Rather than blasting off with a whole series of largely 'cosmetic' changes or uncoordinated improvements, your key task is to review what may be acting as '*brakes*' or '*blocks*' to your present performance, then identify what further actions will provide the greatest impact as business '*boosters*'.

Some further ideas on how you can shape your thinking may also come out of the next section.

MANAGING PROBLEM PRODUCTS

Problems may occur with products at any stage of life, and may be the result of:

● Wrong decisions or actions taken on new products.
● Undetected changes in market environment or customer needs.
● Damaging competitive actions.

A basic rule here is that you should always attempt to identify the **real** cause of the problem before taking over-hasty corrective action.

Checklist for problem products

The following checklist will normally help in this process:

- Has the target market been wrongly or not clearly defined?
- Did you overstate potential or the speed of business build (new products)? Has the market sharply declined from previous levels (existing products)?
- Have the target market or key customer needs changed?
- Is some element of the marketing mix not working correctly? For example:

    vital product feature missing?

    price out of line?

    advertising not working?

    insufficient distribution or trade support?
- Are there deeper problems?

    Some aspect of strategy or positioning incorrect?

    Incorrect, over-ambitious or conflicting objectives set for the product?

The diagram in Figure 5.3 summarizes this visually.

Your so-called 'problems' may have little to do with your offering or your way of operating, in that your potential may have been wildly overstated, or the whole *market* may have dropped and you with it. It *seems* like a problem, compared to what you expected to achieve, but you are not necessarily doing anything wrong now.

Obviously, you need to check this first. Is the problem one of perception or is it a reality?

What the remainder of the checklist requires you to do is to carefully work back step-by-step from the marketplace.

Competitive benchmarking is useful as part of this overall process, but a danger of focusing too much on competition is that you just 'chase your tail' imitating competitor initiatives or apparent strengths. You need to check out whether these are really significant at *customer* level.

Sure, competition has this or that, but are they the *real reason* they are doing better? And are they things you can incorporate and get some real business benefits from – will you be *perceived* as being better if you have them?

Often they are not. You need to go back a level – to **customers** – to identify what is really needed.

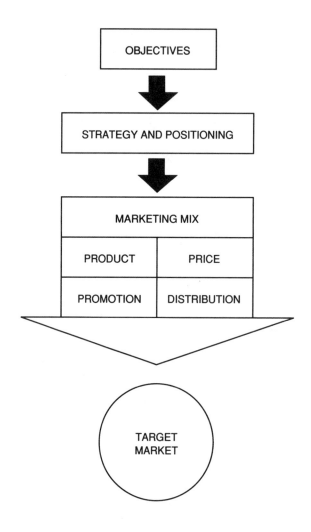

Figure 5.3 Analysing the *real* problems

Do we have a targeting problem?

The fundamental problem may be simply that you are not **'fishing where the fish are'**. You are off-target in terms of where the real business is, or could be. Or you are targeting the wrong segments for this stage of development.

You could also be off-target in terms of key needs, or changes in them you have not previously detected. You do not have a good 'match' and this is leading to rejection.

Do we need marketing mix changes?

When these fundamentals have been investigated, this is the right stage to consider whether specific parts of your marketing mix need improvement or realignment. Any required changes now have a context.

They give you a far better chance of succeeding in a turn-round than any arbitrary 'tinkering' can. They are fixed on a solid base rather than just your own, your boss's or your agency's subjective feelings.

If you are lucky, your analysis will indicate one (or a small number) of key changes are needed. Even then, it may take some time for all the necessary changes to be effected. There are rarely genuine 'quick-fix' solutions.

Do we need to go back to basics?

If you are not so lucky, the real problems may lie deeper than marketing mix, and may demand a reappraisal of the overall thinking behind the product.

You need to go right back to basic strategy, the positioning approach you used, even the objectives set for the product. And then work back through to implementation issues.

This can be quite a painful process, and egos can be severely bruised (including your own) if, with hindsight, you can see that some fundamental aspect of marketing the product incorporates downright wrong thinking or decisions which do not stack up.

PORTFOLIO PERSPECTIVES ON RANGE MANAGEMENT

Where you are managing a number of products, you need to be able to take an 'overview' of product strategy and resource allocation, to give the best results for the resources available. Just like an investment portfolio, you need to make the marketing equivalents of 'hold', 'sell' or 'invest more' decisions.

A number of well-publicized proven techniques are available to help you do this, most based on a matrix setting **market attractiveness** against **strength of product position.**

The Boston Grid

The best-known of these 'portfolio' approaches is the Boston Grid, or Boston Matrix, developed by the Boston Consulting Group. This keeps things very simple by using relative *market growth* as the measure of market attractiveness, and relative *market share* as the measure of product strength.

This gives a matrix of four 'cash quadrants', as illustrated in Figure 5.4, with terms like 'Cash Cow' which have passed into most marketing people's vocabulary. I will run through this briefly now, but strongly recommend that if you are thinking of using it, you read into it more deeply (see, for example, the book by George Day listed in the Further Reading to this chapter).

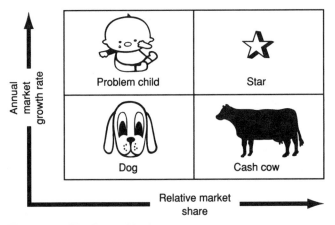

Figure 5.4   The Boston Matrix

Also, do not be surprised if the horizontal axis goes in different directions depending on author. Figure 5.4 has the 'European' way of left-to-right, but most US writers show it right to left.

The basic messages from Boston are that this type of analysis will reveal your range as containing up to four basic types of product situation, each of which need handling differently.

Cash Cows   (high or dominant share/ low growth)

Usually successful older products which are generating more cash than they need to support their position. The basic strategic message is **hold – manage for profit and cash generation.**

These products should only receive enough investment to remain effective as cash-generators. Temptations to invest in product proliferation or expansion should be avoided, unless the market can be grown (but even here there are probably better opportunities in higher growth categories at the top of the grid).

Stars   (high or dominant share/ high growth)

Products with a leading share position but also growing fast will have good profits but probably need cash support to keep the growth going. Part of this is for product improvement, better market coverage, improved production efficiency, etc., and part just to keep pace with growing working capital requirements (more money tied up in stocks and debtors).

The overall strategy message is **build** and invest, particularly in gaining a larger share of key growth points in the business. And use cash generated by the Cash-Cows to fund this. This is not only the right thing to do now, but will also ensure a strong future cash cow, as the business of this product matures.

Problem Child   (low share in high-growth market)

This category is also called 'Joker', 'Dilemma' or 'Questionmark' by some authors. They all convey the same message – you *have to do something*, but this often involves some tough choices.

The basic combination of high growth and poor profit margins is not a healthy one – it can be a 'black hole' which chews up cash without ever giving a return.

The basic strategy approach has to be **selective growth**. This means you have to 'pick your winners'. It is extremely unlikely that you will have the resources to take *all* the products in this category through to full success and Star status.

So which will receive major investment and support? Which should be dropped? (Yes, dropped, even though they are in growth segments!) And which do you want to handle less expensively (and more profitably), via joint ventures or developing a 'premium niche' position?

Dogs   (low share, low growth market)

You may find quite a lot of your products in this box. They are usually at a cost disadvantage and have significantly less 'visibility' than the leaders. Any major investment in them is normally money wasted. But you do have three viable strategy choices – **niche, harvest** or **withdraw**.

You may not be a big player in the overall market, but you can seek to dominate a viable, defensible and profitable niche area of the business. This keeps you in the game as a player.

You can harvest, which is a conscious cut-back of all support costs to a minimum level, often accompanied by price increases. This will at least maximize cashflow for the foreseeable future (usually short, depending on how savagely you implement the strategy).

Or you can withdraw, either by selling the rights to the product on, or by deletion.

How to use the portfolio approach

In positioning your products on the grid, you would normally represent their sales importance by different sizes of circles. The tool also becomes much more powerful if you make it *dynamic*, i.e. you show the direction the products are already moving, by arrows or dotted circles; or overlay the direction you would like them to move.

You can use it at different levels of detail: where your products fit in the company portfolio; in product groups or individual products; or even down to items within product.

You can also develop a grid for your main competitors' products, to develop some understanding of how they are likely to see them, and the broad actions they are likely to take.

However, the Boston Grid, as the oldest approach, does have some limitations. Partly this is because its high-low format largely ignores the issues of products in borderline or intermediate positions. Also, the apparent simplicity of its axes can sometimes be difficult to apply in practice, with different market definitions giving very different strategic prescriptions.

For these reasons, most later approaches (such as Shell's Directional Policy Matrix or the US General Electric Grid, developed by McKinseys), move away from a four-box approach to better defined boxes or zones to cover intermediate positions. They also use a wider base of measures or factors to determine where individual products sit.

If you are going to use this approach, you would also be well advised to think through the factors most relevant for *your* business, but these may include:

Overall market attractiveness factors	*Overall competitive capability factors*
Market/segment growth	Market share
Market size	Technical capability
Strength and behaviour of competition	Cost competitiveness Management know-how
Profit potential	Fit with other business
+/- impact of external factors.	Distribution or sales 'muscle'.

All the portfolio approaches require you to have good external information. In some industries and many smaller companies this is just not available, but you can use a similar approach based on internally available information. In fact, you can use this as well.

Range sales and profit analysis

In this approach, you start by listing your products in *descending sales and profit order*. In most cases, this will be *gross* profit.

Look at their *percentage importance* as well, as this can be quite revealing in terms of how much of a 'Pareto Effect' (80:20 rule) you have present within your range.

Now fit your products into the simple grid shown in Figure 5.5, after deciding where appropriate cut-off points should be made, in terms of 'high' or 'low'.

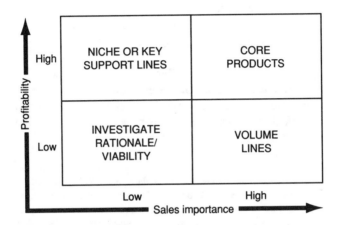

Figure 5.5   Range sales and profit analysis

As well as perhaps giving you one or two surprises ('I didn't realize that second-tier line was so attractive in profit terms !'), it gives some clear perspectives on how you should be handling different parts of your range.

Core products

It will clearly identify your core products. This handful of lines probably accounts for a significant share of your overall sales and an even greater share of profits.

> *When the product management team did this exercise at a speciality chemical company where I was a consultant, it showed six lines – out of more than 1000 – accounted for between 20% and 30% of sales, but **over 50 %** of total gross profit*

Any slippage on these key lines will have a major impact on your overall performance. Any improvement (if this is possible), will be highly enriching.

They are, by definition, the products you should never take your eye off. They demand prime attention and priority in everything: time, resources, advertising spend and salesforce attention.

Volume lines

The analysis will also show up your volume lines. These are usually products in more price-sensitive or price-competitive sectors, where there is good volume available – at a price. In many companies (particularly when the salesforce are rewarded on volume or value sales), such products may get excessive attention. They may be good 'commission-earners' but they can also severely dilute your range profitability, and divert attention away from more profitable lines.

Try to manage them *'selectively'*. Think of them as offering two possible benefits to your range performance:

● The volume they offer can make a useful contribution to overheads; a kind of 'base-loading of production' function, and
● Often they can be useful as 'safety valves'; they offer you some flexibility to step your business in them up or down, depending on how much you need it.

*For example, in glass packaging, major-brand whisky or perfume bottles (because of the final price of the product) offer volume and good margins. They are core products. Milk bottles for the major doorstep-delivery dairies are high-volume 'commodity' business. But as glassmaking is a continuous, round-the-clock production process, milk bottle business can be useful in **both** the ways described above.*

Niche or key support lines

The top left-hand box is an interesting one. It will show up some high-value niche products, that maybe you could do more with, given a bit of marketing attention.

The second category in this box are the **'tag-on lines'**, many of which are much less price-sensitive than the higher-value products they are sold with.

I recently bought a new PC for my office. I 'shopped around' like crazy to get the best price and bundled software package on the PC itself. Then I bought a new printer at the same time, and never even thought of 'shopping around'. I even signed up for a service agreement offering on-site product fix, and never blinked when it cost a third the cost of the computer itself.

If you want another example, *you* may shop around or use promotional vouchers when deciding where to buy your burger or pizza. But think about how much profit the fast food operators make on your side orders of fries, soft drinks or garlic bread.

These are excellent 'tag-on lines' which offer high margins and reasonable volumes *provided they are effectively 'bundled' or system-sold.*

Leave them as free-standing lines, and some will be ordered, but the company will also be missing a major profit improvement opportunity. In fact, link-lines like this often offer one of the *best* opportunities for improving overall *range profitability*.

> *We had an opportunity like this at the chemical company I was Marketing Manager for. In the catering business, we were dominant market leaders in machine dish-washing, but relatively minor operators in all other areas of kitchen chemicals (which represented 60-70% of the overall business available within those customers). We just couldn't get the salesforce to sell the 100-plus lines we had to cover all the other needs.*
>
> *The solution was a combination of a radical rationalization down to a very simple all-purpose product range which was very easy for the customer to understand and buy, and very easy to sell, and a high-profile sales promotion based on a bingo card concept, which required cross-range sales to really earn on the scheme.*
>
> *This three-month incentive was so successful it was extended twice and some big money was earned. But it yielded a 45% improvement in sales/man and a 75% lift in profit/man. Almost all of this dropped straight down to extra net profit.*

Questionmarks

Finally, the analysis will show up the 'questionmarks' – products that look very questionable in terms of sales or profit viability; where you should be looking for rationalization possibilities.

But before you 'get out your red pen', read through the next couple of sections.

HANDLING RATIONALIZATION EXERCISES EFFECTIVELY

Product rationalization is best handled as an on-going 'good housekeeping' activity. Within this, as product manager, you should be regularly checking on the viability and rationale for the lines under your care, and trimming back as necessary.

Unless yours is a very new business, there will almost certainly be some slow-selling older lines or obvious failures which need this kind of review.

In most companies, however, this is not the way things are handled. Rationalization tends to be a 'point-in-time', almost a 'crisis' activity, addressed only when range variety has clearly got out of hand or there are pressures to cut costs.

It is therefore usually a senior management or finance-driven exercise, and often includes the kind of vertical listing of sales and profit performance we looked at in the last section. This may be the *only* analysis done, with the result that a line is drawn, below which lines are not considered viable.

From a marketing point of view, though, such a simplistic approach is likely to cause major problems. It could result in an unbalanced or incomplete range. It may delete some small but important support or 'image' lines, or 'sleepers' (important lines for the future which are not yet selling in quantity).

Marketing and financial issues to check

At the very least, the following questions and issues should *also* be addressed as part of the exercise:

1 *Where is this product in its life cycle?*
 Is its low performance because it is obsolete, or because it has only recently been introduced?

2 *What linkages does it have with other products?*
 Is it an independent line, or does it have to be considered in combination with related items?

3 *What is the effect of its deletion on business coverage?*
 Will deletion have adverse consequences for smaller national markets or segments, or with certain key customers?
 How will it affect our competitive position? Will it leave us with an incomplete range?

4 *What are the full financial consequences of deletion?*
 Will overheads be reduced, or just be reallocated across other lines, damaging their viability?
 Is there dependent stock to be written off, specialized plant or other resources which will become underutilized, suppliers who will need to be compensated? Are there 'opportunity costs' involved?

Apart from these considerations, it is often useful to do some more 'thinking around' the exercise and ask some fundamental questions from two different directions.

What do the market (or individual major customers) really *need*?

It will almost always be *less variety than you are actually offering*, and may cause you to reappraise the requirement for many lines which, with the simplistic 'cut out the small ones' approach, would not even be up for consideration.

Let me give you two more examples from the chemical company we were looking at earlier.

(a) Industrial washing-up liquids (similar to the product in the squeezy bottle by every household sink), are needed in a range of at least three concentrations or 'activity-levels' (measured in % activity of detergent in the formula). But broadly, these run in 5% steps:

10% or 15%	'Cheapies'
20% or 25%	'Regular' product
30%, 35% or 40%	'Premium' or 'super-premium'.

So an absolute minimum of three, or, more realistically, a range of six or seven varieties give full coverage. But we had nearly 40, including most % steps and many 0.5% steps.

Many of these had resulted from individual customer requests or from someone's 'good idea', like 'Why don't we offer an intermediate premium product at 22.5%?'

The cost equation on products like this is very simple. Labour cost does not vary with activity of product and material cost change is very low as a percentage of total cost. What *does* cost significant money is downtime and uneconomic production runs, as does stockholding costs on low-selling lines. So it is actually *cheaper* to supply the 17.5% customer with a 20% product, and let him feel he is getting a bargain in the process.

(b) The same detergents were offered in 26 different shades of green (totally unnecessary, as four or five met over 99% of requirements), and in 48 different combinations of brand, pack size and bottle type (six or twelve – depending on brands retained – give 100% coverage).

I think you get the point by now. The range had 'just growed' like Topsy. No one had looked at it *rationally*, from a hard-nosed market perspective. Over 80% of total variety could be trimmed out and still affect less than 1% of business.

In fact, the tidy-up actually resulted in *more* business, because the range was now so much easier for customers to understand and salespeople to sell. Each product had a purpose and a positioning which could be easily grasped. Instead of 'What do you want?', the approach became 'This is what you need because ...'

What are *we* really trying to achieve?

The standard answer in most companies is 'to save costs' or 'to improve profits' (and occasionally to reduce investment, free up space or release tied-up cash).

How you can seek to reduce range costs

In the standard case of **cost reduction**, you need to dig deeper to see where costs are *really* being incurred, and an approach like Michael Porter's 'value chain' is quite useful in this process.

In the case of most manufacturing companies, the big costs tend to be in materials or components, in the production process itself, or in holding final goods stock.

So areas like key component, raw material, or packaging standardization are obvious targets, as these will save costs of acquisition and in manufacturing – but still allow the necessary variety in final product (e.g. do VW really *need* 26 different gearboxes for four model lines?).

On longer-life products this same standardization also cuts costs of replacement parts stockholding and servicing.

Other important equations to look at are:

- *Production versus stockholding costs*
  Is it cheaper on lower-selling lines to have an 'economic' production run and stock, than to produce in sub-optimal batches?
- *Stock versus made-to-order*
  Should we be stocking lower-selling lines at all? Or perhaps only those which are 'immediate demand' items; the rest become made-to-order and involve no direct cost.
- *Materials versus assembly costs*
  Is it cheaper to standardize your product by 'levelling-up' on features or key components, than to produce a wide variety of 'options'? (This is the reason why Japanese cars have so many 'extras' as standard).

How you can improve range profits

If **profit improvement** is the main aim, there are several lines of thought you can apply:

- Can you *improve average performance by cutting out the loss-makers or lower profit-performers* which will not significantly affect your marketing position?
- Where you have 'alternative' products, can you *switch emphasis to the more profitable lines* and improve your mix performance?
- Can you *replace less profitable products with more profitable ones*?
- Do you have opportunities left to *strip further cost out of less profitable lines* (ideally in ways which will not adversely affect market acceptance), or to *push up prices* without this being wiped out by volume losses?

Looked at in this way, **deletion** is only one option within a rationalization exercise where your prime aim is improved profit performance.

MINIMIZING THE 'DRAG FACTOR' OF LOWER-PERFORMING LINES

In fact, in many companies, you are better to concentrate on minimizing the 'drag factor' of major lower-performing lines than to just go through a largely 'paper' exercise of taking out smaller-sellers which do not significantly affect your overall performance.

Table 5.2 gives an example of a company where you are responsible for five product groups, each of which has a number of items within it. You are charged with the task of rationalizing this range, with the prime objective of improving range profitability.

Study Table 5.2a first, and prioritize the product groups to decide where your overall priorities should be. (What further information would you need before any final rationalization decisions were taken?)

Table 5.2 Minimizing the 'drag factor' of low-performing lines

Table a Prioritizing profit groups

Product group	Sales (£000)	Gross profit (£000)	O'head (£000)	Net profit (£000)	(%)	Investment (£000)	ROI (%)
A	600	120	90	30	5	300	10
B	2251.2	393.6	384	9.6	0.4	480	2
C	1680	420	168	252	15	1008	25
D	210	(30)	12	(42)	(20)	400	(10)
E	120	(18)	12	(30)	(25)	192	(15½)
Total	4861	855.6	666	219.6	4.5	2380	9.2

Table b Assessment of products C and E

Product group	Sales (£000)	Gross profit (£000)	O'head (£000)	Net profit (£000)	(%)	Investment	ROI (%)
C	1680	420	168	252	15	1008	25
E	120	(18)	12	(30)	(25)	192	(15.5)
C+E	1800	402	180	222	12.3	1200	18.5

Table c   Performance of product B

Product group	Sales (£000)	Gross profit (£000)	O'head (£000)	Net profit (£000)	Life stage
B1	180	60	30	30	Growth
B2	420	84	24	60	Maturity
B3	960	120	180	(60)	Decline
B4	480	120	116.4	3.6	Growth
B5	211.2	9.6	33.6	(24)	Launch
Total B	2251.2	393.6	384	9.6	

Product E is a loss-maker, but Table 5.2b tells you that products C and E are almost always sold together as a two-product system. How would you assess their joint situation and what actions does that suggest?

Product B is your biggest selling line but has very low profitability. So study Table 5.2c and think about what rationalization or other corrective actions could improve the performance of the B range.

When you have thought about the issues involved, turn to the Appendix and see if your own ideas agree with what is suggested.

LATE-LIFE PRODUCT ACTIONS

An important, but frequently neglected, area for many businesses is how to effectively handle your late-life products, particularly when you want to ensure a smooth handover to a new replacement.

Handling older lines

As we mentioned earlier, some high capital-cost products can be extremely good cash-generators in late life. They may be full Cash Cows, or at least perform as 'mini cash cows' if niched effectively. So for Boeing, it is very interesting to still sell reasonable volumes of older aircraft like the 747 or 737. And for car manufacturers, it is worth incorporating significant extra value in older models to maintain volume up to the launch of the new one.

Similarly, many companies in defence industries can still obtain worthwhile business in secondary or Third-World markets on fully depreciated products which have become obsolete in primary markets.

It does not always work out that way, particularly if production space or other key resources are required for new lines. This is why

Ford 'killed off' the Capri, even though it still enjoyed good sales in Britain and was making £26 million profit a year. The production space at Dagenham was needed for Sierra, which the company believed it could make far more profit on.

In some high-tech markets, like PCs or certain electronic components, 'old' may be as little as two years, and opportunities for selling earlier lines (like 386 against 486, or Apple Classics) are fairly limited.

The basic rules to apply

However, the basic rules are fairly similar for most product and service businesses:

1 Make sure you have taken every opportunity to *take cost out of the product and related costs of marketing it*. That way, you can still operate effectively on lower volumes, or even (if necessary) lower prices.
2 *Minimize any investment* in the older line to that which is absolutely necessary to keep it viable. This applies to technical effort and to areas like product stocks, advertising, literature or support material.
3 *Reconsider your pricing approach.* Sometimes with lower costs, you can think of bringing prices down to encourage better residual volume. In other cases, you may even be able to creep your price up and improve profitability. Check if the sector has become less competitive (previous competition dropping out). See if the key remaining buying groups are 'laggards' or extreme loyalists, who will stay with you anyway. But don't *overdo* it !
4 *Apply more focus.* Try to avoid wide-angle activities or support. Keep everything tight and well-targeted on the main remaining customer targets and geographical pockets of business. (This is basically the marketing approach being applied by BT with telex.)
5 (Sometimes) *consider repositioning or relaunch.* An example of the former is the BAe Hawk aircraft, which has very successfully made the transition from a 'fighter' to an 'easy to use, easy to learn' trainer and support plane.

   Relaunch is more tricky, and while we can all think of odd successes like Wright's Coal Tar Soap, far more companies have wasted a lot of money trying to recreate past glories.

   It basically depends on the strength of the brand and the continuing relevance of the product. But nostalgia also plays a part, particularly with older age groups. Cadburys have had a number of successes, particularly with old Fry lines. As have Elida-Gibbs with some older toothpaste brands.

Planning an orderly exit

The final area we need to look at is when the old product is about to
be phased out and replaced by the 'new model'. Here, basically, you
must plan the wind-down of the old product as thoroughly as the
build-up of the product about to be launched. You must also be fully
aware of, and managing, a number of difficult balancing acts at this
stage. Key ones are often in the following areas:

● **Production volumes and your own and dealer stocks**

There must be sufficient stock to 'carry over' to the new product
without major stockouts and lost revenue, *or costly clearance exercises.*
Where production is right 'up to the death' of the old product this
is easier. You just need to keep fine-tuning your run-out forecasts
based on latest stock and order data. When production stops
earlier, and in some businesses this may be several months earlier,
the whole process is much more of a gamble. You prepare your best
estimates and hope for the best. If your stocks run short, it is
sometimes possible to 'juggle' dealer stocks to ameliorate the worst
problems. If stock does not move as expected, you are into
clearance exercises.

● **Price and perceived value**

You may have incorporated a lot of 'extra value' into the older line
to keep sales going. So, be careful its replacement does not seem
too 'stripped down'. Likewise with special financing deals; think
about whether some bridging actions are required to avoid a dip in
business with the new line. Also be careful about major 'price
steps' occurring from the discounted old to the full-price new
product, which may cause resistance.

● **Trade support and direction**

The run-out product may also have received heavy discount and
promotional support at trade level. You have to ensure the same
'step' effect does not blunt *their* acceptance of the new product.
Where the older line is not actually being deleted, you also need to
check that excessive 'switch-selling' is not occurring at trade level.

CHAPTER CHECKLIST

How can you improve your management of existing products?

1 Do you consciously think about your *strategic focus* at different life
cycle stages? Specifically, are you anticipating the shift from
volume to value-orientation effectively?

2 Are you effective at picking up 'forced change' factors affecting your products early enough? How could this be improved, so you can keep the initiative and be more *proactive*?

3 Study the checklist on how you can *improve product penetration*. Highlight what you feel are *your* best options or necessary actions.

4 If you have any problem products, use the thinking process recommended to identify the *real* problems, then plan how these can be addressed.

5 Conduct a portfolio analysis of your range. What is this telling you?

6 Look at your range in terms of the suggested sales and profit matrix. Does this require you to consider any changes in priorities, or any actions to improve overall range performance?

7 Review your range in terms of whether, and how, it needs to be rationalized, using the lines of thought recommended. Specifically, look at whether the main issue is *variety reduction* or *improving the performance of larger 'drag-down' lines*.

8 See if you can identify ways to improve your handling of older lines, or the handover process to new products.

Further reading

Baker, M.J. and McTavish, R. (1976) *Product Policy and Management*, MacMillan

Day, G.S. (1986) *Analysis for Strategic Marketing Decisions*, West Publishing Co., ch. 6, 7)

Handscombe, R.S. (1989) *The Product Management Handbook*, McGraw-Hill, ch. 2

Magrath, A.J. (1989) Eight ways to avoid marketing shock. *Sales and Marketing Management*, April

Porter, M.E. (1985) *Competitive Advantage*, MacMillan, ch. 2

6 Presenting, promoting and supporting your product

Packaging and point of sale presentation – Branding issues – Recognizing the in-built problems of advertising and promotion – Using the tools of promotion effectively – Developing effective promotional programmes – Working with your agency.

In this chapter we look at a number of related issues which all concern presenting your product's 'best face' to the marketplace, and promoting the business base of your product in an effective and cost-effective way.

A word of explanation first to avoid any possible confusion. We will be using the word **promotion** or **promotional** throughout this chapter. This is used in the wider sense of encompassing *all* activities which communicate non-personally with the market (known in many organizations as marketing communications) *and* those which help to push or pull the business through (in the narrower sense of *sales promotion*).

PACKAGING AND POINT OF SALE PRESENTATION

Some products of a more 'commodity' nature may not benefit from too much packaging and branding attention, but most products will. So much of what is really important in marketing is about **perception**. The way products and services are **seen by customers**, rather than actuality.

This does *not* mean you can sell a bad product as long as it is well presented. (You can – but probably only once !) But it does mean that a lot of good products are not fully recognized as such, because of image or presentational shortfalls.

Particularly with better quality or 'premium' products, packaging and brand image are almost always a vital element in their appeal and success. For example:

> *Perrier is no 'better' as a product than many other naturally carbonated bottled mineral waters, but its distinctive packaging and aura of 'specialness' helped it to international success.*

> *The L'Eggs brand of tights in the USA are not outstandingly different in quality to leading competitors, but were made special by their unique egg-shaped packaging and distinctive merchandising.*

In both these cases, and generally, packaging and brand image are closely linked, but each involves distinct issues which need to be addressed separately.

Packaging issues

For all physical products, packaging fulfils a number of functions. First, it must meet some **basic requirements:**

- *It must give product protection and offer good utility features.*
  If it needs to be poured, it should allow easy pouring, without waste or mess. If it needs to be opened to allow usage, it should be easy to open. The Tropicana pack is a good example of both these points, as against other fruit juices in standard tetrapaks.
- *It should be of appropriate size, contents or composition for the intended use or user segment.*
  For example, a 32oz bottle of Heinz Tomato Ketchup may be a week's supply to a heavy user family, but a year's supply to a low user.
  If car steering and suspension replacement parts are always fitted in pairs, then this is how they should be presented – kitted up with all the fixing parts needed to do the job.
- *The product's name or variety type, product description and use instructions should all be clear.*
  Print colours used for these purposes (or used generally in a design) should be carefully checked out in a real-life display environment. Some designs which work well in flat art in the studio nearly disappear in certain ambient lighting conditions on display.
  Any labelling copy or layout should also be checked for legal or regulatory requirements.

Secondly, the product's packaging should support any **branding or image requirements.**

- *Common 'house' or range branding colours, logos or imagery may be important, and need incorporating correctly.*
- *The product must clearly convey the 'quality', 'value', etc. image of its own identity.*
  In this respect, it may be under- or over-dressed in the way its packaging is perceived.
- *Every element of its design should be supportive of its imagery.*
  This includes its outer packaging where this will be used in display environments.
- *It should be distinctive but also easy to recognize on display or in use.*

Merchandising issues

Your product may need to be displayed in a wide variety of retail environments.

- Where this is **on-shelf** or **on-counter**, this requires stability, stackability, good display qualities and – sometimes – a simple display or dispense form of intermediate packaging (e.g. toothbrushes).
- Where **rack** or **stand** display is used, you need to ensure your product fits available space or display requirements (e.g. blister packs or eurohooks). You may, in fact, have to provide your own merchandising units for some outlets, to optimize display opportunities.
- For **free-standing** display, you may need pedestals or stands, and header or tent cards. The product may also need supporting with price or product cards, or literature dispensers.

Many multiple outlets strongly discourage some forms of point of sale material which they feel detract from their own branding and merchandising concepts. However, many independent retailers or dealers are very motivated by the provision of a range of branded display items, which may include store signage, door or window stickers, posters, application charts or product display aids.

BRANDING ISSUES

Your product or service branding may be anywhere along a spectrum from pure 'house' branding to individual product brands.

Branding approach	*Examples:*
House branding (company name only)	● Sainsbury ● Autoglym
House branding with product name support	● Vidal Sassoon 'Wash & Go' ● Cadbury's 'Bournville'
Range branding	● John West ● Oral B
Free-standing brands	● Snickers ● Preparation H

Individual free-standing brands are more expensive for your company to develop or support, but allow clearer 'brand identity' and a more exact positioning. This is particularly powerful when a brand name comes to 'own' a particular product category or set of attributes, and becomes a generic name for all products of that type.

> *'Do you have a Kleenex?'*

> *'I want this parcel Data-Posting'.*

This gives your product advantages at the *rational* level. Yours is the name on the 'shopping list' – Nescafé rather than coffee, Lurpak rather than butter – or on the tender, or company buying list.

But this can also work subliminally in your favour, where your brand is a 'known quantity' in many unplanned choice situations, and provides the 'easy' or 'safe' choice.

A strong brand identity can also be limiting or potentially confusing in customer perception terms. We all like to put 'labels' on things to make information retrieval easy. When a brand is 'filed' in a particular category it tends to stick there, together with the key attributes which make it the 'choice' product.

So when the same brand also appears in another category altogether, or is streaming messages at us which are not in line with its own associations (or even overlapping with associations held by other brands), this is a recipe for potential problems.

> *Persil means 'softness' and 'product and family care' in laundry detergents. But does it mean the same in washing-up liquids? Can it, when Fairy already owns 'mildness', 'goes further' and 'caring' in this category.*

> *If you then add the moves of Lever up the concentration scale on the original product positioning, with Persil Power (a super-concentrate which arch-rivals Procter & Gamble claim is harsh and actually damaging to clothes), you can clearly see all these issues taking place.*

Brand extension

You must have noticed that one of the major phenomena in FMCG marketing in recent years has been **brand extension**. This involves stretching the original brand name to cover more and more varieties or even product categories (as with Persil). This may be good for short-term profitability – it does not require the same promotional investment, and sales can be built up quicker – but it can also severely weaken the position and clear identity of the original brand.

Ries and Trout (1993) catalogue a whole series of US brands which have gone down this path, with positive short-term but disastrous long-term results. And the same process is proliferating the variety of many strong British brands.

Think of Oxo, the generic 'beef stock cube', which is now offered not only as Chicken Oxo, but also in Indian, Chinese, even vegetable variants. The logic is understandable, as British consumers adopt different meat preferences and cooking styles. But what started as a very clear proposition – the natural choice to make a *beefy* gravy or hot drink – (which also happened to be in a distinctive, easy-to-recognize red cube and box), is now becoming just a 'well-known stock *cube*'.

Chicken Oxo started the process, but successfully developed its own identity. All the later varieties are just Oxo with the variant description. So what does Oxo mean now? The red box has gone; the newer varieties have their own colours. And none of the newer varieties are at all suitable for drinking. Its 'cubeness' is probably its main remaining brand attribute. But several other brands offer stock cubes (notably Knorr), as do all the major multiples as own-labels – much more cheaply.

The unique 'shopping list' position of Oxo is bound to weaken over time, especially if the own-label equivalents are of good quality. And it will only take one or two below-standard variants to start undermining its 'automatic choice' status with consumers.

Extending house brands

A similar phenomenon has occurred where house branding is used. The big benefit of any form of house branding is again the lower investment required to establish a position in the customer's mind. But the house brand must clearly mean something for this to work. For example: **Johnson & Johnson** have successfully developed a range of babycare products under their house name. This has preserved the integrity of what the Johnson's name means, i.e. 'babycare you can trust'. It has even allowed them gradually to extend these associations to the wider target of 'care for delicate skin' with an increasing share of sales coming from the women's market. The process has been handled extremely well.

But the same cannot be said for many other famous house brands. **Coca-Cola** used to mean 'the original and best cola drink'. Now with so many varieties and Cherry Coke (which is not even a cola drink), what does Coca-Cola mean any more?

Guinness are going down the same path. The house name has extremely strong associations, particularly linked to Draft Guinness's attributes of 'black', 'smooth', 'creamy head' and 'different'. Most people would also think immediately of its quintessential 'Irishness'. Now two of the attributes are also being applied to Guinness *Bitter*, which clearly is not 'black' (a main source of Guinness's uniqueness and identity), nor 'Irish'. Nor is it 'different'. When other brands using the Draftflow cans are already offering 'creamy' bitters (most notably Boddingtons, who have achieved clear leadership in this category), what are Guinness doing?

They will no doubt enjoy some incremental sales, but will have great difficulty wresting leadership in category from Boddingtons. In fact, they are severely constrained from doing this, because the more they stress the link between Guinness and *bitter*-style beer, the more they dilute the distinctive identity of their core product and their company.

RECOGNIZING THE IN-BUILT PROBLEMS OF ADVERTISING AND PROMOTION

When you are new to the job, it is very easy to believe the myths that advertising and sales promotion are all 'glitz and glamour' and 'something that anyone can do'. In fact, these are probably collectively one of the most difficult and demanding parts of your job, and require a high degree of skill and professionalism to enjoy any degree of success.

For a start, you need to learn several areas of vocabulary (almost like learning a new language) to be able to communicate effectively with the various experts in print, production, media etc. You also need to be very clearly aware of certain common problems that any form of promotional activity has to overcome. For example:

It is very easy to spend too much or too little...

There is almost invariably some 'wasted' spending on major advertising campaigns and exhibitions. Most product managers will also at some time go 'over the top' on merchandising aids or literature for products which do not really justify that level of spending.

On many other activities, spending may not be sufficient to get you 'over the sight line', properly support your image, or achieve any result.

...or to spend in ineffective ways

A proportion of limited budgets are frequently committed to 'personal preference' activities (e.g. racing sponsorship), or other activities which may boost corporate ego but do little for business.

Common problems will occur in achieving the right balance between the 'push' and 'pull' elements of your promotion. Too much push gives overstocks and demotivated dealers or salesforce. Too much pull can create unsatisfied demand and maybe help competition if this situation is a lasting one.

Messages may not always be properly 'tailored' to their audiences, or unsuitable media or timing may come into play.

It is often difficult to measure results

Cause and effect are often difficult to connect because of the 'noise' effects of other company or competitive actions. Strategic activities are particularly difficult to measure because of their timescale.

Multiple message sources

Customers receive a wide range of messages about your company and products – not all of which are planned or intended – and some of these may be less favourable than you would like.

You need to appreciate the total information network and sources they use, both in the company and the marketplace, in building a (hopefully preferable) view of your product.

Depending on your product field, this means you may need to plan to communicate effectively with specifiers or influencers as well as buyers or users; maintain active links with relevant trade press; and listen carefully to what competition or suppliers are saying about your product.

In-company, you need to cover not just salesforce or service people, but also other individuals or departments in contact with the market such as Internal Sales or the Help Desk. They all need to be 'singing off the same songsheet' in terms of your product.

Customer indifference

Some customers may be highly interested in your product, but many more will require highly skilled communication to develop any registerable interest or attention, or to influence them to act in the way you would like.

In some cases you may have 'communication overkill' to overcome, as for example in the telemarketing or direct mailing of replacement window organizations. In others, the main problem is the inherently low-interest nature (or postponability) of the product itself, as with many financial services.

One 'acid test' you can always apply is not whether you (or your boss) understand and like an advert, or brochure, or promotion; but whether the intended target group will understand and respond to it. 'Where's the beef?' is the catchphrase from a famous US burger advert. You should be asking 'Where's the benefit?' in everything you do in this area.

Without a **'you' message** (i.e. a message that is clearly intended for a well-defined 'somebody' and contains something *they* will regard as interesting and important), you are just like a party bore. Forever talking about what *you* are interested in and just *talking at* people with 'me' messages. ('I've got this.' 'I've done that.' 'I'm bigger, faster, sexier.' Like a gorilla beating its chest.) Unless you happen to be a lady gorilla, this is inherently a turn-off.

We all know what we do with the party bore. Dump them as soon as possible. The same thing may be happening with your adverts or brochures. Unless they strike a chord in the first quick scan, the page is turned or the wastebin beckons.

USING THE TOOLS OF PROMOTION EFFECTIVELY

Strategic or tactical?

The main promotional 'tools' available for you to support your product can be broadly categorized in terms of their **immediacy** of effect.

Strategic tools

Some forms of promotion are mainly used to improve awareness, image or position. Not to give an immediate business result. They are strategic in nature.

Examples would be most long-life ad campaigns or long-term brand triggers which are used multi-media, such as Silk Cut's purple designs.

Likewise with the Benson & Hedges Cup or the Embassy World Snooker Championships.

Tactical tools

Others seek a more short-term effect, and demand some response from customers or the trade. Usually a fairly immediate one.

For example 'buy now and pay later', 'collect coupons for this special offer before a deadline', 'try this new flavour' etc.

The difference is not necessarily the tools themselves; for example, advertising can be used either strategically or tactically. It is more to do with the objectives being set (limited or broad) and the timescale being applied for results.

With limited budgets, there is often a temptation to concentrate on the tactical rather than the strategic support and development of your product. This may help your short-term results, but can also weaken your product's longer-term branding and positioning.

If all a customer receives are urgent 'close-to-sale' messages, brand attributes may become diluted or undermined, affecting the overall base for preference. This can also encourage a 'sale' or 'bargain' mentality, which may distort purchase patterns or even favour competitors prepared to throw even more short-term inducements-to-buy behind their product.

All you are doing is getting into a dogfight over today's customers – people who are 'in the market' right now, or are close enough to be pulled in. Without sufficient weight of strategic activity, you will not build any lasting position in their minds, or actually *grow* your opportunity and base of business.

You are continually opening the throttle, but not adding any fuel.

If you are not careful, many of your actions in this area will become disjointed, or fail to achieve more than transitory results. To overcome this, you need a better overall structure of what you are really trying to achieve, which is normally a stable (and hopefully growing) base of loyalist customers. These are people who have 'adopted' your product, as it is normally an adoption not just a sales-generating process you are managing.

Modelling the adoption process for your product

We'll run through some general principles of how this process usually works, but you really need to understand this in detail for your kind of product business. You need to take some time to fine-tune this so you are operating optimally for your own circumstances.

The broad stages are:

Awareness/Interest

Evaluation/Preference

Trial/Conviction

Purchase/Adoption

Awareness and interest

Your first task is to ensure all targeted customers and prospects know the product exists, and have a clear idea of what it can offer them.

For any new product, or new form of a product, this is the vital first step: raising your product above the 'sight-line' and on to their agenda of 'products for consideration'.

For existing products, the task is to *maintain* visibility and interest at an optimal level – but to find ways to do this *cost-effectively*.

Evaluation and preference

Particularly with new products, you need to take prospects beyond just being 'interested' to the next stage, where they will start considering it more seriously. Will it really meet *all* their needs? Will it meet their specific situational requirements? How does it compare with other choices?

There has to be some momentum to this stage, even if some of these prospects will not be 'in the market' immediately. Otherwise any initial interest will just dissipate.

The desired end result is to strongly predispose them towards the product: to develop a 'preference position' in their minds, which will positively influence their decision closer to the sale.

Trial and conviction

If it is a major purchase, or the product requires customers to change existing habits or attitudes, or they are just not absolutely sure it is right for them, there may need to be a stage which offers a demonstration or trial – at low cost or low risk – to convince them. For some new FMCG or personal care products, this may require samples or trial sizes as giveaways or for sale (e.g. instant tea or a new mouthwash).

Many software products are now offered on a 'try now, sign up later' basis, and satellite and cable TV together with roadside breakdown services put great emphasis on this to increase their subscriber base.

This stage is more difficult to handle for higher-value or capital items. But we are all familiar with demonstration runs in new cars, or visits to 'showhomes'. And the same principles can apply to industrial products, particularly with the use of in-company 'come and see or try' facilities or by using 'reference customers'.

Purchase and adoption

Finally, some activities may be needed to trigger the sale itself. And others to bring the customer fully on-board as a regular repeat purchaser, interested in buying other things from you, and recommending you to other prospects.

Using promotional tools and actions appropriately to support your product

Figure 6.1 contains a list of some of the major promotional tools which are available. While you are still thinking about the model we have just run through, go through this and consider the application and potential effectiveness of each for your particular product business.

	APPLICATION WITHIN ADOPTION PROCESS			
	Awareness/ interest	Evaluation/ preference	Trial/ conviction	Purchase/ adoption
ADVERTISING Main media (TV, radio, cinema, press) support media (posters, transport)				
DIRECT MAIL OR TELEMARKETING				
SALES LITERATURE Company, range or model leaflets				
PUBLIC RELATIONS Press releases, features, case histories, events (e.g. open evenings, roadshows, sports hospitality), sponsorship				
EXHIBITIONS				
SALES PROMOTION Special offers, premiums, competitions, collection schemes Point of sale material or events Dealer sales activities Gifts or loyalty incentives				

Figure 6.1   Using promotional tools to support your product

Put a star (*) if the tool can help fulfil that particular adoption stage with your end customers. Double-star (**) any which you feel would be *most* effective at each stage. (There may be more than one).

You may now like to compare your own views and experience with the general pattern which is normally found (Figure 6.2).

Advertising

Most forms of main media advertising are primarily helpful at the start of the process. They catch attention and either put you into, or keep you in, the prospect or customer's mind.

Support media basically amplify or extend this process at relatively low cost. Though they can also be used in 'teaser' exercises before the main campaign breaks, as with Vauxhall's highly effective Omega launch.

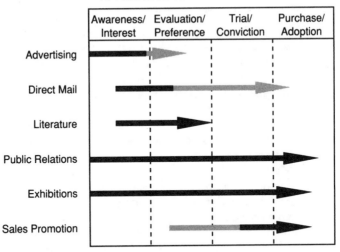

Figure 6.2   General pattern of promotional effectiveness

Direct mail
Direct mail campaigns can be used to generate interest with a wide-angle audience, but they are normally at their most productive and cost-effective when they spill over into the second column.

This requires either an existing owner body or likely user database, or the generation of one through direct response or telemarketing activities.

Literature
The extent of the role of literature does vary. In many industrial, service or specialist retail businesses you need to get into the customer's mind as a credible company or supplier first, before you can get them to consider your products. This may require not only company-level PR and advertising, but also company or 'total capability' literature to support any product-specific leaflets.

Even in consumer durable markets (such as cars or consumer electronics), a range leaflet may be useful in demonstrating total offering and capabilities – even though the customer may only be interested at this stage in one product.

Likewise, many travel companies offer a general 'catch-all' brochure, as well as more specific and targeted holiday destinations or types of holiday.

Sometimes customers don't really *know* what they want. They want to find out what is available. But at some point they will want to find out more, as part of their evaluation process. The right type of product and user-specific leaflet now comes into play, particularly if most of this process will be conducted in private study or discussion, away from any 'sales hassle'.

Public relations

If we think of PR simply in its product-supporting or business-generating function, it offers interesting possibilities in many markets as a multi-purpose tool. It can certainly be used to support advertising at the first stage, via new product editorial pieces in trade and consumer media. Many forms of sponsorship activity are also essentially awareness generators or maintainers. Relevant case histories or user stories, for example, can also extend this into the second stage.

Many staged events (such as roadshows) incorporate opportunities to see or try the product – even to buy it.

And a secondary effect of many PR activities (e.g. case histories) is often to reassure and support existing owner or buyer confidence. In some businesses, major customer hospitality (e.g. at sporting events) also keeps the adoption process lubricated – often literally!

Exhibitions

As with PR, exhibitions (and particularly different types of shows and exhibitions) can be a broad-based tool. This may be to 'showcase' a new product; to provide opportunities for prospects to collect information or discuss specific needs; to actually see or try the product in use; even to buy it.

Moreover, through on-stand or off-stand hospitality activities, exhibitions can certainly help support and extend the 'feel-good' factor of existing customers, i.e. longer-term adoption processes.

Sales promotion

Most forms of sales promotion primarily come into play for the last two steps. Some (such as sample drops or introductory offers) are to pull the product through trial to regular purchase. Incentivized **traffic-builders** are often to encourage seeing the product, or trial itself. Others are more **purchase-specific,** to trigger the sale *now* (as with limited period special offers), or to improve purchase loyalty patterns (as with Air Miles or other collection schemes). Others again are **loyalty-extenders** (e.g. calendars, desktop or personal gift items bearing your product name).

See how this compares with your own views and experiences from when you completed Figure 6.1.

But normally, the 'bottom-line' on this section is that – although there are some multi-purpose tools you can use – most fit more naturally into one (or at most two) of the stages of the process.

So you need to carefully think through your *total promotional requirements* in a sequential way, to make the *whole process* work effectively. Then manage these individual tools or activities as part of a total *coordinated approach* in executing this.

Trade promotional support

In the earlier section on merchandising issues, we touched on the types and uses of display aids which can be used to support your product in a retail or trade environment. But in many businesses where the trade's marketing skills are also well developed, this relationship needs to go much further and involve jointly planned and executed promotional campaigns.

As Figure 6.3 illustrates, normally this will include cooperative advertising activities and special events and sales promotions. These will be organized not only to optimize your selling-in, and share and quality of display, but also to encourage store traffic improvement, demonstration and effective selling-out.

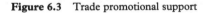

- Cooperative advertising
- Signs, posters and other point of sale material
- Display and merchandising aids
- Sell-in incentives (e.g. bonus schemes or 'one free with' offers)
- Sales training
- Printed or audio-visual sales aids
- Newsletters
- Currrent catalogues and price lists
- Product training
- Technical support
- Market research support

Figure 6.3 Trade promotional support

Equally important, but often neglected, are the provision of basic information flows, together with support activities and materials your trade partner will need, to effectively market your product on your behalf.

As well as newsletters and current literature and price lists, this may need to involve product or sales training, together with commercial and technical back-up. It could even involve sharing existing market research information, or conducting joint studies.

DEVELOPING EFFECTIVE PROMOTIONAL PROGRAMMES

All promotional actions must be carefully planned, executed and evaluated if the problems we looked at earlier in the chapter are to be overcome. For any specific action, programme or campaign, these are the main stages you need to cover:

1 Define the target group

All forms of promotional activity can have their overall and cost-effectiveness improved by being better targeted.

This requires good segment definition of your primary and secondary targets, but, in many industrial markets, needs thinking through in considerably more detail.

This may involve targeting specific elements of the decision-making unit (DMU) you have to deal with at customer level. Or identifying the full network of influences and influencers which can affect your product's acceptance or business performance.

With a new or developing product this can be particularly important, to allow you to achieve full visibility and widespread recommendation. But even an established product may still need targeted actions to reinforce your product's champions or win over the 'doubters'.

2 Define the task and key message

What *exactly* are you trying to do with this particular ad campaign, exhibition, piece of literature or sales promotion action? Is it to reinforce awareness, or to stimulate trial among a low-user group? Or to reinforce or improve repeat purchase patterns?

It could be a whole range of different things, so you must be very clear and *focused* in your thinking. Defining one or two key strategic or tactical tasks you want to achieve, will lead to much better actions *and results* than trying to do too much at one time.

Also, decide on the *key communication points* you want to get over. Again, keep this simple. You can only communicate so much at one time.

3 Define your objective

Go further than task definition, and define the *results* you want to achieve from this action or campaign. Set a yardstick against which you can measure success, partial success or failure.

For some strategic actions, this may be a set percentage improvement in a key image dimension. Or it may be tactical: to generate a certain number of leads or inquiries, organize so many demonstrations, or achieve a targeted improvement in sales to a defined segment.

On extended campaigns, do not just set 'end-game' required results, try to set 'milestone' objectives which you can track throughout.

4 Decide what tools to use

A temptation for busy product managers is just to repeat what has been done before. Your sales manager is pushing for a spring sell-in promotion, so you just pull out the folder to find out what happened before and 'tart it up a bit' for this year. Or your boss is saying 'We normally run an ad campaign prior to our major exhibition'. Does this sound familiar?

It is very easy to get carried along and just keep repeating what may *or may not* have worked before. Which may *or may not* really be in line with what you have defined as your key promotional tasks. Just because 'that is the way we always do it' or your boss or colleague wants it done that way.

If you do not have budgetary control, you are down to using persuasion. But if it is *your* budget you are spending, what you must do is follow the logic of what you are trying to achieve, and carefully review the options for achieving that.

Is advertising really the right answer, or would PR or high-quality targeted mailings be better? Do you *have* to attend that expensive exhibition, or would you be better to organize your own roadshows? Does it *have* to be a travel incentive again, or is there a more appealing sales incentive you could use instead?

Sometimes you will also have to make decisions on *how* you will use a particular tool. For example, should we build a coupon or a freephone number into our direct response ads? Can we have all our existing products on the stand and still give the necessary prominence to our new product?

5 Set and allocate the budget available

When you have decided on the detail of your action or campaign, it is relatively simple to cost this up (or, normally, for the agency concerned to do this for you). This is arriving at the budget by the so-called 'task method'.

If you are wise, though, you will have put some pre-thinking into your available budget; have thought about the business benefits to be gained, and what these are worth as an 'investment'. This helps overcome some of the worst of the 'too much or too little' problem and allows you to optimize spending in line with real needs and likely results. It also puts you in a much stronger position with the agency when they occasionally get carried away with their enthusiasm.

You also need to think through *how* the budget is to be spent. So, **allocations** may need reviewing in terms of areas like:

- 'Push' and 'pull' mix.
- Spending on primary and secondary targets.
- Creative, production and execution splits.
- The timing of any spending (e.g. in advertising, the balance between achieving your initial impact and sustaining the message over a more extended period).

6 Manage all elements of development and execution

We will look shortly at working effectively with your agency. But in the context of managing a specific campaign or action, remember:

- *All* planning and development stages need equally careful attention. Do not take your 'eye off the ball', or be tempted to push things through 'on the nod' because of work pressures.
- If changes do need making, do this as early as possible in the process before they become expensive. Then check that they *have* been done, in line with what was agreed.
- Check *all* sign-offs and bills carefully. Firmly but politely challenge any discrepancies or overruns, and do it while it is fresh.

7 Wherever possible, measure results

This may be possible from company data (as with sales or salesforce performance), or it may require research (as with changes in attitudes or image).

For many activities, the *timescale* over which results are measured can be critical. Many forms of short-term promotion have a 'peak and dip' effect and you need to measure long enough to assess the 'net' effect. Fig. 6.4 illustrates what frequently happens here.

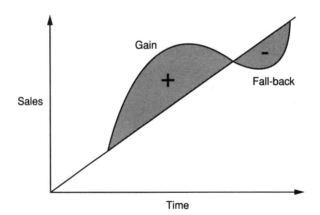

Figure 6.4   Measuring the complete effect

Your tactical ad campaign or promotional action may appear to give some improvement in overall business, but in many cases the effect may have been largely the result of shifting the *pattern* of business (i.e. pulling forward business you would have enjoyed anyway).

If you really want to get 'scientific' here, you need to first establish what your baseline business would be without the action (often just a matter of extrapolating the underlying trend and making seasonal or other adjustments to 'clean' it up). Then measure for long enough (for example, on a one-month promotion you probably need to measure sales for three months afterwards) to establish the peak and dip effect against baseline business. This gives you the **net sales gain** effect.

Even more revealing is to convert that sales performance into extra gross profit generated, then subtract the cost of the promotion to see if it 'paid off' in terms of extra contribution:

Net business result	=	Net GP gain	−	Cost of promotion

This can be a very salutary exercise. Many product managers find when they do it that much of their promotional spending is not really 'profitable'. Or that certain types of action give a much better business result than others, and show the way such actions should be prioritized for optimal business results.

In other cases, you may need to track **substitution** or **'halo' effects.**

Where business is likely to be switched between alternative products, this can usually be anticipated. Both sales and profit effects can then be planned and tracked. The 'halo' effect is sometimes more difficult to see in advance, but a high-impact campaign or promotional action can sometimes have this effect of helping to pull other business through with it. And the extra sales and profit generated offer you the opportunity to build an excellent case for further support, both externally with your trade partners, and internally with your own management.

The role of the salesforce

Many of the promotional actions we have talked about are highly dependent on the support and effectiveness of the salesforce.

Unless you deliberately *plan* for their involvement, all too often this can end up as an 'afterthought'. Or they may not be fully aware of activities on your product, or properly briefed to action them. As a result something will inevitably go wrong, followed by mutual recriminations.

So give some thought to:

● *Planning*
  Involve sales management at the planning stage, where their practical market knowledge and insights can be of great value, in terms of what will really work 'on the ground'. You may also need to plan salesforce availability for some events (e.g. an exhibition in

the summer), or to avoid potential clashes with the programmes of product manager colleagues.

● *Presenting*
When a major promotional event is coming up, cover the wider sales team affected with a pre-event meeting, or do it via their own sales meetings. Ensure you make their role clear, provide any training or materials required, and effectively motivate them.

● *Follow-up*
(This is the part that is most commonly forgotten!) Keep the salespeople fully informed on the progress of the action (via newsletters, for example), and particularly inform them of the results achieved after the event. Where appropriate, thank them for their contribution.

I have made all these points in relation to your own salesforce. But clearly, if you are working with agents, brokers or other trade partners, similar points apply.

WORKING WITH YOUR AGENCY

Most of the activities examined in this chapter will require the high-quality involvement of your advertising agency (or other specialist agency support).

Agency-client relationships can sometimes be problematic, but there are five main areas where problems are *most* likely to occur:

● Quality of briefing and company-generated product information (*your* side of the partnership)
● Communication (two-way)
● On-going working relationships (two-way)
● The creative solutions being presented (agency *and* client)
● Money (and how *they* are spending it)

If you know about them, and have some idea how best to deal with them, it will help to make this important relationship more productive and profitable for you and your product. We will go through each in turn, making a few major points for you to consider.

1   Quality of briefing and company-generated information

Remember the expression 'garbage in – garbage out'? The quality of work your agency can provide is normally in direct proportion to the quality and clarity of the strategy thinking and support information you build into your briefing. And for technical products, this often means you have, at least partly, an 'educational' job to do so that they fully understand your product.

But your agency also needs a good-quality flow of on-going information about your product. Not just sales and shared research data, but also a full update on your other activities with the product (like planned pack changes, new product plans, planned sales actions etc.) which will affect their own thinking or planning.

By investing this time and effort, you will normally get better-quality and more error-free work coming out of the agency.

2 Communication

It may seem strange to list this, as you are both in your own ways professional communicators. But problems frequently occur here.

The answer is normally to *keep communication channels short and simple*.

The agency may want to field a number of people in meetings and various managers from your own company may need to get involved from time to time. But for regular verbal and written communication try to keep everything going through yourself and your account handler. That way, he or she can be fully accountable for managing the work of the various agency specialists and for personally following up any requests or chases you want to make. You *need* that time.

Also, you can act as the prime channel into the company in all matters concerning your product, or the supply of information back to the agency.

If your boss or other managers feel they need to get involved occasionally, brief them fully on what you are doing and ensure that anything they discuss with their own agency counterparts is consistent with this.

Too many cooks really *do* spoil the broth here, and misunderstandings can easily arise and become major problems affecting the overall relationship.

3 On-going working relationships

It is important you strike the right tone here. In all your dealings, be friendly, but be firm and assertive when necessary. Agencies are often very relaxed and informal organizations. Warm personal relationships can, if you are not careful, go too far towards the 'buddy-buddy' end of the scale. So never forget that, though it may be a close partnership, you are the client and it is your (or at least your company's) budget which is being spent.

Do not be swayed into actions or decisions you do not agree with. You can, and should, say no when this is the case. Firmness, when backed up by reason, is a much better basis for an honest relationship than false agreement and later let-down.

4 The creative solutions being presented

Many agency relationships fall foul because of disagreements over creative work. Sometimes, it may be shoddy work from the agency, but more commonly it will be because what they are coming up with does not conform to your preset ideas. Where it is the latter, make sure you **listen** and keep an **open mind**.

Give their ideas a *proper* hearing and stay open-minded on solutions. Not always, but sometimes, their 'off-the-wall' idea is intuitively the right one – the 'big idea' that will really communicate your key message most effectively.

If you are not sure, check it out with research. Or just apply a simple commonsense checklist, such as:

- Will it appeal to the target customer?
- Will the message be understood?
- Is the 'tone' suitable for the target audience?
- Does it conform to agreed strategy, image and corporate parameters?
- Can it be delivered within budget?

If all the answers coming back are positive, maybe it is you who should be re-thinking your position on the ad.

5 Money (and how they are spending it)

This is probably the most common area for effective relationships breaking down, with size of various fees and some areas of cost or expenses being particularly sensitive areas.

In many agency agreements, media commissions or pre-agreed fees cover the main workload, with only 'extras' charged above this. Here, it is often the 'nickel and diming' of expenses which causes aggravation.

For many smaller accounts, though, it is 'pay as you go' and every quote or bill can raise the blood pressure. If you are in this situation, it defuses much of the emotion if you agree an hourly or day rate and quotes are broken down in terms of the time required for that particular job.

When the bills come in, find time to check the invoices against what was quoted. There may be some overruns (many of which will have been verbally agreed by you), but even if the totals look OK still check, as savings in one area may have been wiped out by unauthorized cost elsewhere.

If changes need making, or items challenging, do it quickly.

The following are some of the most common ways in which agency costs can be higher than necessary:

- **Standard of presentation:** e.g. ideas are presented to you as finished artwork, when rough art sketches ('scamps' would be enough at that stage.
  Solution: carefully specify what standard of finish you want.

- **The cost of changes seems too high**
  Solution: if the changes are down to agency error (e.g. literals or factual errors) or because the work is off-brief or not of an acceptable commercial standard, they should cover this. If you want to make changes to what was briefed, you normally pay. So make sure the changes are made early, preferably rough art or draft copy, before change costs start to escalate.

- **The cost of 'extras' is too high**
  Solution: some extras are really 'normal' in the agency business, such as using taxis or couriers extensively (and expensively). Many others arise when you are chasing tight deadlines and overtime rates and surcharges come into play. You can specify or negotiate some of these items (e.g. use post not couriers), but mainly the solution is to plan better and allow more time.

- **Production costs are too high**
  Solution: on many small budget accounts, these can represent 20%, or even more, of total advertising budget. Try to avoid too wide a spread of media, or too many forms and sizes of the ads. Organize film or photographic shoots so all possible options and requirements can be covered at one session. Use library shots whenever possible.

- **Media costs seem high**
  Solution: if you have a sizeable budget, think of operating (at least on a trial basis) through a media specialist and switch the agency to fees. Check that all possible savings are being made (e.g. series or multi-title discounts). Check whether any premiums you are paying (eg. for special positions) are really justified by results.

- **Print costs are too high**
  Solution: any print work placed through the agency will carry a mark-up (in a range normally from 10 to $33^{1}/_{3}$%). If you want to save this, place print work direct. But be prepared to 'shop around', as prices will vary considerably (largely depending on size of run and how busy the printer is). And you will have to do your own quality checking.

CHAPTER CHECKLIST

Checks on how you can improve the presentation and promotion of your product

1 If they apply, check through whether your product fully meets all the requirements covered under packaging issues. Likewise for merchandising. What can be improved?

2 Think about your branding approach, and extend some of the points made here with the recommended reading. Now, are you sure you are using the right branding approach?

3 How many of the in-built problems of promotion clearly apply to you? Can you see how some of them can be minimized or overcome?

4 Think about the total 'adoption process' customers would tend to go through in your product area. Then check that you are covering *all* parts and stages of this process effectively.

5 If you have not already done so, work through Figure 6.1 for your type of business.

6 Check again through the stages of 'developing effective promotional programmes'. Highlight where you can make improvements in the way you operate now.

7 How many of the points in 'working with your agency' apply to you? What are the key actions *you* can take to improve relationships? What should you be pushing the agency to do?

Further reading

Arnold, D. (1992) *Handbook of Brand Management*, Century Publishing

Brannan, T. (1993) *The Effective Advertiser*, Butterworth-Heinemann

Davis, M.P. (1993) *Business-to-Business Marketing and Promotion*, Hutchinson Business Books

de Chernatony L. and McDonald, M.H.B. (1992) *Creating Powerful Brands*, Butterworth-Heinemann.

Hart, N.A. (1993) *Industrial Marketing Communications*, Kogan Page

Kapferer, J-N. (1992) *Strategic Brand Management*, Kogan Page

Kotler, P. (1988) *Marketing Management – Analysis, Planning, Implementation and Control*, Prentice-Hall, ch. 20-22

Ries, A. and Trout, J. (1993) *The 22 Immutable Laws of Marketing*, Harper Collins, ch. 11-13

7 Making the right pricing decisions

Factors impacting on the 'right' price for your product – The influence of these factors on your pricing strategy – Optimizing price/volume/profit relationships – Tactical and multi-level pricing issues – Better ways of delivering value with your product

Price is one of the most important and far-reaching variables within your marketing mix:

- Your product's price is normally **highly visible**, particularly as an 'easy' comparative measure in more competitive markets.
- It can be a **powerful signal** of either quality or value.
- It can therefore significantly **affect your image**, acceptability or credibility within your product category.
- In some circumstances, it can be used very effectively as a **competitive weapon**.
- And it has a major **influence on** the **volume** of sales you are likely to achieve, and thus influences both **sales revenue and profit**.

I want to fully explore these profit links in this chapter, but also think more deeply about not just 'price' in isolation, but also about what makes it the 'right price' and how we can maximize feelings of 'value' for our products.

FACTORS IMPACTING ON THE 'RIGHT' PRICE FOR YOUR PRODUCT

Out in the marketplace, your price needs to work at customer level, has to work competitively and has to be appropriate for the wider market conditions you face.

Customer factors

At end-customer level there are four considerations of particular importance.

1 Ensure your price sits within an acceptable range for its category

This may apply to individual products or product elements, or to the overall price for a multi-part product or system.

The 'acceptable range' you face may be broad for higher quality or performance items, but much tighter at the 'standard' or 'commodity' end of the scale.

In some markets you may also have to recognize 'barrier prices', above or below which it is difficult to operate; or relate to established 'price points' which customers use for reference.

2 Reflect your strength of image, offering and market position in your own price position within category

The message here is, 'Don't sell yourself short.' Customers can handle a justified premium much more easily than a price out of line with their perceptions.

3 Build in any key segmental differences

The 'right price' may not be the *same price* for all parts of your business, and in many consumer markets this may also involve using different brand names or channels to reflect this.

For example, a shirt manufacturer may offer products with only marginal quality or design differences across different retail outlets. Clearly, the price could not be the same in an up-market boutique, quality chain store or 'discounter' environment.

In industrial markets, different vertical markets, or applications or use situations being served, may similarly require major, or more subtle, price adjustments.

4 Accommodate the need for 'deals' or built-in discounts

Some national markets, channels and end-customer segments are more motivated by a 'good deal' (i.e. higher discount) than by a competitive list price. For example, cleaning fluids for carpet extraction machines operate in this way, as did the UK car market for a number of years in the early 1990s. Much of US retail business is heavily influenced by this factor.

Competitive factors

Your overall approach to pricing needs to reflect the **competitive structure of your industry**. Obvious examples are where a monopoly or oligopoly apply. But some highly fragmented industries (e.g. office supply) are the opposite, and are close to the economists' 'perfect competition' in their characteristics.

Generally, it is helpful in your own price decisions if a clear **price leader** or reference product exists, **for overall benchmarking** purposes. You can then reflect your relative strength of position and offering in your own price positioning, and ensure you reinforce the correct 'signals' of where your product sits, relative to competition.

In many parts of the computer industry IBM tend to fulfil this function for follower competitors, as do AT&T (USA) and British Telecom (UK) in telecom network services.

At the micro level, it may also be necessary to get into more detailed **feature or specification comparisons** versus major competition, particularly in more rationally oriented business markets, or in contract or tender work. Most of the car industry 'majors' also work in this way in handling the detailed pricing of their model line-up.

Wider market factors

Getting the price right for customers, and competitively, is usually the major issue you need to sort out. But some products may also require an overlay of wider factors to be built into your thinking. This may need to include:

- The **economic environment** you are facing, and its impact on the elasticity of overall demand, or the price sensitivity of some segments.
- An understanding of where the product category is in **life cycle** terms. How much intrinsic 'added value' does it still have?
- **External** legal or governmental **constraints**.
- Comparisons with **indirect competition**. For example, the relative pricing of cans, bottles or cartons in the packaging industry.

The price you are reviewing or setting also needs to meet a number of company requirements.

Cost and profit factors

We will look a little later at the impact of price on volume and profit. But commonly, you will be tasked with **achieving volume, sales revenue, margin or profit targets** for your product, and price will have a major effect on whether some, or all, of these are attainable.

Generally a 'cost-plus' approach will not work satisfactorily in the marketplace, but your price *may* need to reflect the **recovery of investment costs** (e.g. tooling or network provision) in some circumstances. Or anticipate **expected cost changes** in others.

Company goals and position

In product areas with well-documented markets, your performance objectives are also likely to include **share position** or **growth** targets. These will be directly affected by your pricing approach.

There may also be **wider company goals** you need to be in line with, such as customer satisfaction, lowering 'lifetime costs', or overall company image. Your product's **role in the company's portfolio** may be an important overlay on your thinking.

Main positional issues flow from whether you are seeking to operate in a **niche** or **mainstream** market setting; also whether your product is a **price-leader, follower** or **new entrant**.

In niche markets, you often have more scope to determine your own price level; in more competitive mainstream markets this is often competitively determined.

If you are one of the leading products in your category, it does not normally pay to be too out of line or aggressive in your pricing approach. Particularly in mature categories where there is no extra business to pull in, this will normally just result in competitive reaction and everybody making less money. However, this does not prevent some small share operators or new entrants being very aggressive on price, sometimes with ripple effects through the industry.

In some markets, particularly FMCG, there is also the key issue of own-label pricing versus established brands, which can at times be very predatory in nature. Sainsburys, with their 'Classic Cola', have taken this approach against Coca-Cola. At its attractive price level, the own label lookalike rapidly generated a 60% share of Sainsbury's cola sales, which translates into roughly a 6% national share of the market.

THE INFLUENCE OF THESE FACTORS ON YOUR PRICING STRATEGY

At any time most if not all of these factors will need building into your thinking in terms of pricing strategy for your product.

First, in terms of the market's overall perception of your **price/value** or **price/quality positioning**, you need to consider the options summarized in Figure 7.1. Where do you want the product to sit, or be seen to sit? What will work best, taking all the factors into account?

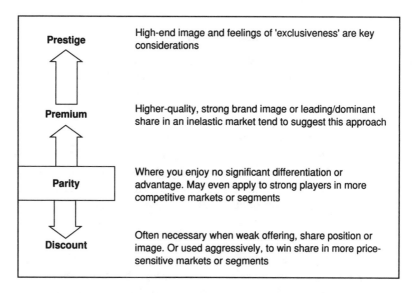

Figure 7.1   Overall price positioning

Many other elements of price strategy thinking may need weaving around this overall framework, to reflect the particular characteristics, requirements or opportunities of your marketplace. Or to meet the company's internal goals, policies or pricing intentions.

For example, you may need to incorporate, or consider the following elements.

Line pricing

Where you set price relationships to reflect market requirements or expectations, rather than cost differences, this may be simple line pricing, i.e. all items priced the same, as with different sizes of clothing. Or it may need to reflect some logical 'step relationship', as with different pack sizes or quality/performance packages.

Overlap pricing

Used primarily where the product is offered in extended price ranges, for example the car market, to allow 'double-hit' coverage and easy migration.

Slot or gap pricing

Where you develop a new price point between established levels and seek to win business from above and below. Piat d'Or has used this approach in the wine market, as did Hirondelle before them, in the 1970s.

Dual (or multiple) pricing

Used when the same (or largely similar) products have to serve different segments or channels, sometimes accompanied by a second (or multiple) branding approach. Consumer electronics manufacturers use this approach very extensively. As do Seiko, with the Lorus brand of watches.

This may also be used to develop a 'fighting brand', to avoid devaluation of your mainstream product. Maybe Marlboro should have considered this in April 1993, when it took 45 cents off its premier market-leading brand in the US, to fight off 'no-brand' price-cutting competition further down the market.

Bait pricing

Sometimes used to develop repeat purchase patterns in a category where business would otherwise be more sporadic. Examples are book or record/CD clubs, where you get the first few very cheap but are then committed to a minimum level of follow-on purchases.

The approach is also commonly used in multi-part products or systems, for example cheap (or even free) film to gain profitable processing business, or the free provision of a storage tank or dosing equipment to secure a chemical contract.

Many forms of retailing also use this approach quite heavily, through 'loss leaders', special offers or 'extra value' own labels.

Skimming

Normally used with new or improved products, particularly with less price-sensitive early buying groups. Unlike premium pricing, this approach requires a later realignment to a more competitive level, to broaden the base of buyers and users.

The aim of a skimming approach is to 'skim the cream' off the market with deeper initial margins, and give an earlier recovery of investment.

Penetration pricing

This is the main alternative to skimming, and is used in similar circumstances.

This approach involves setting prices attractively low, but not so low as to cause concern or resistance. It can be used to encourage trial (as with Bulgarian or Chilean wine); to speed up the process of adoption or market change (as Amstrad are attempting to do in hand-held 'pen' computers); or to develop a high share quickly (as Proton successfully did in the UK car market, and Hyundai are seeking to do in a number of markets).

The strategy clearly only works if you are confident you can *hold* your share, or establish a successful repeat business base, as it relies on taking profit and recovery longer-term.

OPTIMIZING PRICE/VOLUME/PROFIT RELATIONSHIPS

Profits (or contribution) will be maximized where you have the best *combination* of volume and margin:

$$Profit = Volume \times Margin$$

If you put too much emphasis on **volume** only – and sacrifice margins in the process – this may well *lower* the overall profits achieved.

Your salesforce will be happy because their figures improve and they may be doing very well on commission. But anyone can 'sell' if you are just giving the product away.

This may change if the volume improvement is very substantial and sustainable, allowing major savings in purchases, manufacturing or logistics. But often the effect of a short-term step up in volume is to *raise* fixed costs rather than to lower them.

Conversely, putting too much emphasis on achieving, maintaining or improving **margin performance** – regardless of volume consequences – can also damage your overall profit base if it results in your volume base (and share) falling sharply away.

Yet in many UK and US organizations, arbitrary margin platforms are imposed, largely at the instigation of Finance. The 'we've got to make 45% gross for it to be worthwhile' brigade result in many good products, which could be highly profitable overall, not being given a chance.

When looking at this optimizing relationship, it is rare to find a *single* price-point where profits are clearly maximized. Normally, a 'shoulder effect' will apply. Within this range of possible price positions, profits will change only slightly. But outside this range (which for some products can be quite narrow), they are likely to fall away sharply.

In real-life, the hardest part of the exercise is to construct the likely demand curve you face with this product. It will rarely be a simple straight line, as shown in an economics textbook, and will often kink around critical price points.

Your judgement and accuracy can be improved by experience; by taking maximum advantage of other experience around you, particularly senior sales colleagues; or, in some markets by using research or market tests to guide your decision.

Market reactions to different price levels, or changes in price, are one factor. But you also need to take into account the **mix of costs** your product carries. High or low fixed costs, and where you sit in relation to break-even, can also have a big impact on your pricing policy and individual pricing decisions.

Understanding your cost mix

Figures 7.2 and 7.3 show some of the effects of different cost mixes on your overall price thinking. Here, you are looking at dividing the costs of your product or service into fixed and variable:

● **Fixed costs** will not normally change with the level of business you are achieving. They may include cost areas such as premises or facilities costs, fixed payroll, financing costs or plant depreciation or maintenance.

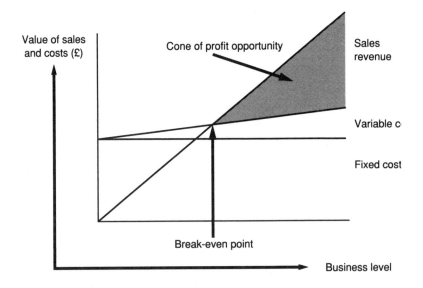

Figure 7.2   High fixed cost product or service

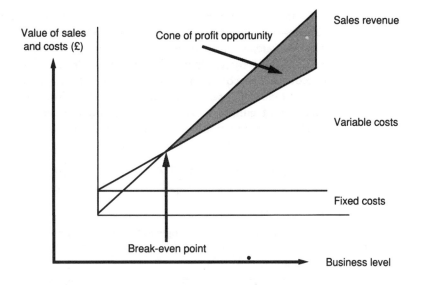

Figure 7.3 High variable cost mix

- **Variable costs** will go up or down roughly (sometimes directly) with the level of business. They will normally include a number of 'per item' costs in the product itself (raw materials or components, packaging, allocated variable labour, etc.) For some businesses, sales commission may be a significant variable cost, or freight where this is handled contractually.

In the simplified **break-even charts** illustrated, both are shown as straight lines.

In reality, your 'fixed' costs could in fact go up in 'steps' as you add extra facilities or people costs to cope with extra volume. Likewise, in some businesses, your variable costs could reduce, per unit, as you achieve economies of scale in purchasing or manufacturing efficiency.

Fixed costs are shown first because you incur them even with zero volume. Then the variable costs are added on top, to show total costs at different volume levels.

The final line shown is your **sales revenue** at different volumes. This starts at zero (no sales = no revenue), and again goes up in a straight line, i.e. it assumes your average achieved price stays constant in this simplified example.

Broad rules for a high fixed cost business

As a general rule, if your product or service is loaded with *fixed cost*, your main marketing emphasis and priority need to be **volume-oriented**.

Examples of such businesses are normally capital-intensive or service-oriented products. These include glass or papermaking, petrochemicals or high-tech manufacturing; hotels and fast food, banking and many financial services; airlines or telecom network operators. The common thread is that a high proportion of costs *have to be in place to operate in that business*, whether these be in plant, financing, facilities or specialist, highly trained people.

The reasons why this type of product demands a volume emphasis are simple when you think about them:

1 With high fixed costs, your product has a high break-even point. So you *must* achieve a fairly high threshold level of business just to be viable.

2 The cone of profit (or loss) opportunity is automatically a wider angle when your fixed costs are high (see Figure 7.2). Lose volume and you are quickly into heavy losses. Gain volume and the profit benefit is very 'rich'.

3 Once your basic costs are covered, it can pay you to optimize volume loading by selective discounting. Hence the airlines offering standby fares to fill the last few seats, or cheap off-peak call-rates from your telephone company.

Fig. 7.4 shows this diagrammatically. You would normally seek to avoid devaluing your base business. But 'at the margin', almost any additional volume and revenue – up to your optimal capacity loading – are very profit-rich, even at apparently highly discounted prices. (You achieve profit **b** rather than **a**.)

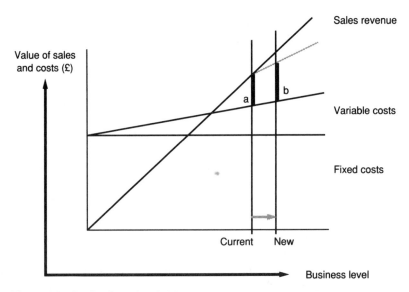

Figure 7.4 Profit effect of optimizing volume loading

Broad rules for a high variable cost business

The approach we were describing above does *not* work if most of your costs are variable. In this second scenario, you need more of a **value orientation** in your thinking.

Examples are products from most simple, relatively low-tech batch or higher volume manufacturing environments. These include many forms of metal, concrete or plastic fabrication, bottling dairies and much of basic food or clothing production. This cost mix also applies to a number of low-tech service products or businesses, such as contract packing, travel agencies or the Betterware-type doorstep selling.

The overhead (i.e. fixed) costs of operating the business are relatively low. Most costs go into the product itself, the services you are buying in and selling on, or other variable labour costs such as salesforce commission.

Here the rules are almost exactly opposite:

1 You achieve breakeven fairly quickly with this type of product or service.
2 Your product's cone of profit opportunity is very narrow, so any form of discounting (unless you can build in significant economies or higher efficiency levels) will not normally give a good profit return.

   For example, my local independent travel agent is operating normally on 6–10% margins. Even the difference between paying by cheque or credit card (with its related commission back to the card company), makes a big difference.
3 You should explore opportunities to add or enhance value around your product. This may be through better design, extra low-cost (to you) features which add to perceived value, or higher levels of service.

   It normally requires you to 'manage your mix' more effectively, with marketing emphasis put on more profitable items within your range, or more effective 'bundling' of higher-earning add-ons.

   And in some circumstances, you can also add perceived value by being a better *niche player*, or being seen as more specialist in certain areas of the business.

There is a danger with this cost mix that just **creeping up prices** (rather than genuinely adding value) can seem to pay short-term. It opens up the profit cone by raising your revenue line and, providing you don't lose too much volume in the process, can put you ahead in profit terms (profit **y** against **x** on Figure 7.5).

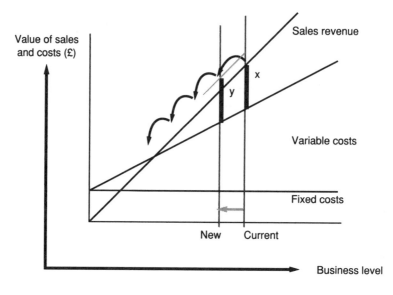

Figure 7.5   The trap of raising prices without adding value

The danger is that as a 'paper' or accountancy exercise, it still appears to pay when repeated several times. But in the process you are losing competitiveness, and probably shrinking your product's sales and share to below a sustainable competitive level. You lose 'critical mass' and become very vulnerable.

TACTICAL AND MULTI-LEVEL PRICING ISSUES

Setting prices involves the assessment of many factors to arrive at the 'right' price – the one that works in the marketplace, given those factors. But in many companies, your involvement in pricing does not end there.

Multi-level pricing

If you market through indirect channels, then policy or decisions need making in terms of the price/discount arrangements for each level of intermediary in the chain.

Broadly, trade margins should reflect the 'added value' the type of intermediary provides. For example, a specialist retailer or dealer may provide advice and service support, may carry a wide range of product variety, parts and accessories, and would therefore require a better margin platform to support this. On the other hand, a simple stockist or sales-only outlet would justify less.

However, other factors – such as the volume each type of outlet can provide – will also need to be taken into account. In many businesses, key wholesale or multiple retail chains control a high share of overall volume and can therefore demand preferential terms – even from major brands.

A common risk, though, is that these outlets may not support the end-customer image and price platform you wish to maintain. Over and above this, any extra discounts they squeeze will have a significant impact on your product's overall profitability, unless they offer significant extra volume to compensate.

The chart in Figure 7.6 shows the extra percentage volume you would need merely to sustain present profitability. To use it, start on the vertical axis and read off your product's normal level of gross profit or contribution. Then go along the horizontal axis to read off the extra discount being proposed (as a percentage of selling price). Go across and up from these two points, and where the two lines meet on the fan scale gives you the percentage extra volume you would need just to stand still in profit terms.

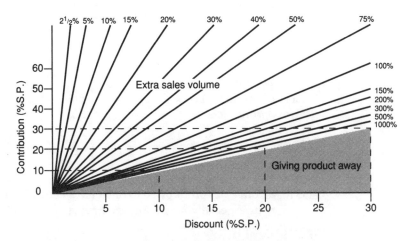

Figure 7.6 Extra percentage volume requirement from discounting

The impact of discounts on extra volume requirements

It is not only with major channel partners where discounting issues will come into play, so we need to think more generally about the impact of discounts on your product's profitability.

If we work through a simple example together, you will see how this chart works for *any* kind of discounting activity.

1   You produce 100 items at £0.6 and sell them at £1. Your overheads are £30. So you currently make a gross profit of £40 and a net profit of £10 (see simple P&L below).

	£
Sales revenue (100 x £1)	100
Cost of product (100 x £0.6)	60
Gross profit	40
Overhead (or support) costs	30
Net profit	10

2   If you discount (say, by 10%) without achieving any extra volume, what happens is that your sales revenue drops to £90 (100 x £0.9). As the cost of product remains the same, your GP goes down to £30 and, after overheads, your profit is wiped out. It is now zero.

3   Many sales people mistakenly believe that as long as they match any discount with a similar percentage of extra volume, they are OK. The reworked P&L below shows you what *actually* happens:

	£
Sales revenue (110 x £0.9)	99
Cost of product (110 x £0.6)	66
Gross profit	33
Overheads	30
Net profit	3

Going from a net profit of 10 to one of 3 is *not OK,* however you look at it, especially when you are having to sell 10% more to achieve a worse result.

4   In fact, *providing the overheads or support costs do not change,* you cannot get back to a profit of 10 on the bottom line until your gross profit is back to 40. You do not need to be a mathematical genius to see that at the discounted price level (£0.9), getting 30 up to 40 requires a percentage volume climb

of $33^1/_3$%, not 10%. If we go through the P&L again you will see how it works out:

	£
Sales revenue ($133^1/_3$ x £0.9)	120
Cost of product ($133^1/_3$ x £0.6)	<u>80</u>
Gross profit	40
Overhead	<u>30</u>
Net profit	<u>10</u>

So, when we discount the price of a (normally) 40% gross profit line by 10%, we need a third extra volume just to earn the same profit as before. Think about it:

- This is actually a worse result. We are now earning our 10 on sales of 120 (8.3%), instead of 10 on 100 (10%).
- How many products can realistically sustain a 33% growth rate, except in the extreme short term? Can yours?
- Also, we have made a big assumption: that our overheads and support costs will remain the same. In reality, both may need to rise to support this growth. And if the 30 goes up, so does the required gross profit, and this cranks the sales growth requirement up even higher... just to *stand still* in £ profit terms!

Understanding Figure 7.6: the implications for your product

All Figure 7.6 shows us is the extra percentage volume climb required to maintain profits, assuming other costs do not rise, when we apply extra discount activity behind our product.

So, if we use the chart to repeat the little exercise we have just done mathematically, we go to 40% on the vertical axis and 10% on the horizontal. Go across and up and you will see the two lines come together just to the right of the 30% line on the fan scale. (That is the $33^1/_3$% we have just worked out in the exercise, but the chart gives you an easy 'shorthand' way of arriving at the approximate volume climb needed.)

If other costs *are* likely to rise, the chart does not help you. You need to do this with your accountant as a second-pass exercise.

What the chart *does* clearly show you is that:

1 Any percentage extra discount you offer requires a higher percentage of extra volume to even stand still in profit terms. There is *always* a **multiplier effect** at work here.
2 If you have the good fortune to manage a product with a high percentage GP (usually a high fixed cost business or a product able

to sustain premium or prestige prices), then the multiplier effect is more modest.

3 However, if you normally operate on lower GPs or in a commodity business, be very careful of *any* discounting activity because the multiplier effect is much more severe. For example, if you were to discount a 20% GP line by 10%, you would have to *double sales* to stand still in profit. Not a healthy game to play!

4 Smaller discount steps penalize you less than big ones. Many product managers and sales people automatically think in 5% (or at least 2 1/2%) steps. What's wrong with 1%? If you turn it round and look at the **profit benefit to your dealers** of that 1%, they also enjoy a multiplier effect on their own margin. You will see this if we look at another simple example.

Let us say the dealer normally enjoys a 25% margin on your product. So they buy from you at £75 and sell at £100, giving a £ margin of £25. An extra 1% discount from list (25% to 26%) drops their buying-in price to £74 and raises their £ margin to £26. If they continue to sell at £100, this gives them a 4% better trading margin.

$$\frac{26}{25} \times 100 \quad = 104\%$$

Similarly, if you give them an extra 2% (really generous, this!), this is worth an extra 8% as an improvement on *their margin*.

$$\frac{27}{25} \times 100 \quad = 108\%$$

You don't have to 'give it all away' for your offer to be attractive to them.

Tactical price or value adjustments

In most businesses, the issue is not just simple discounting. There are also likely to be a wide range of further price or business support activity adjustments which may be brought into play on a tactical basis. Many of these start as short-term or promotional schemes but, once offered, are often difficult to take back.

This applies particularly to any activities which affect your trade partner's cashflow, such as extended payment offers. Most dealers or retailers suffer constant cashflow strains. If you offer later payment for a period, when you go back to normal payment terms they will face a 'double-hit' – two payments together – and most will not be able to cope with this. *Everything* may then be extended.

Price activity	Manufacturer to dealer	Manufacturer to buyer	Dealer to buyer
Cash discount			
Volume discount			
Seasonal discount			
Free delivery			
Trade-in allowance			
Ad/promotional allowance			
Price hold			
Longer warranty			
Extended credit			
Lower/zero interest			
Sale or return			
Package deals			
Retrospective rebates			

Figure 7.7   Tactical price and 'extra value' adjustments

Figure 7.7 is an exercise it is very useful to do for your product area. Down the left-hand side are a selection of some of the more common tactical price or business support adjustments. You need to add any further schemes your industry uses which are not covered here. The three columns are because some of these will be offered: by you to intermediaries, some direct to customers (normally only major customers), and some (with or without your support) by your intermediaries to end-customers.

The first two clearly affect your own profitability (*you* are giving the money away, or covering the funding). But you cannot ignore the third column, as this could also affect your end-customers' perception of your product's image, quality, value etc.

However, if we concentrate on the profit angle here, the best way to complete the exercise is to run *down each column*, and identify which adjustments apply to your product at each trade level. Some will currently be used promotionally (mark 'P'), some will have become part of normal trading (mark 'N'), and some will not apply (just put a dash).

Checks you need to make

● First, check whether the adjustments which apply are properly being **negotiated** or just being **taken** or **'given away'** with no obvious business benefit for your product.
● Secondly, check with your colleagues in Finance how much each of these schemes are **actually costing** you to operate, in terms of 'lost profit'. Look at this as a percentage of sales value and the absolute amount involved in each scheme.

Now, either yourself or with your sales colleagues, try to estimate or establish what **sales benefit** each scheme offers. (This can be difficult, as often these schemes are 'bundled' for certain types of trade partner or customer. But have a go anyway, even if you can only do it crudely.)

You will normally find that some incur very high cost for little apparent return. Others may be good negotiating points, offering high 'perceived benefit' and good business results, but at relatively little cost to you.

Then check the **total cost** to your product of all the adjustments used, in terms of their overall percentage dilution of sales value and 'lost profit'.

Unless you already do this kind of exercise, you are probably in for a shock! It will be much more than you realized.

But the good news is that improved management of how they are being offered, plus the phased withdrawal of less productive schemes (with more emphasis on the high-return options), can have a very significant positive impact on your product's profit performance.

In my own experience of handling profit improvement programmes as a manager and consultant, two of the most immediate and high pay-off ways of enhancing product profitability have almost invariably been:

1 Better management of discounts and other price/value tactical adjustments.
2 Improved range management. (Better management of mix, including the effective 'bundling' of profit-rich support lines, which we covered in Chapter 5.)

A third area, which will be covered in Chapter 8, is to seek to manage your customer or trade channel mix more effectively, as a way of optimizing overall profitability.

All these are also likely to be key focus areas for improving your own product's profit performance.

BETTER WAYS OF DELIVERING VALUE WITH YOUR PRODUCT

Pricing is rarely the only – or even the major – factor in customers' assessment of **'value for money'**. Normally, when going through a buying process, a whole range of objective and subjective factors are brought into play.

If we think of buying a car, these are likely to be some examples of each:

Objective factors	*Subjective factors*
Price	Manufacturer's reputation
Running costs	Product's brand image
Likely depreciation	Styling and design
Availability	Interior colour and trim
Convenience of	Personal attention
dealer location	given by dealer staff

Objective factors are things which are more measurable, tangible and easily comparable on a rational basis. **Subjective factors** tend to be more intangible and personal to the individual. Sometimes, they are also partly hidden or disguised. (For example, the factor in some markets of 'Can I understand/handle the technology?' or techno-fright.)

When to use these factors

With early-life products, there are often significant objective factors which can be brought into play. Your product may be discernibly faster, smaller or in some other way measurably more effective.

For example, the new generation of low-temperature 'power' detergents have an extremely good 'performance plus economy' case to make.

In many mature product areas, though, objective factors will normally have been largely levelled out by competition, and the subjective factors can become the main battleground.

In your strategy thinking for your product, this normally means you need to anticipate this process, and ensure you develop a superior position in customers' minds in terms of key subjectives, ahead of actually needing them as your main value-generating proposition.

Using subjective factors

The right **company credibility and brand image** can be very powerful in preference decisions where products are similarly priced. Handled well, they can often support a premium even when the objective factors are only equally met, because of the higher **perceived value** these factors generate.

For example, if we go back to the car market, both BMW and Rover rely heavily on 'massaging the subjectives'. This includes stressing non-functional styling elements such as chrome grilles or wood inserts, which enhance feelings of quality or 'specialness'.

Jaguar do a very similar job, but Volvo stress the subjective factor of 'safety'. (How do you *measure* this as an individual customer, other than crashing the car and seeing what happens?) Ford and Renault emphasize the subjective of 'sportiness', based on their track success, and so on.

With cars now looking and performing so similarly, the only weapons left (other than very transitory product advantages) are stressing the subjectives and price itself. As we saw in the last section, treading down the discount path is not a good option. So the right 'image' emerges as the favoured option.

In many markets, **design** and **styling** can be major factors in developing or supporting high value perception, as with Bang & Olufsen, Braun and many major perfume brands.

In a wide range of (particularly service) businesses, **customer care** which is *relevant and personal,* greatly adds to feelings of satisfaction and value. Allied Dunbar do not necessarily offer the cheapest life insurance policies, or the highest-return endowments, pensions or investments, but they are extremely successful at building trusting and apparently 'caring' relationships with their customers.

Little touches like the Singapore Airlines hostess asking 'What would you like to drink before your meal, *Mr Collier*?' clearly work – with me, at least!

Researching value perceptions for your product

There are so many factors that could come into play in your product field, it is important to identify *which are the key factors* which offer most leverage for your product. It is dangerous to guess or rely on established assumptions. There is no need to, because research (or even an internal brainstorming session), can give more definition to the process. Use the following three-step approach.

1 First identify who is involved in the total 'consider – recommend – buy – use/assess – rebuy' cycle for your product. Particularly in business markets, you need to know who can *influence the value feeling* (for example, relevant consultants), as well as all the members of the organization's own DMU (decision making unit).
2 Then, for each of the 'players' you have listed, identify the key objective and subjective factors they use and their perceived priority. You are likely to find some common threads, but also some differences of emphasis, or even totally different factors, emerging. These need building into your thinking about the product and into aspects of your marketing approach.

3 Finally, look at this comparatively. Establish where your product stands against this external scale of values, particularly as compared to key competition.

As well as providing valuable input into pricing decisions, such a study can also reveal:

● Areas where we offer 'superior value', which can be stressed in the way we promote the product,
● Opportunities for gaining an edge in perceived value which competitors have not recognized,
● Problem areas or negatives, which are pulling down our perceived value and need some attention.

Offering value rather than just lower price

A final summary point in this area is a generalization, but almost always true. When delivering 'extra value' to customers, an improved offering is a better and more attractive option in most cases than just simply 'extra discount'. This may simply be 'more – or better – product'. Or it could involve a number of further aspects of your total offering, such as better warranty, better service or free or subsidized add-ons.

> *I recently bought a new fax machine from a local dealership. I had 'shopped around' on price and knew I could buy it around £25 cheaper from the discounters. But this dealer successfully struck two chords with me which swung the decision his way:*
>
> *First, he mentioned **service**. I knew from experience of him servicing my photocopier, that if there were any problems these would be dealt with quickly and effectively. He offered trouble-free ownership and minimum downtime. (That was definitely **not** my expectation with the discounter).*
>
> *Secondly, he offered **extra value**. He could not match the discounter's price, but he bundled in an armful of fax rolls as a way of making up the difference. I rapidly calculated what this 'year's supply' of fax rolls would cost me retail, and this put me well ahead of the hardware price difference. I was 'sold'.*

In this example it did not matter that the cost to the dealer was considerably less than the retail value. He had hooked the customer (me) with better perceived value.

Think about when you have had similar personal or business experiences, and not necessarily bought the 'cheapest available'. Outside of pure commodities, the 'extra value' route works far more often than it does not.

The odds are with you in taking this approach. The customer is usually happy, sometimes even delighted. And you enjoy more profit in the process, as the impact of the 'value-generator' will normally only be a fraction of 'giving it away on price'. It represents a true win–win scenario.

CHAPTER CHECKLIST

Some issues to consider in your pricing

1 Are you building enough 'market-side' thinking into your pricing, or is this largely determined by company issues? Are there some specific factors for your product you ought to investigate, or think about a bit more?

2 Review the full range of price strategy options, in terms of their suitability for your product and market. You will probably find you are using some already, but could possibly weave others into your thinking.

3 Do you have an optimal balance between volume and margin currently? If the answer is 'no' or 'don't know', think about how you can investigate or improve this.

4 Check your 'cost mix' and think about the implications of this in terms of the way you currently are, or maybe should be, operating.

5 If you have not already done it, check whether some of your current discount arrangements make sense, when you use Figure 7.6.

6 Again, if you haven't already done it, fill in the exercise in Figure 7.7 and talk it through with your accountant and sales colleagues. Then decide what you are going to do about it.

7 Review the 'value' you are building, or could/should be building to support your product in achieving a 'fuller price'. Think particularly about the 'subjectives' you could work on.

Further reading:

Corey, E.R. (1982) *Note on Pricing Strategies for Industrial Products,* Harvard Business School Teaching Note 9-582-124

Cowell, D.W. (1993) *The Marketing of Services,* Butterworth-Heinemann, ch. 8

Hatton, A. and Oldroyd M. (1992) *Economic Theory and Marketing Practice,* Butterworth-Heinemann

Kotler, P. (1988) *Marketing Management – Analysis, Planning, Implementation and Control,* Prentice-Hall, ch. 17

Levitt, T. (1980) Marketing success through differentiation – of anything, *Harvard Business Review,* Jan.Feb. [Some ideas on maximizing 'added-value' opportunities in commodity products.]

8 Optimizing sales, logistics and aftersales service support

Links with the salesforce – Directing or influencing sales activities – Providing sound forecasts for your product – Stocking and supply decisions you may be involved in – Ensuring the right level of after-sales support – Handling feedback, problems and complaints

This chapter groups together a number of activities which are often considered 'secondary', but which can be vital in the support of your product. These are summarized visually in Figure 8.1.

They are mostly 'internal', in the sense that they involve your links with different parts of your own organization. But each also has important business, profit or customer-related aspects which need to be at the forefront of your thinking.

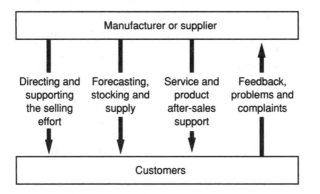

Figure 8.1 Key contact and support areas

LINKS WITH THE SALESFORCE

In most companies, product management has a major role to play in supporting sales activities.

This may involve you in providing **training support** on your product to internal or field sales, which may also spill over into similar activities at customer level. Particularly in high-tech or more specialist product areas, this is a very necessary element of your 'product expert' role.

In such organizations you are also likely to be involved in supplying or updating **product information** sheets or newsletters on product developments, new applications, new customers or technical support data.

In all organizations, you will be fighting for share of salesforce time and effort for your product. So as well as any product updates or newsflashes you send out, the 'hearts and minds' battle also needs to include regular **direct contact with sales management** and the fieldforce.

Much of this contact will be informal, but is also likely to involve more formal **presentations at sales meetings or conferences**, where the motivational element of your input will always be a high priority.

Think of the salesforce as your *'first customers'*. You have to win them over first to get maximum field effectiveness for your programmes. And you need to keep them 'loyal' and enthused in their support for you and your product.

You will need to provide, or at least contribute to, the provision of any **sales aids** required by the salesforce or intermediaries, and to optimize their practical usefulness and sales effectiveness This may be simple leaflets or sales folder inserts, but in some businesses could also involve survey or cost comparison forms, or relevant case histories.

In most companies also, you will be handling most of the activities which **improve the selling climate** for your product. As well as advertising, PR and promotions at end-customer level, this may also involve parallel activities at trade level.

In some more targeted businesses, database marketing, involving telesales or selective mailings may also figure strongly, to **generate** a quality flow of **leads** for the salesforce.

Where intermediaries are used, there may again be a liaison function, for example in **sharing marketing information** or the **joint planning of promotional activities.** You will probably be expected to contribute ideas to support selling in–selling out, display and the right point of sale environment for your product.

Finally, you are likely to be drawn, in varying degrees, into a whole range of **direct end-customer contacts** in support of sales colleagues.

Particularly in industrial markets, this may involve both a **technical** and a **commercial** element. You may be involved as a central member of the 'selling team' throughout this process, or just 'wheeled out' as the 'expert' at key stages.

DIRECTING OR INFLUENCING SALES ACTIVITIES

The title of this section suggests the possible range of your involvement. It could be a full **lead role** if you have your own specialist salesforce, or have Mini-MD level authority, where directing the selling effort behind your product is a major area of management for you. But in the majority of cases your relationship with sales will be **staff rather than line,** or at best 'dotted line'. Somebody else will call the shots, but you have to supply the bullets and the direction they should be aiming.

The regular analysis you are doing will provide much of this direction. For example, identifying slippages or low-performing areas which need specific corrective action. Overlaying these tactical activities, you need to maintain a clear **strategic overview** of where and how sales activity should be applied.

Strategic sales direction

Part of this will relate back to your **customer strategy** decisions, particularly your targeting emphasis on key segments or channels. In businesses where you are selling direct to end-customers, it is particularly vital you maintain this focus, and avoid 'scattergun selling'.

Part will also relate to your **competitive strategy,** and may require specific selling focus on vulnerable or 'softer' competitive targets. Or blocking more threatening competitive moves by appropriate field action.

But the major overlay will be to successfully execute key elements of your overall **business development/improvement strategy**. This may, for example, involve the successful launch and consolidation of key new products or variants, or the opening up of new segments.

It is also likely to include actions to manage your product's sales/profit mix more effectively, by putting greater sales emphasis on specific customers, segments or channels which offer greater opportunity in one, or both, of these measures.

Managing your product's sales mix

The issues are very similar to those we looked at in a product mix context in Chapter 5, except you are cutting in from a different perspective. Here we are concentrating on the 'market' rather than the 'product' side of the mix equation.

So instead of analysing individual product (or item) sales and profit, we now do the same for your key segments or channels. And for some highly focused businesses, or those with heavy Pareto (80:20) characteristics, we need to take it right down to individual major customers.

Figure 8.2 is developed by first doing a vertical listing of sales and profit (again, normally *gross profit*) importance, then deciding where the cut-off points should be between 'high' and 'low'. And from this, positioning segments or customers in the appropriate box on the grid.

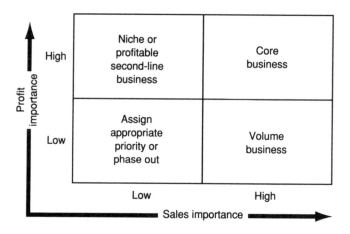

Figure 8.2 Sales direction matrix

The conclusions, when you have decided 'what fits where', are fairly similar.

1 It will clearly identify your **core business** which, because of its sales *and* profit importance, must always be given **top sales priority**. A very high proportion of your sales, and (particularly) your overall profit, will be coming from this box.

2 **Volume business** can fulfil a 'base loading' function, but does normally need some policy guidelines from you on acceptable price/profit parameters and the maximum share of mix this type of product should represent.

Without such guidance most salesforces will tend to concentrate too much on volume business (easier to sell and a bigger payoff if they get it), to the detriment of your profit mix. (One change which 'self-polices' this tendency better than anything else is to switch commission, or at least bonus payments, to a gross profit rather than a sales base of measurement.)

Key **priorities at company level** can also have a direct bearing on your business mix emphasis. Normally you would be managing for optimal profit and you need the controls in place for the category of business in the bottom-right box. However, if the key requirements switch to volume, value sales or share improvement, then this is almost certainly the area on which to concentrate to achieve this.

3 Under normal circumstances, where profit improvement or maximization is the key requirement, you also need to concentrate significant sales effort in the top-left box. This means exploiting **profitable niche areas** of your business mix, or **second-line customers, segments or channels** which are less price-sensitive, or generally offer better-than-average margin possibilities. Clearly, though, this has to remain secondary to your emphasis on core business. It is 'additional to', not 'instead of'.

4 Earlier uncontrolled selling effort, traditional areas of business which have petered out, or business development failures are all likely to be found in the bottom-left box. Also here may be some key elements of your future business development strategy which, at the moment, are small-scale and may still be requiring heavy subsidy.

Each 'pocket' of business in the bottom-left box needs **regular review** and **appropriate sales priority** assigning to it. You may also have to take some tough decisions on **phasing out** or even making an **early exit** from some of the 'going nowhere' areas.

Do it together with Sales

Rather than doing this analysis in isolation and seeking to *impose* it on the salesforce, it is better to actively seek their involvement, to ensure full understanding and commitment when it comes to be implemented. You can do this with sales management only, or with the wider involvement of the salesforce.

(A word of warning: this type of exercise often generates a lot of heat and emotion from some salespeople. You need to be fully prepared for this and be certain you can take it through to a *positive outcome*. Two things can help here:

● Do the exercise *yourself* first, so you have fully mastered all the relevant facts and arguments. But do not present this as a *fait accompli* for their endorsement. Keep it in reserve and only produce it if it will catalyse the process in a positive way.
● Do not try to force the exercise through in one pass unless it is going extremely well. Secure agreement and commitment where you can, but leave any contentious areas for later review when your arguments have been absorbed or tempers and emotions have cooled.)

PROVIDING SOUND FORECASTS FOR YOUR PRODUCT

Some companies actively involve their salesforces in 'bottom-up' business forecasts, but usually the main forecasting load will fall on you, as product manager. In doing this, you are acting as a 'bridge' between the market and the organization. There are important requirements on both sides of this:

- You have to ensure you effectively match the **market demand pattern** for your product or service; and
- You are also providing a vital **internal planning framework** which will be the base for many other functions' ability to effectively supply that demand.

The critical stage is developing your **annual forecast** for the product, though in some long-lead or high-growth businesses, your longer-term forecasts will also be important input for the resource planning of other functions.

In many companies, however, these are really little more than **projections,** i.e. a roll-out of *what has been happening* to product sales, with some additional lift for planned activities. Normally it takes a bit more thought to arrive at a reasonably sound forecast.

Separate volume and value

At the very least, you need to forecast volume and value separately. Rolling forward a value sales requirement or forecast and then 'making volume sales fit' is not a good way to do it.

Normally, you would concentrate on the **volume** forecast for your product *first*. Then overlay the value pattern of this expected business, taking into account both expected business mix changes (where different parts of the business are at different price levels), plus any planned price adjustments over the year, to arrive at your final value sales figure.

Getting your volume forecast right

Look at the 'big numbers'

The starting point is normally a smoothed projection of overall underlying product sales trends – a **'top-down'** view. To do this, you need enough back-data (usually at least the last three years), which has been smoothed (often using a 'moving average' technique), and any non-repeating irregularities (like one-off export orders or special promotions) taken out. Then you roll this underlying trend forward as a projection, to give your overall 'baseline forecast'.

At this stage, you can check this out against market projections, to make sure it looks sensible in projected share terms.

Slice up the big numbers

Next, you need to introduce a **'bottom-up'** element, which means breaking your product's sales down into individual product elements (e.g. pack sizes or varieties), segments, regions, channels or major customers – whatever is useful to allow you to see what is happening at the detailed level. Again you look at trends and likely projections, but now at the 'micro' level.

When you build it back together, this may support the overall top-down view on trend, or suggest a different (and normally more accurate) picture of what is really happening and likely to happen.

Any differences need reconciling before you go on to the next stage.

Build in all the 'influencing factors'

This third stage requires you to carefully review all company, competitive and market factors which are likely to push the actual forecast line up or down from the baseline you have projected. This needs to cover:

● The impact of your own planned activities.
● Any known competitive actions (e.g. new launches).
● Changes in the market, or factors impacting from outside the market on the likely demand for your new product (e.g. growth/decline in the customer base, import restrictions etc.)

It is important that you think this through from all angles, then keep a record of the **assumptions** you have made. This will be important later, in checking why any variations from forecast have occurred, and to give you a base for your next cycle of forecasts.

Final checks and adjustments

When you have developed your 'informed best guess, taking everything into account' forecast, think of doing two things:

1 Apply some final checks that it *does* make sense and that it is *attainable*, particularly in sales terms. For example:

● What growth in customer base does it assume? Is that realistic with the resources available?
● What about average order size, order pattern or average customer size?
● What does it require in sales or sales growth per salesperson? Is that asking too much?

Remember, your forecast is going to be translated later into sales targets. Most companies apply a 'lift factor' to these, to give an overall company sales target for your product higher than your forecast. So you need to ensure the forecast these targets will be based on does not already set unrealistic or impossible requirements, and result in salesforce switch-off when it reaches them 'in the sealed envelope'.

2 Take a little bit out in areas where it won't be noticed. This sounds like 'heresy' when you are trying to develop an accurate forecast. But there are two very practical reasons for doing this:

● If you put in a very 'full' forecast, this might come back to haunt you as a budget requirement too high to realistically attain.
● Secondly, in most companies, your management will come back asking for 'a bit more' during budget negotiations. Doing it this way, you now have something to put on the table without, again, making your task impossible. (But practise your eye-rolling and hand-wringing technique well in advance. And *don't offer until asked, or forced.*)

STOCKING AND SUPPLY DECISIONS YOU MAY BE INVOLVED IN

As was mentioned in Chapter 1, these are normally low-key areas for the majority of product managers, but they are important for some. They are also clearly more relevant where it is a *physical* product you are managing.

Read on if these decisions apply to you or just skip to the next section which *does* apply to everyone.

The most common areas where you are likely to be involved are:

● Deciding which products should be held in stock and which 'made to order'.
● Determining the stocking level of service which should be maintained by product, or what cover stock level should be held. This may need to vary by segment or major customer. Some may require 100% 'supply on demand' or a 'just-in-time' arrangement. Others may have less urgent requirements, and their orders can take a slight delay.
● Deciding on special delivery arrangements for parts of your business. This may apply only to certain customers, or to vital spare parts, for example.

And sometimes:

● Developing special programmes to shift slow-moving lines or clear out deleted or obsolete items.

Except for the last point, you are basically involved in trying to strike the right balance.

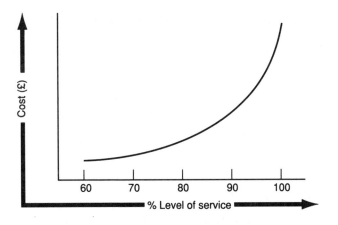

Figure 8.3   Cost of different stocking levels of service

On one side, you need to ensure that customers' genuine needs in these areas are being met, and that you are operating 'competitively'. On the other, you need to be very conscious of the cost and profit implications of these decisions. For example, as Figure 8.3 shows, operating a 100% level of stocking service (i.e. *every order met immediately from stock*) is very expensive. And significant savings can be made by dropping this to, say, 95%, if this is all that is really needed.

ENSURING THE RIGHT LEVEL OF AFTER-SALES SUPPORT

Just as you are likely to be drawn into 'pre-sales' (i.e. developmental) customer contacts, an important element of many product managers' jobs is to organize (and sometimes personally provide) key aspects of after-sales support. In many less tangible product areas, such as specialist software, your availability on the telephone or on-line to answer queries or resolve problems can be an absolutely central role.

In other settings, you may not have continuous contact personally, but would need to interface effectively with any field service or technical support teams, or with staff manning internal help-lines.

Very often, you will be the 'back-stop' in this process. When other people cannot cope, you will be called in.

This may well involve you in some further training activities, or ensuring any technical teams were supported with the right technical or problem-solving information.

With longer-life products, you may also be drawn into issues of warranties, or parts and service provision.

HANDLING FEEDBACK, PROBLEMS AND COMPLAINTS

If you are in the 'front-line' of after-sales support, you already have a very direct line of feedback. The requirement here is to ensure that the right kind of logging and analysis is done, to identify the common patterns coming out of this. To be able to 'see the wood for the trees'.

Many product managers, though, do not have constant or regular contact with the customer body (this particularly applies to most 'consumer' goods), and need to organize their tracking of customer satisfaction some other way.

Using surveys

Increasingly, this is done by surveys, either on a self-selection, self-completion basis (as with the guest questionnaires left in hotel bedrooms). Or doing this proactively as, for example, a number of banks, telephone and car companies are now doing.

One of the most comprehensive of these is Ford's CSP (Customer Satisfaction Program) scheme. This involves a 100% sample (i.e. a full census) of all their new car buyers, with questionnaires just after they received the car then again some months later. As well as being useful in quickly picking up and resolving any minor product or 'service' niggles, this also acts as a powerful lever on the overall 'service performance' of the dealer body.

Customers are asked to rate their dealer's performance across a range of key measures, and the statistics from this, together with any 'verbals' (i.e. specific comments customers wanted to make) are fed back to dealers by their Ford Zone Manager to trigger improvements.

A measure of the seriousness Ford are applying here to customer satisfaction with their dealers (apart from the millions of dollars the survey is costing), is that the attainment and maintenance of a minimum CSP rating are now built into their franchise agreement. Dealers and their key staff are also incentivized on CSP, including a so-called 'President's Award' luxury travel incentive.

But with research for this industry showing that fully satisfied customers are *70% more likely to rebuy that make*, they clearly believe this is money well spent.

Other ways of handling feedback

Other feedback mechanisms you may be able to use include warranty claims, service records and customer complaints.

In Tom Peters's *'In Search of Excellence'* he cites a New England grocery store – Stew Lennard's Dairy – which bases much of its considerable success on positively encouraging customers to pass on their complaints. The store even provides an oversized suggestion box in the store to encourage this, and it is full every day.

However, the key is not just getting the feedback (particularly the 'negatives' or 'niggles' that reduce satisfaction, but also ideas on how the store can be improved), but in being fully committed to rapidly and effectively **doing something about it**. It is exactly because customers at Stew Lennard's Dairy know this is the case that they provide the feedback in such numbers. They very quickly see *their ideas* for product or store improvements being implemented.

In a fast-moving business like retailing, the chain is very short and the business fast-moving. It accommodates this type of change, improvement and renewal very well. In your business, getting the direct feedback from end-customers may be difficult, and the process of responding to it may be much more extended in time. But that does not mean that you should *not* try!

Handling complaints

One 'open channel' from your customer body is often the flow (or hopefully, trickle), of direct customer complaints. As the 'dumping ground' for everything to do with your product, they are likely to end up *on your desk*, and join the rest of the pile there gathering dust. All too often, these are accorded low priority (low importance and low urgency) by product managers. They are seen as a 'chore'. They are answered in a desultory or self-justifying way which does not at all answer or meet the customer's genuine complaint.

A personal case history

As a normal 'Joe Soap' customer, I received a letter from a product manager with a well-known British small appliance maker. My complaint had been that I had wanted to buy one of their products under a special promotional deal, but the product was out of stock in my area for the whole of the specified promotional period. One week later, it was in stock everywhere and I actually bought it at full price.

I had (more in hope than expectation) sent in my sales receipt and the voucher, complaining about the problem and requesting they honour it even though I was a few days overdate on the promotion.

All I got back, after some delay, was a two-page monologue of a letter from the Senior Product Manager (whom we will call 'Jeremy'), which told me in detail what a tremendous success the promotion had been and implying I obviously hadn't looked hard enough to buy the product.

The basic content was 'We're OK, it's *your fault*'. No word of 'sorry'. No offer to do anything about it. Any kind of reasonable reply and I would have been satisfied. Not completely happy perhaps, but at least not *dissatisfied*. As it was handled, the outcome was a *very dissatisfied customer*.

That company is now completely off my shopping list. I do not care how good or how cheap their products are, I will *never* buy them again.

I must also have indirectly put dozens of other people off the company. Not just friends and neighbours. I have frequently used the contents of the letter as a case history of how not to do it when training several hundred product managers over the last couple of years. I make no comment on the letter. I give the factual background as I saw it and then ask my trainees for positive and negative comments on the letter and the way the complaint was handled. So far, there has not been one positive comment in support of it, but a mountain of criticism, usually including some comment along the lines of 'I know how I would feel if I received it!' 'Jeremy's' ill-considered and unsatisfactory letter may have cost his company hundreds, perhaps even thousands of pounds in lost business.

You may perhaps think this a little vindictive on my part, but it serves to illustrate what research consistently shows – that unhappy customers tell more people about problems, than happy ones do about satisfactions. And conversely, research also shows that an unhappy customer turned around can become one of your greatest advocates and loyalists.

So, look at that pile on your desk in a new light. It is *not* a 'chore'. It is a vital 'ambassadorial' element of your job. Don't be a 'Jeremy'. Make time. Do it properly. It pays.

CHAPTER CHECKLIST

Some points to consider

1 How strong and active are your links with the salesforce? Can you see any ways these could be strengthened or improved?
2 Are you being **strategic** enough in the direction you are providing to sales, or is it largely reactive? Are you applying something like

the Sales Direction Matrix (Figure 8.2) to provide overall direction and emphasis?

3 How good is your forecasting? Can you now see ways this could be improved? (Think of doing some further reading in this area.)

4 Check out that everything is as it should be, in terms of your stocking and supply, and after-sales support decisions and level of involvement.

5 Think about how you could help improve existing feedback mechanisms from the marketplace.

6 Think particularly about how well you are currently handling any complaints in your product area. How good an 'ambassador' are you – for your product, and your company?

Further reading

Chambers, J.C., Mullick, S.K. and Smith, D.D. (1971) How to choose the right forecasting technique, *Harvard Business Review* (July/Aug.)

Christopher, M. (1992) *The Customer Service Planner*, Butterworth-Heinemann

Christopher, M., Payne A., and Ballantyne D. (1993) *Relationship Marketing*, Butterworth-Heinemann

Cowell, D.W. (1993) *The Marketing of Services*, Butterworth-Heinemann, ch. 11

Handscombe, R.S. (1989) *The Product Management Handbook*, McGraw-Hill, ch. 6

Hill, R.W. (1973) *Marketing Technological Products to Industry*, Pergamon, ch. 8

Peters, T., and Watermann, R. (1982) *In Search of Excellence*, Harper & Row

Streward, K. (1993) *Marketing Led, Sales Driven*, Butterworth-Heinemann

9 Channel management

Reviewing your product's route to market – The main options: direct and indirect – Multi-level and multi-channel issues – Your role in trade marketing and developing trade relationships – The continuing rise of own-branding – Coping with increasing 'retailer power'

In this chapter we want to focus on a number of major issues which tend to be of most importance to product or brand managers. If you want a wider view, there are a number of useful references in the Further Reading section.

Let us start by trying to define what is involved in this area of marketing. If we had done this a few years ago, it would have read something like:

> channel management is a set of actions involved in analysing, planning, coordinating and controlling channel members, tasks and environments.

Now, as we will see later in the chapter, the word 'controlling' rings rather hollow for many product managers.

REVIEWING YOUR PRODUCT'S ROUTE TO MARKET

Few issues you will be involved in will be more strategic, or more influential on other aspects of your marketing, than your decisions on 'route to market'. By their nature, many commitments to a particular channel strategy involve significant set-up and support costs, will directly affect your product's level of share, sales performance and profitability, and can be difficult to change when change is required. But change is very likely in most markets, particularly when your product is subject to life cycle effects.

Life cycle changes

Particularly for products going through relatively short life cycles, it is vital you reflect your developing customer base and your customers' changing needs by planning an **evolutionary channel strategy**.

Most innovative **new products** have intrinsically high added value, but may only appeal initially to early adopter groups (hobbyists and trendsetters). They need enthusiastic and knowledgeable specialist retailers or dealers who will actively promote them to these groups; who are attuned to their needs, can spot trends and advise on possible improvements.

In return, they will probably require deep margins and exclusivity (for a period), to justify their own support and investment.

As interest in the product develops and it moves into **growth**, initial channels may not provide sufficient coverage, facing you with two options:

- Creating a denser network of specialist outlets, where you believe it will remain a limited-market product for some time;
- Moving it out into other high-quality but also higher-volume outlets, which may not provide the same service level but offer broader coverage for new buyers coming in.

As the product enters **maturity**, added value is being eroded and competition is likely to intensify. The resultant downward pressure on prices tends to force a reappraisal of whether you should swing your main channel emphasis into lower-cost mass-market channels.

Finally, in late maturity and **decline**, even lower-cost channels come into play, such as mail order or discount outlets, or sometimes handling sales in-company, e.g. via telesales.

Kotler (1988) cites the case of PCs as a classic example of this process, moving through their life cycle from hobbyist stores to dedicated chains (e.g. Computerland) and department stores, to mass-merchandisers like Sears, then finally to mail order and low-cost company direct supply.

Some of you managing early-life products may need to plan just this kind of channel evolution yourselves, but the majority of you will be managing relatively mature products where other issues tend to arise.

THE MAIN OPTIONS: DIRECT OR INDIRECT

For many mature business-to-business or service products in particular, one key area which tends to come up for review is the balance between what should be handled as 'direct' or 'indirect' business.

In theory, the 'rules' about which is the more appropriate way to handle your product's business are fairly straightforward, with normal 'deciding factors' including:

Best direct by company	*Best by intermediaries*
Technically complex products requiring high levels of support	Simple products with basic service requirements
Made-to-order or customer-specified products	Standard, stocked lines
Small customer base	Large customer base
High volume or value customers	Smaller customers
Geographically easy to cover	Geographically difficult to cover
Large-scale or planned deliveries (e.g. JIT).	Small, random delivery patterns, often requiring rapid fulfilment

But these factors are not absolute in their application. Many technically complex products or major customers are handled by specialist distributors. And conversely, many large and complex markets are handled directly by companies, as with IBM Direct, First Direct in banking or Tjaerborg in holiday travel.

Defining the boundaries of direct and indirect business

Where the whole operation is single-channel, as with Tjaerborg, this is fairly simple. The problems start to occur when business could fall into either channel, where 'mixed systems' are used.

Historically, most business-to-business products have developed via a direct sales organization (at least in their home market). So whereas most consumer products have been sold 'indirect' at least since the 1960s, their industrial counterparts are often still in the painful process of change and realignment to new channel patterns.

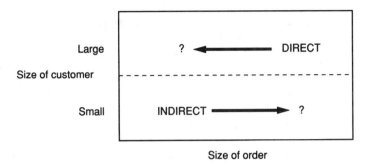

Figure 9.1   Using a mix of direct and indirect channels

A very common scenario in this process is illustrated in Figure 9.1.
Looked at in this way, some business appears to be fairly self-defining: 'We want to keep the larger customers direct, and use our developing dealer network to focus on smaller-account coverage'. However, often it is not so simple, as Fig. 9.2 illustrates:

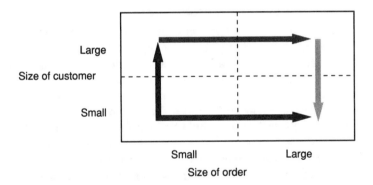

Figure 9.2   'Mixed' systems – what tends to happen

1 Most direct salesforces will not take the trouble to chase or look after the more fragmented business of major accounts (top-left box).
2 However, they will want to pick up major orders which arise occasionally from intermediate or smaller customers (bottom-right box).
3 Dealers will, quite legitimately, also want to operate in the bottom-right box, to improve the attractiveness and profitability of handling your product.

4 Over time, the better dealers will also have the confidence and credibility to want to move up into the upper half of the grid: probably top-left first, but ultimately into direct competition with your own salesforce on their major business.

The Harvard case on Wang and the problems they encountered in developing their PC business in the USA is a classic example of this process taking place. Unfortunately, they never resolved the issues fully or satisfactorily, and so were in a vulnerable position as the industry changed and temporarily turned down.

What many companies have found is that the first conflicts are in terms of 'who can sell to whom'. But these often resolve themselves by separating out order taking and order fulfilment, or account control and account servicing.

Thus, there may be some strategic accounts where you wish to always maintain direct sales links, but choose to use intermediaries to service and supply this business.

If all business goes to intermediaries, the main problem is that, after a time, they cease to be *your* customers. You lose control, but also direct feedback on business patterns and changing needs.

End-customer requirements

For your channel strategy to really work, not only you (i.e. your company) need to be happy with the arrangements made. As first-line customers, your trade partners also need to be happy and you need to ensure you take their full needs and motivations into account (even though this may involve some compromise on both sides, in reality).

But as Figure 9.3 shows, the final part of the equation is the key one: the end result should be happy end-customers.

What frequently tends to be forgotten is this last piece: *what the end-customer actually wants, needs or prefers.*

There are many customers (not all of them majors), who actually prefer to deal directly with a manufacturer, who may, in fact, regard having an intermediary serve them as an affront, or a kind of 'demotion of interest'.

There are others who value the accessibility, service level and more complete range an intermediary can offer. In many fields also, dealers are more prepared to sacrifice margin and 'do deals', so buying through them can be cheaper than direct from the manufacturer. (If uncontrolled, this can cause major conflicts.)

Key **customer motivations** also come into play. Some common ones tend to be:

● 'I want to **deal with a specialist**; to talk to the organ-grinder, not the monkey.'

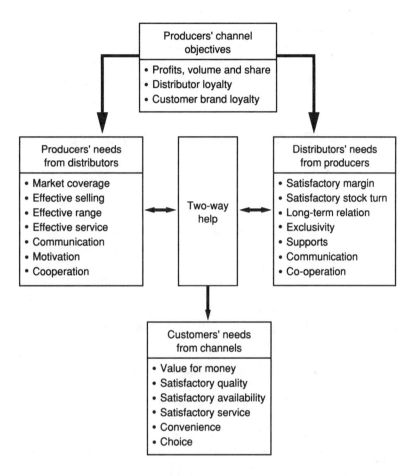

Figure 9.3 Needs satisfaction through channel cooperation. (With acknowledgement to Dr David Shipley, from the original ideas of Dr Martin Christopher.)

Unless your intermediaries are sufficiently knowledgeable and specialist themselves, this may mean you need to back their efforts up with your own sales or support links.

● 'I want to **buy comparatively** (or competitively); to have a choice of supply and not feel tied to one source'.

This may need a dual system (direct and indirect), or sufficient density or variety of intermediaries to allow healthy local competition.

● 'I want **maximum convenience and flexibility**; to get what I want, in the quantities I want, where and when I want it'.

This level of service is extremely difficult and often impossibly expensive to provide directly (except for some services, like telephone banking). It demands intensive distribution, to keep the product and related services local to the customer. In some fields, it may even require some kind of vending machine facility, to cover 'on the move' or 'out of hours' provision.

MULTI-LEVEL AND MULTI-CHANNEL ISSUES

Difficulties can arise when the market being served is very extensive, particularly when different segments or market areas have different sets of requirements.

Traditionally, the way to resolve scale issues was to operate through a multi-level channel structure, where distributors, wholesalers or brokers handled the complexity of the trade for you. Many national markets still operate in this way. But in some markets, notably the UK, traditional channels have been badly squeezed by the growth of multiples and specialist chains, where relatively few buying points at retail level offer access to a large share (sometimes the majority) of available business. Table 9.1 shows the extent of this concentration for most European markets.

Table 9.1 Shares of total domestic retail sales held by large[a] multiples in European countries

	1982 (%)	1988 (%)	1995 (%)
Austria	21	31	36
Denmark	13	16	22
Finland	N/A	11	11
France	17	18	20
Netherlands	26	28	32
Norway	24	34	38
Spain	N/A	14	18
Sweden	21	20	23
Switzerland	15	19	23
United Kingdom	56	59	65
West Germany	22	24	30

[a] Ten or more outlets
Source: Institute of Retail Studies

Wherever concentration occurs, this inevitably leads to potential **conflicts between suppliers and retailers**. Successful chains have their own marketing policy, actively develop their own trade-brand, and believe they have the best view on what *their* customers need.

This may or may not coincide with the requirements of your product or brand, and usually leads to difficulties over how much of marketing policy is determined and controlled by you as the manufacturer, and how much by the dominant channel players.

Where different channels are required to cover the whole market, further issues come into play, particularly potential **conflict between channels**.

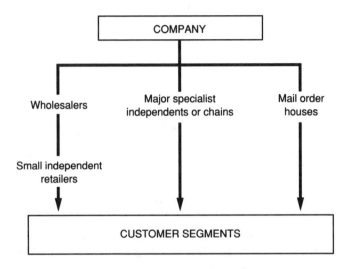

Figure 9.4   Example of a simple channel structure

Even with a relatively simple channel structure, as in Figure 9.4, price competition may arise which is harmful to your product's image and to relationships with other channel members. In this scenario, you may sometimes need to consider dual or multiple branding (sometimes involving 'own-label' supply), or at least some separation of product, to give each channel some 'exclusivity of offering'.

The real problems occur, though, when channels have become more complex, and some difficult choices need to be made in terms of where, and how, you should be concentrating your marketing effort.

Channel choices: an example

Figure 9.5 illustrates the typical complexity of many business-to-business markets, and shows the 'route to market' issues for industrial cleaning equipment in the UK.

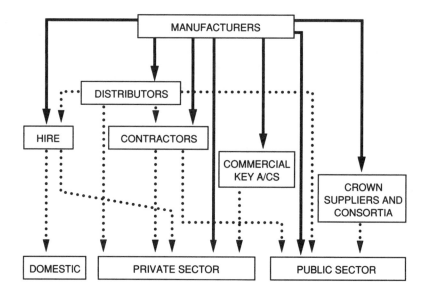

Figure 9.5 Channel structure for the UK cleaning equipment market

Looking back from the marketplace, at end-customer level the business is split roughly 45% private (industry and commerce) and 55% public sector. But each has very different characteristics:

- The **public sector** has a higher density of major buying points, most of whom prefer to buy direct, or through their own dedicated supply chains such as Crown Suppliers (mail order), or bulk-buying consortia (effectively acting as wholesalers).
- The **private sector** is much more aligned to buying via distributors, or to contracting out their cleaning (roughly 60% contracted out). But some major groups, for example certain supermarkets and hotel groups, do buy direct via a tightly-managed central purchasing function.

Other than direct selling (either territory salespeople or key accounts), manufacturers' routes to market include:

- **Distributors** specializing in cleaning materials and equipment. There are a large number of local independents but a number of key groups dominate, who tend to be 'sister companies' to the major contractors, and supply them on an 'in-house preferred' basis.

- **Cleaning contractors,** who have made their main penetration on the commercial side (primarily retail and office cleaning), but are being encouraged to seek an ever-increasing share of public sector work under the government's privatization policy.
- **Tool and machinery hire outlets** form a relatively limited channel, tending to handle larger 'industrial' type machines but also carpet extraction cleaners (which overlaps with the consumer market).

The choices for manufacturers

Any manufacturing company operating in this market faces some difficult choices:

- Whether to concentrate on **direct or indirect** business, especially in the public sector where, at user management level, you cannot be seen as an acceptable partner if you are 'working with the enemy', i.e. the contractors.
  (Public sector direct business – other than major contracts - offers high profitability, but is expected to reduce significantly as cleaning is outsourced.)
- This also involves a **public v. private** dimension, as working through distributors and contractors is essential to address the major volume segments in the private sector.

(These are summarized in Figures 9.6 and 9.7.)

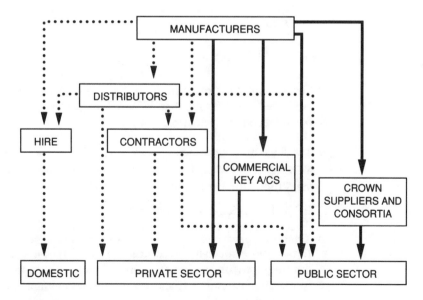

Figure 9.6 Focus on 'direct' business

- If you go the distributor/contractor route, **choice of distributor partners** is critical, as some of these companies are happy for you to supply some competitors but not others.
- Further either/or decisions involve choices of whether to supply key **buying consortia** at heavy discounts but no guarantees of sales volumes, **or** selling **directly** to their member organizations, where discounts are not so damaging to margin performance and you have better control of sales effort.

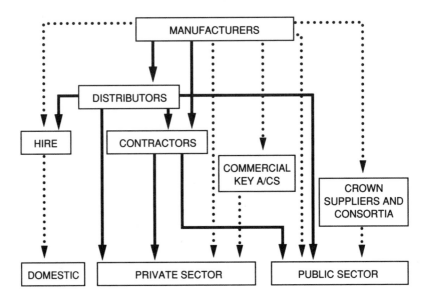

Figure 9.7   Focus on 'indirect' business

For a manufacturer with a full product range, this is further complicated by the fact that *different product groups require different channel patterns*. For example:

- Small vacuum cleaners as a commodity 'off-the-shelf' product, are supplied primarily via distributors, but are also bought in bulk (often by tender) by some contractors and major customers.

  In such a price-competitive market, there is no room for high direct-sales costs.

- Larger more specialist vacuums and other special-purpose heavy-duty equipment are bought almost totally direct from manufacturer, after extended trials or demonstrations and high levels of sales involvement.

Distributors are often not willing to stock such lines and cannot usually provide the required specialist selling effort. In any case, this is the opposite formula: low unit sales, high unit profitability but high selling costs required.

One set of channels will not work for all product groups – each needs a tailored channel approach. But clearly, this can lead to problems when handling these issues at company level.

Profit implications of channel mix

In the example we have been looking at, and in multi-channel choices generally, there are are usually major volume (and share) implications in the choices you make. You also have to consider **channel dynamics**: i.e. not just where the business is now, but how this is likely to change. What are the relative growth patterns likely to be? Or, could relatively new or unimportant channels now be the key ones for the future?

However, the factor which can often be overlooked is that there may also be major **profit implications** to the choices made.

With different prevailing price and discount levels, alternative channels, or channel members, will often offer widely differing gross profitability (or gross contribution).

For many businesses, however, this only gives a partial picture, as selling and other support costs also need bringing into the equation, to give an idea of the **net profitability or contribution** each offers.

If we look at an example this may be clearer:

	Channel A	*Channel B*
Prevailing discount level.	−22.5%	−10%
Ave. achieved gross contribution.	17.5%	30%
Less sales/support costs as a % of sales.	−5%	−20%
Yields achieved net contribution of:	**12.5%**	**10%**

Channel A demands higher discounts but costs little to serve and support. Channel B delivers richer gross profitability, but when high sales/support costs are taken into account, is actually less profitable.

This type of equation commonly applies between dealer and direct business, or between major channel members and smaller volume outlets. You need the **full equation** to really see where you should be putting emphasis to enhance overall profitability for your product.

YOUR ROLE IN TRADE MARKETING AND DEVELOPING TRADE RELATIONSHIPS

Your role in trade marketing can involve you in a number of areas right across the marketing mix, and in parallel to your end-customer -oriented marketing activities:

- **Information gathering and analysis** of overall trade business patterns and performance. As well as desk research or working with Nielsen-type data, this may also involve some direct contact, by telephone or personal visit, with trade partners to collect more qualitative assessments, or to negotiate information exchanges.
- **Product-related activities**, which could involve own-label supply issues, ensuring you meet the trade's product shelf-life, display or packaging requirements, or developing special pack or product variants for their outlets.
- **Pricing**, stocking incentives and discount arrangements where, if you are a full Mini-MD, you will be negotiating or at least setting these yourself. Otherwise, you will be contributing to any discussions in these areas with relevant sales colleagues.
- **Promotional activities**. You are likely to be involved across the whole spectrum from 'you to the trade' or joint advertising and PR, to specific selling-in schemes, merchandising aids or stock layouts, through to agreements on in-store trialling, special offers or other selling-out promotional actions.
- Occasionally, you may get involved in liaison on **administration or logistics arrangements**, or in product after-sales support. You may also be drawn into developing or modifying major customer sales forecasts, or managing dedicated stock levels.
- **Contacts through sales meetings or presentations**. Very few product managers have an 'open-line' direct access to their trade counterparts. Normally, your links will be via sales colleagues (often key account managers or trade sector managers), or on accompanied visits with them.

From time to time, you may also be involved in preparing and making trade presentations, either formally at trade conferences, or more informally to specific trade partners or prospects.

In all of these, unless you have had equivalent sales experience yourself, you need to be prepared to take guidance from sales colleagues on the style and content required to achieve a positive business result. Often this will mean cutting down on the detail you would *like* to cover, and keeping your points very short, simple and persuasive.

● **Planning**. If trade business represents a significant share of business or targeted potential, you will also need to cover this as a separate section of your product marketing action plan, and carefully monitor its execution.

Your involvement in trade marketing may vary considerably, depending on the industry or product sector you operate in.

Industrial and service sectors

Many industrial businesses still remain largely direct-sales oriented, with either embryonic dealer activities (often with a 'Cinderella' status), overseas distributors, or just a controlled slice of 'low-end' business being handled indirectly. Process chemicals and many 'capital' products fall into this group.

In some businesses of this type, however, you may also need to maintain links with consultants, public servants or managing contractors, acting as intermediaries on projects your product is feeding into.

Other industrial products, for example power tools, office supplies or small office equipment (like fax machines), are heavily – sometimes completely – dealer oriented. Others again, such as many IT products, can have fairly complex mixed systems, involving relationships with original equipment manufacturers (OEMs), value-added resellers (VARs), as well as more conventional retail trade channels.

Service businesses likewise are found right across this spectrum, from virtually 100% direct (as with banks) to 100% indirect (as with holiday tour companies working through travel agents). In between, are also a number of mixed systems of varying complexity, such as are found with airlines, telecom network providers or hotels.

In service markets in particular, it is quite common to find different providers of similar services adopting quite different channel strategies, as in the life insurance, motor insurance or pensions sectors.

As such, the trade marketing element of your job may be almost negligible, or may be a very significant element – as it is for your consumer market counterparts.

Trade marketing in consumer markets

Developing specially tailored programmes and events for key trade partners occupies a significant share of time for most brand managers in markets like the UK. ('Standard packages' work less and less well across the different demographic profiles and store-branding policies of larger, more sophisticated multiples.)

In FMCG in particular, your interface profile with trade counterparts (who may be called category manager, product merchandising executive – even product marketing manager), is likely to be more frequent and more extensive. Much of this contact will be to review the major flows of information you both have available on your product category's performance and your own brand's position within this. Planning contact may be annual or quarterly, but monitoring activities are likely to be much more frequent.

With bar-coding and electronic point of sale (EPOS) checkouts, your trade partners will often have performance data very considerably before you get your Nielsen (or equivalent) figures. This speed of data response also means they are able to check out marketing mix or display initiatives very quickly, and require an equivalent speed of decision response from you, in agreeing or implementing any changes.

Although most companies have considerably sharpened up their professionalism in trade marketing, a Mintel trade survey as recently as 1992 still showed your trade partners looking for improvement in a number of key areas. Among these were:

- More fully incorporating trade thinking into product marketing strategies.
- Providing product support which recognizes the retailer's uniqueness.
- Objective competitor analysis.
- Range review input.
- Exclusive below the line activity, either in technique or timing.
- Better new product launch liaison and coordination.

You may be thinking, 'Well, they always like to bitch, don't they?', but first check that you (or the colleagues you are working through) really are 'up to scratch' in all these areas.

The swing from advertising to sales promotion

In some advanced markets, trade sales development and product promotional support programmes are growing to the point where they dominate as a share of total promotional spending, and in terms of the share of product management time they demand.

In the USA, for example, relative spending on brand advertising shrank from 43% to roughly 25% of budget over the decade 1981-1991. Over the same period, trade promotion grew from 24% to around 50% of spending.

This swing has been brought about by the increasing negotiating power of major retailers and their **blocking power** in allowing you to achieve distribution coverage, unless they feel your product is heavily supported.

The development of category management

To get away from this 'mincing machine' of ever-increasing trade promotional spending, the latest trend in the 1990s is away from individual brand support activities and more into 'category management'. This involves building joint marketing programmes (with related store layout and planogram input), to *improve sales of the whole category* your product belongs in, *not just your own brand's relative position*.

The idea is to work in a 'win-win' partnership of increasing overall business, rather than just the 'zero-sum' equation of fighting competition for fluctuating brand emphasis and shares within the outlet.

Having gained ground in the USA, this concept is now gaining in interest in some European markets (notably the UK).

Making category management work

For your product to take advantage of the increasing interest in this approach normally requires as many as possible of the following factors working in your favour.

1 It helps if you are already **category leader** (or at least No.2) in the market, or occupy the position or perception of category leader within this partner's business.
2 It adds urgency if your category is **underperforming** within this partner, relative to the market generally.
3 You have a stronger case if your category offers **higher than average growth** or trade profitability.
4 You have to be **positive**, either **in taking the initiative** yourself, or responding enthusiastically if the opportunity is offered by the partner to you.
5 You need the **resources and expertise** available in your organization (or through agencies) to support this effectively.

To work successfully, the approach needs commitment and shared aims, together with a much higher than normal level of shared information.

It must be tailored to the end-customer profile and business approach of the retail partner. It also requires flexibility and adaptation, to make it work right down to regional or even individual store level.

Increased promotional delegation

In the USA, this last group of functions has triggered some companies (notably Campbell's Soups) into an organizational response of increased local promotional delegation. Here, the management of detailed programmes has been handed to regional or even territory-level trade promotional executives, to give the necessary flexibility and avoid the log-jam of all this detail being handled by a central product management function.

You may also have a personal interest in knowing that this has involved stripping a major slice of promotional budget from national product managers, and re-allocating to this delegated level (i.e. effectively under 'sales' control).

At present, a number of companies are still climbing the learning curve in this area. But in addition to providing the necessary marketing training for these executives (in practice, often relatively short and 'functional'), the one change which has to happen to make it really work is to change their performance measurement from volume objectives to profitability. Otherwise unscrupulous trade partners may take advantage of a scenario of working with uncoordinated low-level manufacturer partners with low know-how and big budgets to spend. Not to mention the impact on your overall responsibility for product profitability, if others are spending 'big bucks' from what was your budget, but without the same overall goals.

THE CONTINUING RISE OF OWN-BRANDING

Own-branding involves supplying your product (or something similar), to form part of the offering of a re-seller, and sold on under their own name as if it were their product. As such, 'own-branding' occurs in a wide range of businesses, whether this be:

- petrol companies pooling supplies from refineries
- value-added re-sellers adding your product element into their bundled offerings
- Mercury or others selling branded telephone services based on other carriers' networks
- Barclaycard handling the administration for most other UK credit or retail card schemes.

In most cases, the customer does not know and does not care. But the supplying and trading companies can both gain from any in-built economies. Handled well, it can be mutually beneficial.

However, in FMCG and some other highly concentrated consumer businesses (such as consumer electronics), this mutually beneficial formula does not always apply. There can sometimes be an element of coercion by retail groups, and common accusations that the store own-labels are substituting (or even replacing) branded product sales, but not making any investment in growing the market for their categories. In short, they are often seen as 'parasitic' and a threat.

Articles have been written along this theme for at least the last couple of decades (particularly during a hysterical period in the late 1970s, when Sainsbury's mix of own-label grew to 65% of their total turnover). However, more recent articles in the 1990s are generally more balanced, and have some messages which are more positive for branded goods manufacturers.

Latest trends

A good example is a 1993 article by Stephen Buck, of Taylor-Nelson. After reporting that UK own-label sales had grown from around a fifth of grocery sales in 1981 to around a third a decade later, he goes on to point out that this is not a consistent picture.

There is nothing inexorable or overwhelming in the progress. In fact, the latest figures show considerable variation by retailer (with many chains remaining predominantly branded-product based); by region (where the South of England is main own-label territory), and by consumer demographic group (where own-label acceptance is higher for mid- and high-income groups).

Other significant variations occurred by product category, with the following being among those with highest own-label penetration (more than 50% of category sales) in 1991:

Hard cheese
Frozen vegetables
Kitchen towels
Cooking oils
Evaporated milk
Fruit juices
Frozen fish
Instant milk.

At the other extreme, the same AGB Superpanel data was still showing some extremely low own-label shares in June 1992. For example:

Dietary bread	0%
Scouring powders	3%
Detergents	6%
Cat food	7%
White sugar	8%

Why is there such variety by category?

Further evidence revealed this pattern was *not* just price or discount-related. Many own-labels were roughly 20% cheaper than their branded equivalents. But kitchen towels, for example, where own-labels hold a 56% share were, on average, 8% more expensive than brands.

Similarly, baked beans with a 29% own-label share, were only 2% cheaper.

Buck suggested that certain characteristics typified markets with high or low own-label shares:

High own-label markets
● Surplus manufacturing capacity
● Commodity status
● Low technical barriers to entry
● Little product differentiation
● Low levels of manufacturer investment.

Low own-label markets
● Extensive manufacturer interest
● Technological investment
● Customer reluctance to accept own label

COPING WITH INCREASED 'RETAILER POWER'

The factors outlined above have strong messages for product managers of any company facing increased retailer power, and especially own-label substitution.

Let us add to them a little from points made elsewhere in the book, and put together a checklist of how you can most effectively cope, and perhaps even strengthen your position, against 'retailer power'.

First, you have to **keep the product initiative** through sufficient genuine innovation, product development and improvement. In doing this, you need to concentrate on improvements you can keep 'proprietary' in some way, or those which give your product a more lasting (and less easy to imitate) advantage.

They should also be real improvements (i.e. with benefits customers can appreciate and value), rather than just 'cosmetic' changes.

Secondly, our products need effectively **positioning and branding**, to differentiate them from copies, and make or keep them 'customer choice' lines.

Thoroughly check whether your marketing actions are really strengthening and **supporting your core brand values** and its fundamental 'proposition' (or reason for choice).

Be extremely careful about dissipating brand equity in a flood of minor changes and brand extensions. (Re-read the section on branding in Chapter 6 if you need convincing.) When your brand ceases to 'mean' anything, or tries to 'mean everything', then you are wide open to potential substitution by a reasonable quality retail brand, which does have consistent brand values (those of the retail brand).

Thirdly, you need to **invest enough in advertising and related PR** to give your product regular visibility. Even better if you work to develop your product's appeal via long-running campaigns which enhance easy recognition and the right 'warm feeling' towards it.

Ideally, this advertising job should be done on TV, but where this is a misfit with your buying profile, then do it through some other high profile medium which will support trade credibility in the product.

Above all, you should a**im to win on quality**, both perceived quality via your packaging and imagery, but also the real discernible quality of your product itself.

As recent battles, such as that between Coca-Cola and Sainsbury in the cola category clearly demonstrate, *both* are important customer choice factors. But product itself is ultimately the key. Ask yourself: can your product stand up to (and beat!) own-label challenges in 'blind' taste (or user) tests? Can customers really discern your superiority?

Before you rush to answer, you might like to know that a recent *Which?* survey resulted in a very poor showing for brands. In only two of the eight categories tested (cornflakes and – ironically – colas), did the branded products emerge as 'superior' when blind-tested.

Finally, can the use of a **category management** approach take you out of the 'fight' mindset into a more genuine and mutually beneficial partner relationship, where you and your key trade partners can both 'win'.

The future

The Retail Research Unit in 1991 listed some of the key retailing trends forecast for the year 2000 as:

- More concentration
- More internationalization
- Better management
- More share fighting
- More marketing orientation
- More data sophistication

- More specialist chains
- More channel power
- More demands on suppliers
- New user needs
- New ways of shopping
- Shorter shop life cycles

Clearly, the majority suggest a further rise in retailer power.

Other forecasts suggest that the trend of retail concentration is continuing in many other European countries (as we saw earlier in Table 9.1), so the issues faced by product managers in the USA and UK will soon be shared by product managers in many other markets.

But other trends suggest more of a natural 'balancing process' may be about to take place. After brand manufacturer dominance for a number of decades, retailers in more advanced markets have now enjoyed around two decades of 'calling the shots'.

If we look at the UK as to how the balance may start to be restored, I would suggest a number of factors may be 'ones to watch':

- The major multiples who have built the largest shares and pushed along the own-label challenge are now themselves under threat from simpler lower-cost retailing formulas. In a 'European' market, they are being challenged very effectively not only by Kwik Save, but by Netto (Danish), Aldi (German) and others. They are clearly also alarmed by the entry into the UK of Costco, and the prospect of other US 'warehouse clubs' following them.
- The major retailers themselves have 'brand extended' towards one-stop shopping operations. They are moving towards being unfocused 'generalists'. Just like so many department stores before them, they may find they ultimately start to lose out to better-focused retail concepts and chains.
- Finally, major retailers have benefited greatly from improved technology, particularly the information and control benefits of EPOS.

But other new technology in the home could start to have an impact by the late-1990s through improved on-screen interactive 'home shopping' services and the development of linked 'home delivery' services.

In an age of street crime, rising fuel costs, pollution and ever-increasing congestion, for how long will driving to the city centre or out-of-town retail park remain 'fun' and attractive when a more convenient and trouble-free option is available?

But, for the moment, a quotation from Mintel best summarizes the present situation:

> Although the 1990s is dubbed the era of the consumer, the fact remains that retailers hold the keys to reaching these consumers. In that respect, the battle for market share is not a consumer one, it is also one of retailer power and will be won or lost in the buying offices of the major retailers.

CHAPTER CHECKLIST

Some areas to think about in channel management

1 Do you regularly review channel strategy, either as a free-standing exercise, or as part of your formal planning process?
2 Think particularly about whether any of the following apply for your product:

- Are you effectively anticipating channel changes, to match life cycle and changing customer requirements?
- Do you have a clear policy on 'channel boundaries', especially where you have a 'mixed' system?
- Are your channel choices fully aligned with end-customer preferences and requirements?
- Have you resolved, and are you regularly reviewing, strategic and operational issues affecting potential conflict within and between channels?
- Are you taking the profit implications of 'channel mix' fully into account?

3 Use the points on your role in trade marketing (and the Mintel list of retailer-required improvements) to check where your own role could be expanded or improved.
4 Think about whether a 'category management' approach could be beneficial.
5 Use the points in 'coping with increased retailer power' to check whether you are operating as effectively as you could in supporting and improving your own product's relative power.

Further reading:

Books

Hardy, K.G. and Magrath, A.J. (1988) *Marketing Channel Management – Strategic Planning and Tactics*, Scott, Foreman & Company

Kotler, P. (1988) *Marketing Management – Analysis, Planning, Implementation and Control*, Prentice-Hall, ch. 18

Randall, G. (1990) *Marketing to the Retail Trade*, Heinemann

Stern, L.W. et al (1989), *Management in Marketing Channels*, Prentice-Hall

Articles and reports

Buck, S. (1993) Own label and branded goods in FMCG markets: an assessment of the facts, the trends and the future. *Journal of Brand Management*, 1 (1)

Buckingham, C. (1991), New databases and forecasting techniques for trade marketing, *Marketing Intelligence and Planning*, 9 (1)

Buckingham C. (1993) Onset of the Category Management Phenomenon. *Admap*, July/Aug.

Buzzell, R.D., Quelch, J.A. and Salmon, W.J. (1990) The costly bargain of trade promotion. *Harvard Business Review* (March/April)

Egan, C. (1992) Spreading the Word. *Marketing Business*, Dec./Jan. 1991/92

Grover, J. (1992) Own label closes in on the big brand names. *Marketing*, 19th March

Heller, R. (1993) Brand loyalty no longer works. *Observer*, 26 September

Marketing News (1992) Category management – marketing for the 1990s. 14 September

Mintel Retail Intelligence (1992) *Growth in Retail Branding Heightens Need for Trade Marketing*, Volume 2

Urbanski, A. (1987) Repackaging the brand manager. *Sales & Marketing Management*, April

10 Developing a sound product or brand plan

Putting planning in a company context – What your plan needs to cover – How this may differ for a strategic or annual plan – Stages in developing the plan – Specific issues of action planning, budgets and controls – Final checks to make on the soundness of your plan – How to successfully present your plan at approval stage

Many companies and product managers are intimidated by the whole planning process. They are often put off by past mistakes, or concentrate too much on the form (i.e. documentation) of the plan rather than ensuring they are following a sound process.

In this chapter we will look first at the kind of company environments in which the planning needs to take place, then go through what needs to be covered in the process itself to ensure a sound plan for your product.

We will not be looking, as such, at the actual documentation you should be using. There are many books which will give you this (see McDonald (1989) for example). In any case, many of you will be working in companies which have good documentation already in place. You have only to ensure you use it in the best way.

PUTTING PLANNING IN A COMPANY CONTEXT

In my experience and that of many researchers (see the article by Leppard and McDonald (1991), for example), marketing and product planning tend to fall into three distinct groups of companies, as in Figure 10.1.

The 'Planners'

In a relatively small number of multi-product (and often multi-national) companies, planning systems are extremely well developed and documented. At product level, this means individual product or brand managers are constrained not only by the 'system' itself, but also by the levels of planning which have already taken place above them (Corporate, Regional, National, Divisional, Etc.), to which their plans have to conform.

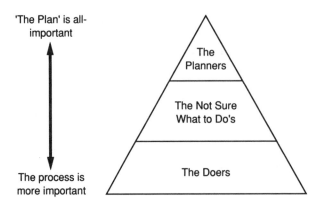

'The Plan' is all-important

The process is more important

The Planners

The Not Sure What to Do's

The Doers

Figure 10.1 Approaches to marketing and product planning

Alongside the planning process, particularly in major-brand FMCG companies, there is also likely to be a controlling policy document (often called the 'Brand Strategy'), which lays down required conformity in most key aspects of how the product should be marketed.

Generally, this type of planning tends to be highly centralized and **convergent** in its thinking (rational, straight-line, concerned with reconciling detail and numbers). It will be 'sound' in terms of the factors it concentrates on. But often it lacks the opportunity for **divergent** thinking at key stages (e.g. identifying new and fresh ways of operating, adding value for customers, or developing competitive advantage).

So plans developed in this environment tend to have a very strong 'formula' theme, where likely actions are very predictable and easy for competition to discern. 'The Plan' and its preset routines and requirements have taken over, sometimes at the expense of a healthy process of planning, and the strongest possible planning options emerging at the other end.

The 'Doers'

In many smaller or newer companies, often still based on one product, area of technology or specialist service, the 'product plan' is often, in effect, the company plan. It may or may not be formalized in a fairly simple controlling document, but even where it is, is likely to be changed quite frequently 'on the run', as the business changes.

Planning as such is largely an intuitive on-going process rather than a ritual annual event. It involves constant inputs of divergent thinking (What if we do this? What is likely to happen if this variable changes?). But may be fairly light on convergent thinking, particularly where 'reconciling the numbers' is concerned.

The 'Not Sure What To Do' group

In between are many medium-sized and larger companies (where probably the majority of product managers are employed), which are not too sure how to handle this area.

They may have tried the more formalized or sophisticated approaches and had problems in making them work. But they recognize they are too big to operate effectively without planning, so have some kind of (often incomplete) system in place.

What they often tend to use is again basically a convergent type of approach, where some type of document has to be produced by each product area – but basically just to support the 'numbers' of the budgeting process.

WHAT YOUR PLAN NEEDS TO COVER

Whatever your company circumstances, there are certain key elements any sound product or brand plan needs to cover. These are summarized in Table 10.1 along the lines of Kotler, but they basically fall into two areas:

- To be **effective**, your plan needs good analysis, clear objectives and well-thought-through strategy for your product
- But it also requires detailed action planning (including key financials), good implementation and feedback (or 'controls') in order to be **efficient** in operation.

Whatever documentation you use, you need to go through all these steps as a 'process', to arrive at a sound plan.

The reality of planning in many UK companies

It all sounds so logical, easy and straightforward. But a study in 1991 by Laura Cousins of the London Business School showed that the reality for many UK companies is a long way from this:

- Only 61% of the 385 medium–large (£10m+) UK firms she contacted claimed to prepare any kind of formal marketing plans at company or product level.

- Over 90% of companies planning only produced annual plans: there was no longer-term strategic framework for these to be set within or against.
- Only 11% claimed to include *all* the key elements of the 'textbook' approach (as in Table 10.1).
- The plans were dominated by objective setting, with some strategy thinking and action planning a poor third

    55% of plans were centred around financial objectives (for budgeting and control purposes);

    42% included some strategic analysis and/or a statement of strategy;

    only 26% covered a comprehensive programme of marketing mix actions to support the plan.

It is clear from this fairly large sample that a great many companies are not planning at all. And that most are, at best, only doing a partial job and so are unlikely to be developing plans that will:

- Really help to improve your product's performance in the market-place; and
- Provide the kind of integrated company 'team effort' behind their execution, needed for full success.

Table 10.1   The textbook contents of a marketing plan

	Section	*Purpose*
1	Executive summary	A brief overview for management skimming
2	Marketing audit (or situation analysis)	Background data on the market, product, competition, distribution and macro environment
3	Opportunity and issue analysis	The main opportunities/threats, strengths/weaknesses, and issues facing the product that the plan must deal with
4	Objectives	What this plan seeks to achieve. May be expressed in sales, share and profit terms, or using other measures
5	Strategy	How the plan will be achieved in overall terms – the 'game-plan'
6	Action plans	The detailed planning of marketing mix and other actions required to effect the strategy
7	Projected P&L statement/budget	The expected financial payoff from the plan
8	Controls	How the plan will be monitored

After Kotler, 1988

This is clearly not the most conducive environment for you to operate in, so any improvements you can suggest or effect will be in your own interests as well as your company's. Think about this as we go through more of the detail in the next and the following sections.

General principles of good product planning

1 A good plan should be rooted in reality

So an essential preliminary is to conduct a full review and issue analysis *before* committing to objectives. Those organizations which lay down preset objectives (or even fully developed budgets) as the starting point of the process risk:

- Dislocation from the 'real world' the product will have to perform in.
- 'Ivory tower' or 'fit the numbers' plans.
- Very little commitment from the product managers who need to effect them.

2 The plan should be very clear in its objectives

Not only you, but everyone else involved in the successful execution of the plan, should know exactly what is expected of them: what they have to do or achieve with the product over this planning period.

It is even better if these are expressed both as longer-term goals and shorter-term 'milestone' objectives, then all concerned can 'buy in' to where you are trying to take the product.

3 Strategy thinking should be clear, complete and purposeful

It should not be mixed in with objectives. The 'what' and 'how' elements are much better kept separate. Nor should it be buried in the detail of marketing mix planning.

Strategy is your overall 'game-plan', the consistent and considered direction you are taking in all your thinking and actions to achieve your objectives. If you don't pull your strategy thinking together in a separate section of the plan and express it simply and clearly, your action planning has no context and may be uncoordinated and therefore ineffective.

Your strategy section should summarize all the key elements we covered in chapter 3:

- The steps you will take to consolidate and develop your product's business base.
- Your customer strategy (who you are targeting, how your actions will vary by segment and what image or benefits package you will base your 'winning appeal' on).

- Your compete/co-operate strategy (who you are working with or against, how you plan to strengthen competitive position or any advantage your product enjoys).
- Your overall positioning of the product (largely defined by the previous sections).

Your strategy thinking should also be *purposeful*, in the sense that it is carefully developed to be the best overall approach to achieve your objectives, after a careful consideration of all the viable options you have available.

(There must be some 'divergent' thinking at this stage, otherwise you risk being stuck in historical 'tramlines'.)

4 The product or brand plan should be a 'working document' for the organization and you as its manager

This means the plan needs to cover all key aspects of planned perfor-mance (expressed as broken-down budgets or targets) and all key execution issues (marketing mix, timing and responsibilities) in sufficient detail to be able to constantly run alongside this throughout the period of the plan.

Plans which are written then 'put in drawers' are a total waste of everyone's time. Instead, key elements you need to track should be on your wallchart and in your diary, PC or personal organizer, and referred to constantly.

5 Finally, good planning should be a 'learning process'

Something will always occur which means that certain assumptions or planned actions do not work out as you planned. Fine. This offers you an excellent learning opportunity.

You should be constantly striving to improve the internal and external information available to you, to improve the quality of your assumptions where hard data is lacking, to actively develop and use every form of feedback which will allow you to build a better plan next time round.

Without a good plan you are 'rudderless' and reactive. You should aim to be as proactive as your particular business allows, and that means not just scanning ahead but learning from mistakes and improving your personal experience base.

HOW THIS MAY DIFFER FOR A STRATEGIC OR ANNUAL PLAN

One of your personal aims, whether your organization demands this or not, should be to have a strategic plan for your product. Whether it is a new or existing product area you are managing, you need to

Table 10.2 Strategic and annual plans

Section	Strategic plan	Annual plan
1 Executive summary	In as few words as possible, covers all the key points from below. (Try to do this in one paragraph, or as a maximum, 200-300 words).	In a one-page summary format, outlines the key issues and changes in your product's market and recent performance. Highlights key objectives, strategy refinements and actions for this year.
2 Marketing audit	Covers fundamental analysis and research on the product's market, including projections on longer-term trends.	Reviews shorter-term marketplace trends and factors to put our product's performance in perspective.
3 Opportunity and issue analysis	Uses a longer-term and wide-angle SWOT approach to underpin the rationale for the overall marketing approach being adopted.	Uses SWOT as a fine-focus tool to highlight key current and short-term issues which need to be addressed in this year's plan.
4 Objectives	Your overall goals or mission for the product over a 3-5 period (longer if appropriate).	This year's required levels of performance expressed in sales, share and profit. Plus any further significant events or achievements this plan must cover.
5 Strategy	The core elements of strategy and positioning you intend to follow over the longer-term in achieving your goals.	Key strategy developments or refinements for this year, including strategic aspects of marketing mix actions.
6 Action plans	Not applicable, though some companies use this section to outline broad marketing mix parameters, or list key planned actions for following years.	Covers all necessary marketing mix, support resource and operational actions. Includes key timings, responsibilities and itemizes costs.
7 Projected P&L statement	Outline financials for the whole period under review.	This year's P&L, normally supported by commentary on how the 'top-line' will be achieved, mix and product cost assumptions, and proposed spending to support the product this year.
8 Controls	Outlines key future milestones for tracking annually.	Lays down in more detail how this year's performance will be monitored.

have at least an outline view of both performance and positional goals, and the strategy your plan needs to follow beyond a one-year horizon. (This may be three to five years, but for some high-investment or high-technology products may need to be longer.)

For products with shorter life cycle patterns, it is particularly vital that you are planning ahead on 'next-stage' actions or developments (even though the business impact of these may be outside the one-year planning cycle). But for all products, you need some 'strategic intent' to guide your shorter-term actions.

If we go back to the basic sections of any complete plan, then Table 10.2 outlines how these two types of plan will tend to differ, in terms of what is covered as contents.

Fundamentally, the **strategic plan** looks at issues which are:

- Related to longer-term environment, performance and actions.
- 'Core' to the way the product is positioned and managed, and therefore unlikely to be changed significantly year-to-year.

It ensures effectiveness in the overall management of the product.

The **annual plan** updates and refines this overall thrust, incorporates shorter-term issues and next-step objectives, but is specifically concerned with planning detailed actions and their successful execution across the whole team involved.

So it also relates partly to effectiveness, but is much more concerned with the efficiency of delivering this year's required results.

STAGES IN DEVELOPING THE PLAN

Some of the stages of the planning process closely follow what we have already covered in depth in previous chapters. Where this applies, I will just highlight key points, but concentrate mainly on other areas which have not been covered so far or so fully.

Marketing audit

This is basically a comprehensive and up-to-date review of the key external and internal information flows we covered in Chapter 2. Some of this will be basic trend, share or performance data, but it . should also include brief coverage of key changes or developments in the marketplace affecting your product. Any significant new research findings should also be incorporated.

Table 10.3 outlines some of the forms of external analysis which can be useful. In each case, you need to relate your own position and performance to this. For example:

Market size and trends	Our product's size, share and trends
Changing customer needs and requirements	How well we have kept aligned to these changes
Key competitors' strengths and weaknesses	Our own product's strengths and weaknesses

In this last example, in more competitive or sophisticated markets you may need to roll this out into more detailed comparisons, such as:

- Product range line-up, features, quality
- End-customer or trade price competitiveness
- Image/reputation
- Promotional budget available and success of activities
- Salesforce/dealer capability
- Achieved customer or distribution base
- Product availability and supply efficiency
- Parts, accessory, service and aftercare provision.

Table 10.3 Key external factors to build into your analysis

Market situation and external influences on the product's business	<ul><li>Present market size and trends</li><li>Stage of market development including review of further potential</li><li>Market structure – channels and segments – business importance and trends</li><li>Impact of external factors or wider market trends on our product area</li></ul>
Customer analysis	<ul><li>Detailed customer segmentation</li><li>Key target customer needs, requirements, satisfactions and dissatisfactions</li><li>Variation by market or segment</li></ul>
Competitor analysis	<ul><li>Overview of competitive environment (including cooperative issues)</li><li>Review of each major competitor in terms of: comparative strength of offering market reach, share, position by segment, strategy and way of operating competitive advantages employed, resource base and commitment</li></ul>

Depending on the type of market you are in, you may be well-served (even over-burdened) with information, or find gathering this very difficult.

In both cases, though, there are likely to be at least some areas where you need to close key gaps in information with assumptions, until hard or soft information becomes available.

Opportunity and issue analysis

This next stage takes your review or audit information and 'digests' it to pull the key messages out.

Commonly, this will involve some form of **SWOT analysis,** to identify the main opportunities/threats, strengths/weaknesses and issues facing the product, which the plan must deal with.

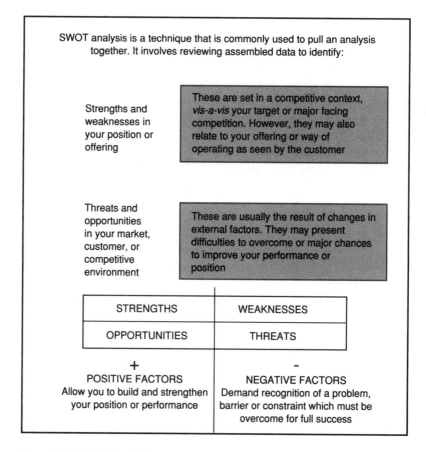

SWOT analysis is a technique that is commonly used to pull an analysis together. It involves reviewing assembled data to identify:

Strengths and weaknesses in your position or offering

These are set in a competitive context, *vis-a-vis* your target or major facing competition. However, they may also relate to your offering or way of operating as seen by the customer

Threats and opportunities in your market, customer, or competitive environment

These are usually the result of changes in external factors. They may present difficulties to overcome or major chances to improve your performance or position

STRENGTHS	WEAKNESSES
OPPORTUNITIES	THREATS

+	-
POSITIVE FACTORS	NEGATIVE FACTORS
Allow you to build and strengthen your position or performance	Demand recognition of a problem, barrier or constraint which must be overcome for full success

Figure 10.2 SWOT analysis

Although SWOT is an easy acronym, in practice you are better to look at opportunities/threats first, as they give a more complete, wide-angle view. Strengths/weaknesses then apply finer focus and provide more specific issues to consider. Figure 10.2 summarizes how this works.

In more sophisticated companies, this stage may be extended to include further 'overview' perspectives, such as portfolio or gap analysis, to give further focus to key issues.

Objectives

If you have a strategic plan, part of the function of this section of your annual plan is to incorporate key 'milestones', which must be achieved this year.

Objectives may also be guided by overall company or corporate requirements, for example, the company portfolio priority of growth or profit from your product area.

Other objectives may be needed to highlight critically important actions or achievements this year. For example:

- Secure 10 high-quality reference sites (in a new segment which will form a main area of development next year), or
- Ensure a key new product is successfully launched by a certain critical date.

So your objectives may include:

- Key performance elements
  Sales value/volume
  Desired share
  Gross or net profit
  Productivity measures or improvements.
- Key events, actions or timings which are critical to the success of the plan
- Wider company or corporate requirements (e.g. to raise company image or credibility in this product field, improve 'lifetime costs of ownership' or improve customer satisfaction ratings).

As such, they may be **external** or **internal** in their requirements.

Objectives cover *where you want to be and what you want to achieve;* they should *not* cover the detail of *how* you are going to achieve it – that belongs in the strategy and action planning sections – unless certain actions are so critical to overall success that they need 'flagging' as specific 'what' requirements.

Remember also the following guidelines for setting the objectives themselves (see Figure 10.3).

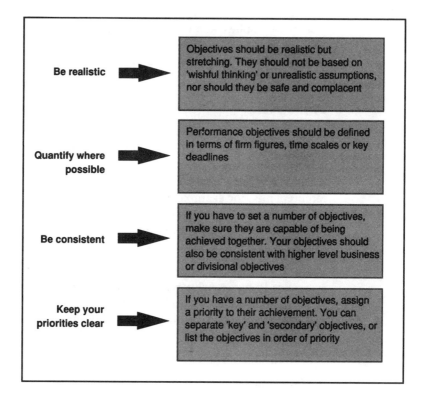

Figure 10.3 Guidelines for setting or assessing objectives

Strategy development

Chapter 3 covered this whole area in considerable detail.

When first developing a strategy plan, or the first-year plan for a totally new product, *all* aspects of the detailed strategy thinking need fully exploring and developing.

In the context of a rolling one-year plan, however, the main lines of thinking should already be in place. So you basically need to ensure all core aspects still hold good, but concentrate mainly on the detail of strategy execution for that period.

You should avoid planning too many separate strategy actions, though, and concentrate your effort and key resources on the small number of key developments or refinements which your options analysis suggests will deliver the best results.

SPECIFIC ISSUES OF ACTION PLANNING, BUDGETS AND CONTROLS

Sound analysis, objectives and strategy are the 'keystones' around which everything else is built. But to make you plan a fully effective **working document** for you and the whole team, detailed **action or implementation plans** must be developed.

What action plans require

Each major marketing action, development or support programme must be planned in terms of:

- Timetabling key actions or activity stages.
- Identifying responsibilities for these.
- Making decisions on the mix of resources (i.e. marketing mix) to be used.
- Setting overall and detailed targets for results.

Many companies lay out their detailed planning visually (as a spreadsheet across the months or quarters of the year), to show linkages and related deadlines. This can be handled very effectively using relatively simple tools such as Gantt charts.

Always try to plan your actions to a calendar (rather than just listing them), as this greatly helps the process of putting a 'through the year' budget together and any later monitoring activities.

Cover the linkages

At this stage (if not before) it is vital that you liaise effectively with all colleagues who will be involved in 'making the total plan happen'. Their collaboration and commitment need agreeing up front, not just left as hopeful assumptions on your part.

This particularly applies to **sales** colleagues. It is vital you ensure that their business targets, priorities, key deadlines and trade/end customer development plans are fully in line with, and supportive of, your marketing plan for the product.

Fine tuning

Only after this stage, with all the detail negotiated and agreed, can the overall plan be pulled together again for fine-tuning, making decisions on conflicting priorities and locking into budgets.

Much of this fine tuning will be concerned with specific decisions or resource allocations across your marketing mix. For example, you will be unlikely to be able to afford *all* the product support resources you would ideally like. So you may have to take some tough decisions on the balance of advertising and trade marketing spending, or be reviewing in detail ways of making your available spending more cost-effective or productive.

Kotler (1988) has some points to make on thinking about relative 'response rates' to different levels of spending in each area, and managing resource mix issues. These may be of more interest to those of you with larger budgets or more spending discretion (see Further Reading).

Building the budget

An important implementation aspect of your plan is to express this in budgetary terms, as a projected Profit and Loss (P&L) Statement.

The business as a whole will probably already have set an overall operating budget, but for your product area what you particularly need to think through and quantify are:

1 How you plan to achieve the required business levels, i.e. how your 'top-line' will be made up.
2 What marketing or support costs you will require to achieve this.

Building the 'top-line'

Working only with annual sales as a total figure is not very helpful. It does not tell you what your *'mix'* of business will be (which could have significant gross profit implications). Nor does it tell you *when* that business is likely to come in. You need *both* to effectively track your product's performance through the year.

This requires you to go back to your 'bottom-up' forecasts, where you broke the likely business flows down by area, channel, segment or major customer. Look at this particularly in terms of the year-on-year growth this implies, in terms of judging budgetary realism.

You also need to consider the expected business pattern over the year, so your monthly budget requirements are as accurate as you can make them. This may involve looking at:

● Seasonal patterns
● The impact of major shows or promotions
● The timing of new business from development activities.

A simpler way of building up elements of top-line budget

In companies that lack good quality market or management information, but where Sales have a good view of likely business flows, a simpler way is as follows.

(1) Start with **existing business due to repeat over the budget period**. This should be the most reliable element, as Sales have fairly firm information on booked or planned requirements from existing customers. Some 'rolling contracts' may also need to be included here.

(2) Then look at **new business from existing customers**. Try to avoid woolly promises or over-estimates of this. To go in the budget, it should be fairly certain. For example, the customer may be part-way through product trials showing very positive results, or have expressed a firm intention to buy a new form of the product when it is available. When this business falls part-way through the year, this should be reflected in the figures (not the 'whole year' value !).

(3) Add in **new business from new but identified customers**. Basically, the same rules apply as for element 2. But many companies try to 'qualify' this element by applying some form of 'probability factor', so that only part of the likely value is actually included.

(4) You may also need to add some balancing item for **new non-identified business**. This may be an element of 'windfall' business, or something may need including for planned developments where some activity has already occurred but not yet reached the point of firm orders from identified customers.

This element could be dynamic once it takes off, but in budgetary terms should be handled very conservatively until this actually happens.

(5) Also allow for any **existing business not repeating**. One of the most frequent errors in building top-line budgets is to ignore this element and carry it over without thinking.

Some previously enjoyed business may be coming to end of contract. But some allowance normally needs putting in for known or estimated 'lost business' over the period.

As Figure 10.4 illustrates, all the first four elements need plussing up, but this fifth element is a minus.

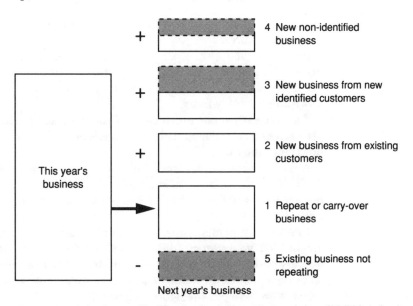

Figure 10.4 A simple way of building top-line budget. (By permission of Neil McArthur.)

Leave some room for negotiation

As we mentioned in the forecasting section, it is very unusual for senior management simply to accept your first-pass budget. There is usually a period of negotiation where they are calling for better figures. It is important, therefore, that you build some 'caution' into your initial top-line and keep some of the impact of developments 'in reserve'.

When and where you are obliged to improve your figures, negotiate hard, and make it clear where you believe this is going beyond reasonable expectation, so this is 'on record' if shortfalls occur.

Managed cost budgets

It depends on your own level of responsibility, but in most companies, product managers are expected to at least contribute to the development of specific areas of cost budget to support the planned level of sales.

This is handled to different levels of detail. For example, promotional support budgets may need developing in considerable detail, to cover:

● Advertising – production and media
● Planned PR
● Exhibitions
● Literature or other point of sale material
● Trade or end-customer promotions
● Salesforce incentives

Other areas may be treated more simply, for example, one line for MR expenditure.

As with your top-line, all major areas of cost under your control need to be planned in terms of *when* they are likely to occur, so they can be effectively monitored. This may be on a quarterly, or right down to a monthly basis.

This is clearly made much easier if you have developed your action plan across a calendar spreadsheet, so relevant costs can drop straight down into the budget.

As with your top-line, try to build in a small amount of 'fat' which you can concede if pushed, and leave a small amount of 'contingency' budget to cover the unexpected needs or opportunities which may arise.

In some companies, your P&L will also carry cost elements which are outside your direct control, like salesforce, warranty, R&D or delivery costs to be set against your product. The assumptions behind all these items need carefully checking out with colleagues or departments who have put the figures together.

Finally, if your product is measured right down to net profit, there will be some general overheads and allocations it will have to carry. Many of these may not be 'negotiable', but at least check out the assumptions or 'rules' by which they have been applied, should you want to build a case for 'fairer treatment'.

As with the top-line, part of the process of budgeting is that you will have to 'justify' your overall level, or specific areas of, spending, so be prepared for this. The ultimate form of this is 'zero-cost' budgeting, where you start with a 'clean sheet' each year and have to justify every item of spending – not easy when you are doing this with 'bean-counters' who can only think in simple 'cause and effect' terms like: 'What *extra* business will we get from this brand advertising, Miss Jones?' Or in an organizational climate which does not fully understand, and is not sympathetic to marketing.

Controlling and monitoring implementation

For successful implementation, you need to define in advance your requirements for monitoring and control. This is likely to involve you in decisions on:

- **What** needs to be tracked, and what is the priority?
- **When** i.e. at what interval (weekly, monthly etc.)?
- **Who** will be responsible for providing and analysing the data? (Probably you, so have you got access to all the information and reports you need?)
- **How** will you handle this in managerial terms? (Some activities will be 'track and report'; others will require direct action from you; others again will require you to liaise effectively with others, or handle the monitoring within groups or committees.)

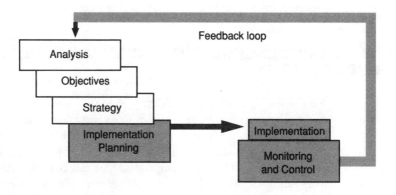

Figure 10.5 The feedback loop

With this well thought through, you are much better placed to not only track, but effectively 'drive' your plan right through the planning period.

This process also maximizes the 'learning benefit', with various elements of feedback contributing to your on-going analysis, quality of assumptions, and experience of 'what works' to feed into action planning next time round (see Figure 10.5).

FINAL CHECKS TO MAKE ON THE SOUNDNESS OF YOUR PLAN

You will have checked out various strategy options and action plan alternatives along the way. But before you get into a presentation or approval environment, there are some further, final checks you can make on your plan's basic soundness.

The **Ansoff Matrix** is a useful tool in strategy option development. It also has a secondary use at this stage, by making you think about the 'development package' you are proposing *before* you lock into final planning and budgets.

Often this will show you that you do not have a very balanced plan, or that too much of your required development is planned to come from high-risk options. In either case, you may want to re-evaluate or re-prioritize your options.

Secondly, before finalizing your plan, and particularly before presenting, see where it fits (objectively!) on the **risk/return grid**.

(Both these approaches, together with some relevant points on the type of risk your plan may contain, are covered more fully at the end of Chapter 3.)

Finally, go right through your plan using the checklist in Figure 10.6, to try to identify any 'weak spots' or 'loose ends' which need working on before you 'go final' and present your plan.

HOW TO SUCCESSFULLY PRESENT YOUR PLAN AT APPROVAL STAGE

You have probably spent weeks, perhaps off-and-on even months, in the development of your product or brand plan. Along the way you have carefully reviewed the product's market, performance and position; have considered all the issues and options; and have finally planned in detail how any improvements can best be achieved.

Psychologically, at this point you are committed – like a sprinter at the starting blocks – ready to go and get the job done. But nothing happens until the starter fires the gun. And, in your case, this means successfully steering your plan through perhaps a series of review and approval stages, and achieving the 'go ahead'.

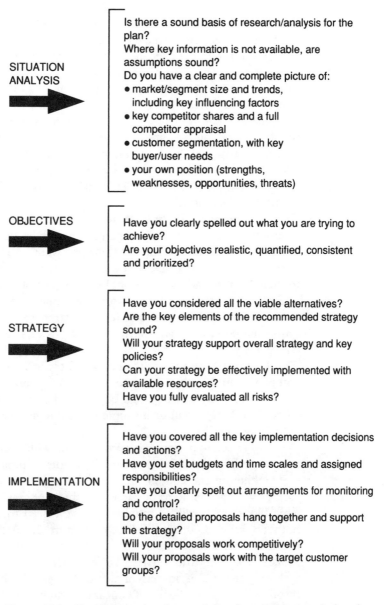

SITUATION ANALYSIS

Is there a sound basis of research/analysis for the plan?
Where key information is not available, are assumptions sound?
Do you have a clear and complete picture of:
- market/segment size and trends, including key influencing factors
- key competitor shares and a full competitor appraisal
- customer segmentation, with key buyer/user needs
- your own position (strengths, weaknesses, opportunities, threats)

OBJECTIVES

Have you clearly spelled out what you are trying to achieve?
Are your objectives realistic, quantified, consistent and prioritized?

STRATEGY

Have you considered all the viable alternatives?
Are the key elements of the recommended strategy sound?
Will your strategy support overall strategy and key policies?
Can your strategy be effectively implemented with available resources?
Have you fully evaluated all risks?

IMPLEMENTATION

Have you covered all the key implementation decisions and actions?
Have you set budgets and time scales and assigned responsibilities?
Have you clearly spelt out arrangements for monitoring and control?
Do the detailed proposals hang together and support the strategy?
Will your proposals work competitively?
Will your proposals work with the target customer groups?

Figure 10.6 Checklist to review the soundness of your product marketing plan

Now you need to do as good a 'selling job' on your plan as you can. Like all forms of selling, preparation is often just as important as how you handle the selling situation itself.

The following approaches and actions are generally found to be helpful to this process.

1 **Step back** from your intense involvement **and look at your plan objectively,** as your manager or a senior management audience will. (Go through the checklist in the last section again if it helps.) How does it look? Does everything really 'gel'? Would running through it with colleagues and getting their views help?

2 **Think about where your audience are coming from**. How is the company culture likely to affect their views or perspectives on the plan? Are you prepared for questions from all the functional specialists you may have to convince? If your product is off-line from historical business, or your audience's own experience, can you find some way to make it feel familiar or 'related' to what they are used to looking at?

3 Try to **anticipate likely questions, objections** or key **discussion areas,** so you are well prepared. You are probably going into a 'pressure situation', so the last thing you want is to be caught off-balance or unprepared. Do you want your boss (or his or her boss) to do a bit of sounding out or lobbying as part of this process?

   Presenting at senior level is often a 'confidence game'. They want to test your mettle, not just the strength of the plan. So remaining cool, calm and having all the answers ready helps this enormously.

4 **Think about how you will present**. This will vary in different companies in length, style and content. In some, you will be expected to deliver using high-quality slides and sample ads on video. In others, it will be a simple talk-through, perhaps with the aid of a few OHPs.

   Do you need to preface your presentation with some 'headlines', to set a positive tone? Or leave time for a brief summary at the end?

   Think about the content of any visual aids you use and make sure they are as **visual** as possible (i.e. charts or graphs rather than large blocks of words or numbers). If you need to use words or numbers, keep them simple (but have more detailed breakdowns in reserve, for if needed).

5 Make sure you **allow time to rehearse** your presentation, including the use of any visual aids or 'props'. Again, doing run-throughs with an audience of colleagues can be helpful.

6 **Think about the way you will be seen when presenting**. Many

companies have a standard of appearance which is part of the culture, or at least expected from you, particularly at senior levels. Look the part.

Act the part too. You have an excellent plan to present and your confidence should shine through when presenting. Judge the level of overt 'enthusiasm' you should show and how you should do this. Don't go 'over the top'.

Remember, psychologists tell us 80% of communication is **non-verbal**. And of the 20% only around half is the words themselves, the rest is the 'tone' or 'music' with which you communicate. So listen out for your voice being pitched too high or low. Avoid talking in a flat monotone. Maybe practise using an audio recorder (or even a video) to check how you come over.

7 **Take your lead from your audience**. If they stay formal, then you must also. If things become lighter and more informal, relax a bit yourself. But not too much! Remember you are selling yourself as much as your plan and, above all else, you need to maintain credibility.

CHAPTER CHECKLIST

Some points about product planning

1 Does your product planning approach fully include both **divergent and convergent** thinking approaches in its process? Which element most needs strengthening?

2 How **complete** is your present product planning system? (Use Fig. 10.1 as a checklist.)

3 How many of Laura Cousin's findings apply to your company?

4 Go through the 'general principles of good product planning' and identify where improvements most need to be made in your present product planning system.

5 Do you have a strategic plan for your product? Think about how this could be handled, or handled better.

6 Start from 'Stages in developing the plan' and work right through the chapter again up to the end of the following section. Highlight stages and specific areas needing improvement. Jot down what needs to be done.

7 Apply the suggested 'final checks' (especially Figure 10.6) to your *last* plan. What does it show you?

8 Identify *at least two ways* you could improve in plan presentation.

Further reading

Books

Bureau, J.R. (1981) *Brand Management – Planning and Control*, Macmillan, ch. 1-4

Kotler, P. (1988) *Marketing Management – Analysis, Planning, Implementation and Control*, Prentice-Hall, ch. 3, pp. 76-99

McDonald, M.H.B. (1989) *Marketing Plans – How to Prepare Them: How to Use Them*, Heinemann

Wilson, A. (1982) *Aubrey Wilson's Marketing Audit Check Lists*, McGraw-Hill

Articles

Cosse, T.J. and Swan, J.E. (1983) Strategic marketing planning by product managers – Room for Improvement, *Journal of Marketing*, Summer

Cousins, L. (1991) Marketing plans or marketing planning? *Business Strategy Review*, Summer

Ginsberg, S.G. (1981) Negotiating budgets: games people play. *INC. Magazine*, September

Leppard, J.W. and McDonald, M.H.B. (1991) Marketing planning and corporate culture: a conceptual framework which examines management attitudes in the context of marketing planning. *Journal of Marketing Management*, no.7, pp. 213-35

11 Internationalization of markets and brands

Factors influencing the regionalization or globalization of markets – How these factors impact on branding and other product marketing issues – Implications for a branding approach and brand portfolios – Branding and advertising standardization or adaptation – Issues of standardizing strategy and other elements of marketing mix – Organizational implications of operating regionally or globally.

There has been a steady stream of 'hype' developed by books and articles since the 1970s, along the lines of: 'It is not a case of whether markets globalize, only when.' Moving into the 1990s, the slow but inexorable progress towards a European 'single market', and the formation of new trading blocs in North America and the Pacific Rim have switched the emphasis to 'regionalization'.

In this chapter, I want to look, with latest research, information and views, at how this is affecting product marketing and particularly branding in the middle and later 1990s. We will look at some of the main factors (or 'drivers') of this process, how they have impacted on different types of product and market, and the issues they pose in terms of brand, advertising and other areas of standardization or adaptation. Finally, we will look briefly at some of the organizational implications for companies affected.

FACTORS INFLUENCING THE REGIONALIZATION OR GLOBALIZATION OF MARKETS

Looked at from the most basic level, for globalization (or even regionalization) of markets to take place, at least three factors have to be in place:

1 Customers' basic needs, requirements or aspirations have to be fairly homogeneous, so the same (or largely similar) offering will succeed wherever it is marketed.
2 There has to be some economic or corporate rationale for companies to want to do it.
3 They must be able to operate in this way.

1 Customer needs

Some of the least discussed but most developed areas of common customer needs are in **industrial** markets. Many forms of IT-linked components (e.g. semiconductors or monitors) have a truly global market, as do laboratory analytical equipment, marine paints and petrochemicals.

Services, such as telecom network facilities, international news services, shipping or many investment activities, have been global for some time.

In **consumer markets**, common customer needs emerge at several levels:

- Many 'basic need' products like cigarettes, petrol, soft drinks or fast foods can serve a 'global customer'.
- Products driven by technology (as in hi-fi or computer games), or by mass-market style and fashion (as in music or training shoes) can do so likewise.
- More up-market 'style' also knows no borders, particularly when this is overtly geared to a cosmopolitan lifestyle or to 'old-style class' aspirations.

The 'shrinking world' factor

In consumer markets in particular, the feeling of a 'shrinking world' is clearly heightened by:

- The growth of international media like CNN.
- The internationalization of many retailing operations (Benetton, Body Shop, IKEA, for example).
- The use of international corporate imagery (as with BP's worldwide forecourt designs).
- Global communications and much wider travel patterns.

Market fragmentation and 'localization'

At the same time, but working in the opposite direction, many previously 'mass markets' are fragmenting as customers become more selective or discriminating, or are looking for products which allow more 'individuality' to be expressed. This allows the development of 'alternative' or niche brands, but these normally have to work on a broader international scale to justify their investment.

Some product ideas just do not catch on outside their 'home area', as with karaoke, which has never reproduced the same extreme enthusiasm outside its Asian heartland.

While other markets still stay firmly 'localized', as with French language entertainment (films and music), German beer tastes (own town or local regional beers still predominate), or some aspects of house design, fittings and furnishings across Europe.

2 Company economic or 'corporate' motivation

There is clearly a strong sense of 'chicken and egg', but overall this has probably been a greater driving (or at least initiating) force than the consumer 'shrinking world' factors, particularly in technology or scale-driven businesses.

Economic pull

Economic motivation comes through in several ways:

- Some high initial R&D investment products, such as pharmaceuticals or civil or military aircraft, need a global (or at least major regional) base of business to justify this.
- Similar factors apply in many processing industries involving major capital expenditure (as with pulp and paper, steel or many basic chemicals). In most cases, higher capacity facilities also offer very considerable advantages of scale.
- Many assembled products, such as consumer electronics, 'white goods', office equipment or certain types of clothing or footwear offer not only economies of scale in purchasing and manufacturing, but also tend to show major 'experience curve' effects when produced on a regional or global scale.
- Regardless of product type, there are also significant cost advantages available in standardizing the product itself, packaging, branding and related advertising for most businesses.

Corporate push

Over and above this, for many large companies (particularly US multinationals), *strategy tends to follow structure*. So if the company has a 'global' head office and global policies, it tends to seek a global image through its products and marketing operations. To keep tight control, and enjoy related cost savings, this also often means working with a global advertising agency partner, as with IBM or Ford.

Likewise with companies operating regional HQs. These tend to develop from 'reporting centres' to full-blown regional marketing centres over time.

Particularly with Japanese multinationals (but also more recently with those from Korea or Taiwan), globalization is a logical extension of their highly ambitious 'strategic intent', to dominate a particular technology, product category or end-use, or topple the present 'top dog'.

3   Barriers to globalization or regionalizing

Many barriers to full globalization still exist. Frequently these are in the areas of 'national standards' or 'approval procedures' (Japan being notorious for this). And even with all the efforts of various GATT rounds, there are still significant tariff or quota restrictions affecting some businesses.

National or regional interests often arise, as in favouring 'home-grown' technology systems, or the political protection of state-owned businesses.

Telecoms, especially mobile systems, are a good example of this. Logically, this is a 'natural' for a global business (common customer needs and aspirations and massive potential economies of scale). But different systems and standards still persist. And protected national PTTs (post, telephone and telegraph), as in Italy, are failing to provide the required infrastructure or are blocking outside provision and the competition that comes with it.

Other barriers are more subtle, being linked to cultural differences (as with 'Latin' and 'North European' sub-regions in Europe), or national (rather than political) attitudes, language or traditions. These can have an effect in several areas.

- **Pack designs** or **colours:** symbols and colours vary greatly in their significance between regions, or even national markets. For example, white to most people of European extraction means 'pure', 'wedding', etc. In Chinese culture, it is the colour of 'death'. Red, as in Ferrari or Marlboro means 'macho', 'excitement', but in many Eastern cultures is the colour of 'wedding'.
- **Product** (or **ingredients**): many religious taboos come into play with food products in particular. So beefburgers need to become 'lambburgers' in markets like India. Ready-meals and fast food need to reflect preferences on what goes with the main meal, like KFC providing mashed potatoes and gravy (USA and Australia) or french fries (elsewhere) with its chicken pieces.
- **Branding:** many of you will know of examples of unintended humour or offence from brandnames which have difficulties crossing languages or cultural norms. My children derive great amusement from Bimbo bread and Bonka coffee in Spain, and from Pschitt soft drinks (France) or Bum bubblegum (from Scandinavia).

   But such problems can be more subtle than this. Toyota slipped up by launching the MR2 in the French market (hear what happens when you pronounce the letters and number aloud in the French way); and the British market brand for GM's small car

(Nova) would clearly not work in 'Latin' markets (no va – it doesn't go).

Numbers can have similar problems: 69 and 13 have certain unfortunate associations in Europe, but 4 (even as in Alfa-Romeo 164) will not work in Chinese cultures. It is the most 'unlucky' number possible, in a culture very conscious of such things.

Brand name and trademark legislation can also be a 'minefield', even though in Europe this is being simplified. (See the article by Isabel Davies (1993) on Mueller's experience.)

- **Advertising:** not only is this rife with different regulations across markets (for example, no 'comparative' advertising in Germany), but dominant media, media access and relative cost also vary significantly across markets. (Similar factors can affect aspects of 'below the line' activities also.)

And while some emotions or appeals are universal, the way they are treated creatively, or whether they are felt to be appropriate can get very different reactions. For example, most small car advertising in Italy or Spain uses heavy sexual innuendo as its appeal. This would clearly not work in the 'green' markets like Germany, nor in those more geared to 'features and offers' like the Netherlands or UK.

Some humour is notoriously difficult to internationalize. And many slogans or headlines which work extremely well in the 'home' language lose a lot in the literal translation.

HOW THESE FACTORS IMPACT ON BRANDING AND OTHER PRODUCT MARKETING ISSUES

In spite of all the remaining difficulties and pitfalls, there is a clear 'megatrend' towards international branding, with varying degrees of standardization being applied to the total marketing approach put behind this.

It is probably not an overstatement for Richard Zambuni of Craton, Lodge & Knight to claim that 'international branding is the make-or-break success factor for most large marketing-oriented companies in the 1990s' (Zambuni, 1993).

Megatrends affecting global or regional branding

Chris Macrae (1993) outlines three major megatrends at work:

1 Problems of scale

Increasingly, one-product or 'one dominant market' brands are losing minimum critical mass. And in markets like the UK, 'local' often fails to differentiate the product from strong own-label competition (which is also 'local').

2 The pull of international lifestyles

There is tremendous 'fashion' value in being seen as part of a 'global club' and this is no longer confined to clothing, young people or up-market goods.

For example, food products or more everyday drinks (traditionally a strong area of local tastes and brands) are also strongly moving to international offerings. Even the appearance of 'international' can be appealing, as with Gino Ginelli ice cream in the UK.

3 Brand effectiveness

Media costs are now so high in many markets, that developing traditional free-standing brands internationally on traditional media like TV can be prohibitive.

One impact of this is an increasing move towards other (or new) communication platforms which offer high levels of international exposure more cost-effectively. Some of the approaches Macrae cites are:

- Ownership of own media, such as Disney.
- Coke's presence on international promotional 'stages', whether linked to sport, entertainment or cultural or leisure stages such as the Seville World Fair or EuroDisney.
- Gatorade and Isostar using top sporting clubs' training kit as endorsement (in fact, Puma used similar football star endorsement for their 'Predator' brand at the 1994 World Cup).
- Making the brand's packaging visibly more fashionable than competition (e.g. Becks Beer), or
- PRing the brand, as with Benetton, Body Shop or Virgin.

IMPLICATIONS FOR A BRANDING APPROACH AND BRAND PORTFOLIOS

These trends collectively are forcing more and more major companies to concentrate on company name (i.e. 'house' branding) where this is suitable, or a relatively small portfolio of umbrella megabrand platforms which can cover all key business areas, and be developed to be highly appealing to the global club (as with Gillette or Lever).

The other popular option is a combination of house and 'power' brands, each of the latter with a separate focus and positioning (as with Kelloggs or many car manufacturers).

This kind of concentration, particularly where house brand is involved, demands a powerful, consistent, convincing and clear corporate or brand 'stance' (or overriding image), which normally derives from a combination of:

● *Where it is originally from* – its national heritage. Examples would be the 'Frenchness' of Perrier, cognac or Janet Reger lingerie; the 'Italian-ness' of Ferrari or Gucci; or the 'American-ness' of Coke, MacDonalds or Jeep.
● *Who or what it is linked with in terms of other imagery* – its association heritage. This could be Porsche or Jaguar with motor racing success; Ralph Lauren and polo; Marlboro and the rugged, independent cowboy.
● *What the brand 'stands for'* – its motivating appeal. Examples would be Volvo and 'safety', Mercedes and engineering excellence, Body Shop and 'green values', Haagen Daz's and luxurious self-indulgence. Sometimes this is simply that it is 'oldest' or 'the original' (Coke), 'biggest' (Budweiser or IBM) or 'best' (Gillette).

The need for absolute conformity and consistency

To make the approach work, every aspect of marketing must be 'right', i.e. totally consistent. And this needs to be ferociously guarded against imitation or dilution, to preserve the uniqueness of this highly valuable brand 'platform'.

Hence the corporate role in policing this, not only externally against predators, but also internally through the brand strategy, other policy documents on use of trademarks, etc., and, in some businesses, through franchise partners' operating standards.

BRANDING AND ADVERTISING STANDARDIZATION OR ADAPTATION

It is a commonly held view that branding and advertising are inseparable in this process. And we can all think of many high profile examples where this is the case (Coke, Levi's etc.). But a study by Sandler and Shani (Sandler, 1992) of 300 brand managers operating in Canada showed a different picture. Of a 2 x 2 matrix offering four different combinations of standardization and adaptation (see Figure 11.1):

Strategy 1 standardizes both (as with Coke or Nike)
Strategy 2 standardizes branding, but adapts advertising locally

(they cited Volvo, but this applies to many car makers).

Strategy 3 uses different brand names (or slightly different forms of them), but standardizes ad campaigns internationally (they cited Procter & Gamble's Camay marketed, for example, in Sweden as Dunn, but Oil of Ulay also has many variants internationally).

Strategy 4 standardizes neither and allows locally-based decisions on branding and advertising.

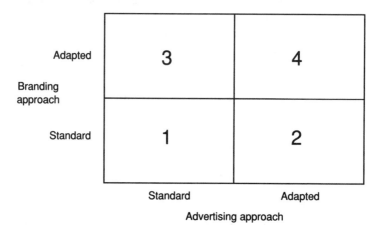

Figure 11.1 Branding and advertising options. (Based on the research of Sandler and Shani, 1992)

A key finding from this research was that Strategy 2 emerged as the most common approach, not Strategy 1. The recurring theme which emerged was *'brand internationally but advertise locally'*.

ISSUES OF STANDARDIZING STRATEGY AND OTHER ELEMENTS OF MARKETING MIX

This was researched by Kapferer (1993) with 210 brand-owners in a European context. In the study, he basically looked at the trade-off between country or customer requirements for differences, and companies' willingness to adapt or desire to maintain conformity.

Four basic positions or 'types' emerged:

● **Type 1** (29%) were hypersensitive to **customer differences** from one country to another, and thus adjusted strategy significantly (customer targets, positioning, promise, creative idea). Examples were Yoplait, Persil, Porsche and Swissair.

- **Type 2** (21%) maintained the same basic strategy, but did change the **allocation of resources** from country to country. They were particularly sensitive to media mix, the ratio of above and below the line and the use of promotions. Examples were a number of major car brands.
- **Type 3** (27%) were hypersensitive to the **competitive environment** and **differences in distribution channels**. They were far more likely to get into a number of tactical changes, such as packaging, promotions and distribution variations. The health and beauty sector was notable here.
- **Type 4** (23%) were the main advocates of **overall standardization** (but are clearly in a small minority). These companies and their brands refuse to take account of inter-country differences in any significant way (other than minor price or promotional adjustments). Examples were many luxury brands, together with a high proportion of US brands operating in Europe such as Playtex, Apple, Mars and Coca-Cola.

ORGANIZATIONAL IMPLICATIONS OF OPERATING REGIONALLY OR GLOBALLY

What Kapferer's study shows is a picture a long way from (and a lot more subtle than) the normal impression of the Head Office ('We want to globalize i.e. to standardize') versus local organization ('we are different – you need to adapt to our market') debates which run through so many companies with international organizations.

It does depend, of course, on how centralized the organization is in its overall management, in its marketing operations, and also to some extent in its staffing policies.

'Home market' mentality at the centre

One of the factors in some multinationals is that products or marketing programmes that work in the dominant market tend to be recommended, or even imposed, elsewhere. And those required by other regions or markets are ignored, or given low priority.

This is amplified if most of the central product managers are of 'home' (i.e. dominant market) nationality, and do not have any real experience outside what works in their own, familiar, surroundings.

This factor certainly played a part in the late entry of Philips into the booming Asian karaoke market. Local product managers saw it as their largest growth area and were screaming for it, but to the Dutch central product marketing team it was 'below the sight line'.

In this context, it does not matter if the international product managers are American, Dutch, Japanese or Swiss, although the phenomenon of applying 'own market perspectives' can sometimes be amusing to an outsider.

I remember one problem in a Swiss multinational I was working for, where the (Swiss) international product manager for weighing machines just could not believe that no other national product manager in Europe was interested in a new portable machine for cafes, canteens – even roadside stalls – which he was trying to impose on them. 'What's wrong with you people' he said, 'don't you *weigh* your meat and cheese when you make sandwiches?'

The cycle of change

Many organizations regularly go through cycles of 'centralize everything' (it doesn't work in most cases – it is too inflexible), then 'delegate everything' (this doesn't work either, without either direction or control of at least some key aspects of brand policy).

IBM have just been going through this the other way round. After two or three years of 'loose-rein' management in the early 1990s which almost led to anarchy (for example, more than 20 different ways of presenting and positioning the IBM brand in the UK alone), they have centralized branding policy again and have adopted a 'world-wide ad agency' approach to make this stick.

Team approaches

Rather than allowing these 'battles' to develop, other companies have deliberately avoided 'us and them' situations arising by various forms of 'team' approach. Normally these co-opt product managers (and others, from R&D for example), from the national organizations into a central coordinating or marketing decision-making unit. Henkel did this successfully with its Sista sealant programme in the mid-1980s.

Lever have also adopted this approach successfully with their European Brand Group (EBG), comprising fully 'Europeanized' teams working together on, for example:

● Key innovation products.
● Strategic direction and long-term 'vision' for each brand and its category.
● Conducting pan-European market research.
● Applying what they call 'clever harmonization', i.e. the right balance between standardization and local variation based on differences that are *vital to the customer*.

Use of local nationals or 'international' managers

The action of involving a good cross-section of local nationals, or true 'international' managers is often the key to international marketing success. Zambuni (1993) cites the case of Wedgwood.

> *Historically, Wedgwood had a major business base in the UK and operated two key 'export' operations in the USA and Japan staffed by highly autonomous British expatriates. Although in a sales role, they were effectively acting as market 'product managers', making range selection decisions and handling all local marketing.*
>
> *When Wedgwood wanted to tackle the underdeveloped markets of continental Europe, however, they put together an international team who were not British (or even Wedgwood employees), but who were experts on the product and marketing requirements of the customers in these markets.*
>
> *Over the past five years this has been Wedgwood's most successful and fastest-growing business area, and moves were made to set up a fully international marketing-led management team to replace the previous UK-dominated 'export' mentality.*

Many Japanese multinationals, although often retaining Japanese nationals in key positions, are very 'consensual' and adaptive in their approach, and tend increasingly to use local (or regional) product management and design set-ups; and value their input on local requirements and tastes.

The Nissan Micra and Toyota Carina E are recent examples of this in Europe. As was the Miata (MX5 in Europe) from Mazda, which was developed by a US design and marketing team, based in California.

CHAPTER CHECKLIST

Issues to consider on internationalization

1 To what extent has your brand or product area been affected by regionalizing or globalizing factors so far? Jot down some key points to remind yourself what they were.

2 How is this likely to change through the remainder of the 1990s? Identify the key issues this means you will have to address.

3 How regionalized or globalized is your current branding and marketing approach? Does this apply to all products or only some?

4 How relevant are Macrae's megatrends to your business? See if you can identify any further ones.

5 What are the key attributes on which you base your international appeal? Do these need reinforcing or refreshing, to maintain future appeal and relevance?

6 How standardized are your branding and advertising approaches across your international business? Are both equally standardized, or do you fit into one of Sandler and Shani's other strategy boxes? Will this change, or does it need to change?
7 Review other aspects of your standardization or adaptation and check which of Kapferer's four 'types' you belong in. Again, fully consider whether this will remain the most appropriate approach for the future.
8 How well are you handling international marketing issues in organizational terms? Are you still in 'battle' mode? Or are you using team approaches and local input fully and effectively?

Further reading

Books

Arnold, D. (1992) *The Handbook of Brand Management*, Century Business, ch. 11
Griffin, T. (1993) *International Marketing Communications*, Butterworth-Heinemann
Kapferer, J-N (1992) *Strategic Brand Management*, Kogan Page
Paliwoda, S. (1992) *International Marketing*, Butterworth-Heinemann

Articles

Davies I, (1993) The international implications of branding: part 2 – An international brand launch – the Mueller experience. *Journal of Brand Management*, vol.1
Kapferer, J-N. (1993) The challenge of European branding: facing inter-country differences, *Journal of Brand Management*, vol.1
Macrae, C. *et al.* (1993) Brand reengineering – why and how? *Journal of Brand Management*, vol.1
Riesenback, H. (1991) How global are global brands? *McKinsey Quarterly*
Sandler, D.M. (1992) Brand globally but advertise locally. *International Marketing Review*, April
Seth, A. (1993) Organization for international brands at Lever Europe. *Journal of International Marketing*, 1(2)
Zambuni, R. (1993) Developing brands across borders. *Journal of Brand Management*, 1(1)

12 The future for product management

Some key trends in consumer, industrial and service markets – Product, market, category or business development management – Strategic involvement and profit responsibility – Social and organizational issues and their impact on the role in the 1990s.

> The future is never clearly known. The past and present provide tantalizing hints, but surprises always exist. (George S. Dominguez, 1971)

These are the words with which Dominguez summed up his own thoughts on the future for product management in 1971. Since then, nearly two and a half decades of 'todays' have become 'yesterdays'. Over that period, product management has become firmly and almost universally adopted as *a management system that works* and that delivers better performance for companies adopting it.

This does not mean it will not change and further evolve. Nor that the titles used to describe the function will not also change over time. Any management system has to be appropriate for its time and its internal and external circumstances, and these are clearly changing.

In 'life cycle' terms also, various business sectors are still at different stages in the adoption and use of product management, and this will lead to a necessary focus on different issues and priorities, depending on the type of business you work in.

SOME KEY TRENDS IN CONSUMER, INDUSTRIAL AND SERVICE MARKETS

FMCG and other consumer markets

Consumer goods markets pioneered the system (around 70 years ago in the case of Procter & Gamble!), then evolved collectively to a more narrowly-focused 'brand management' form of product management from the 1950s onwards. In this setting, product management is clearly a very mature management system and is probably in need of rejuvenation and refocusing. It is not, however, as some authors in the late 1980s (e.g. Howley, Mazur) would have you believe, in terminal decline. Paraphrasing Mark Twain: 'reports of its death have been greatly exaggerated'.

So what of the future here? And how do more recent events impact on some of the trends which have been present?

Indisputably, some consumer product manager roles have diminished from the 'golden age' in FMCG of the 1960s and 1970s, where brand managers were the pivotal point and 'powerhouses' of their organizations. A number of main factors have been at play here, all of which are still changing and evolving. These are summarized in Figure 12.1 and discussed in further detail below.

Main trends of the 1980s

- Decision-making power moved upwards to senior management
- Some decision-making moved to corporate or regional level
- Some decision-making went to other functions, as business became more cost- and trade-driven
- Brand visibility down as budgets cut and media became more expensive
- Era of low-cost, low-risk development and almost universal line extension
- Brand management not linked directly to business and 'the trade'

Most likely trends for the 1990s

- Upper layers of marketing management being stripped out
- Greater involvement in international issues on a project or team basis
- Need for more genuine innovation and strategy thinking to support this
- Core brand values rethought and restored
- Use of more cost-effective media platforms
- Fuller business development role, combined perhaps with a move to 'category management'
- Wider experience and more job rotation
- Responsible for more brands, with 'less hands' to support you

---

Figure 12.1 Trends in FMCG and consumer markets, 1980s–1990s

Decision-making moved upwards

In the 1980s some decision-making power moved upwards to more senior management. But in the 1990s, many large FMCG companies (such as Procter & Gamble) are already in the process of actively stripping out layers of marketing management. General cost pressures are likely to make this the 'norm' for this sector.

These new, leaner, senior management teams cannot possibly get involved so fully in all the strategy development and policy detail required for all brands. Much of this thinking and decision-making *will have to be delegated back down*, or will be handled more internationally.

Decision-making moved to corporate or regional level

As major brands became more fully international in their business base, and consistency and conformity of branding became a key issue, some decision-making power moved to a different level. But this cannot be handled in a vacuum. It needs the vital link of local input and involvement to remain fully coupled to the market. As Chapter 10 suggested, this is likely to involve more teamwork through the forming of international brand groups, or similar coordinating developments at regional level.

Many key aspects of branding policy may thus still be set at the centre, but the execution of supporting strategy and marketing mix adaptation will *have to* reflect local (i.e. regional or major national) conditions and market realities. Otherwise, in most cases, it will clearly not be effective.

To a large extent this has already happened. In Kapferer's European study (cited in Chapter 10), 77% of the international brands were already reflecting this in different ways. Less than a quarter were using the 'no adaptation' sledgehammer (with over a half of these being US companies).

So the role of many consumer brand managers is likely to involve *increasing* input or participation in the international management of the brand as the 1990s unfold.

Decision-making went to other functions

As mature brands became more driven by cost issues and subject to increasing trade power, some decision-making power was given to other functions.

There are some signs that this will reverse, or more fully involve product management (i.e. you), in the 1990s:

1 The all-pervasive 'bean-counter' mentality of cutting support budgets and stifling all forms of genuine innovation or development (other than low-risk, fast-return options like brand extension) has patently *not worked* for most of the organizations following this course. It is a 'long-term loser'. And it *will* not work, as it diminishes overall brand clarity, appeal and perceived added-value (average brand premiums have declined from 25% to 17% over the past decade). It is just playing into the hands of the own-labellers.

2 At the same time, trade marketing has taken an increasing share of your budget, and key account management (still largely a Sales function) has been calling the shots in markets with more concentrated retail buying power, particularly in terms of required 'deals', pricing and hence brand profitability. But simply 'giving the trade what they want' (like ever-increasing control over product, share of support cost and share of available total margin) is not an answer

either, and can be crippling to brand profitability if handled weakly and not involving you as the brand's profit guardian.

Key 1990s trends likely to affect brand managers

Several welcome, and very necessary, trends (listed in Figure 12.1) are likely to emerge out of this which will revitalize and maybe significantly change the way you are expected to do your job in the 1990s.

There will be a greater brand-owner recognition of the need for more genuine **innovation** and **new product development** which adds value for the customer, and moves the brand away from the 'copycats'. (This is long overdue, because in some fields own-labellers themselves have been the prime innovators in the category.)

There will be less dissipation of brand equity through uncontrolled extension and the restoration or rethinking of core brand values and *real* **strategy thinking**.

Support for the brand is likely to happen more and more through the use of more **cost-effective media platforms** than the conventional media.

Your role will widen again to a **fuller business management involvement.** This will require fuller 'share of voice' and decision-making participation in trade marketing issues though not, perhaps, as far as Turner's view that a new breed of 'Major Account Product Managers' will develop, to mirror their trade counterparts. To accommodate this, brand managers will need **wider** (particularly key account sales) **experience**, and more **job rotation** in early career. (A 1994 Booz, Allan study showed only 15% rotate to other experience fields during their first six to eight years in the company.)

Category management is likely to figure much more strongly, as the vehicle for your increasing trade involvement, and again to parallel the way major retailers are managing their side of the business.

Finally, one (perhaps unwelcome) aspect of job widening is likely to be **responsibility for more brands** (as foreseen by Morein in the 1970s) caused in the short-term by headcount reductions, particularly at the brand assistant or assistant brand manager level.

(The same Booz, Allan study showed that 'one-brand' brand managers had dropped from 45% three to five years previously to 33% in 1994. And those working on three or more brands had grown from 30% to 46%).

Industrial and service markets

Overall trends in role, image and responsibilities

As the role here is far less mature than for consumer counterparts, the main trends (see Figure 12.2) are likely to be a continuation of those picked up by the 1991 CIM survey. That is, we will see a continuing move up through the four stages of role outlined in Chapter 1, with Product Champion and Mini-MD type roles increasingly becoming the 'norm'. As a consequence of this, the role will take on **greater strategy involvement** and **more, genuine, profit responsibility**.

- Continuing upgrading of role to full 'business managers' of the product

- Greater strategy involvement and more, genuine, profit responsibility

- More emphasis on 'the brand'

- More specialization and focus, perhaps to 'single-product'

- Development of matrix structures in larger organizations

Figure 12.2 1990s trends in industrial and service markets

Overall, this means these product managers will pull away from any remaining perceptions that they are only in a 'support', 'coordinating' or 'planning' role, and will assume job responsibilities more akin to the brand managers of the 1960s and 1970s. They will become **full business managers** of their **product area or business sector**.

Just as happened earlier in consumer markets, other trends are likely to be **more emphasis on 'the brand'**, as a key element to effectively manage. (This is coming through strongly already in many service markets, particularly financial services.) And there will be **more specialization and focus,** i.e. a move away from the 'many products, many markets' approach which has predominated to date.

Already some service organizations (in particular) are moving much closer to the 'single product' focus of traditional brand management. (They are also even using the 'brand manager' title on a more widespread basis, to reflect this and the previous point.)

Matrix management

Moving in a different direction, many larger organizations in industrial and service fields are moving to more of a 'matrix' structure involving more narrowly-defined **product managers** (i.e. technology, product improvement and new product development specialists) and **market or application sector managers** (who represent or support the sales and business management side of the process).

Increasingly in large industrial organizations, the 'product' element is being concentrated at regional or corporate level, to allow better coordination and less duplication of expensive research effort. Business targets are still frequently used to judge performance, but based on the larger unit's sales or profit performance.

Normally, the 'market' or 'industry' manager element make their input at national organization level, with sales and profits achieved also measured at this level. The only exception is if the business in a sector is highly concentrated within international company clients. Then this element can also go international.

PRODUCT, MARKET, CATEGORY OR BUSINESS DEVELOPMENT MANAGEMENT

In all market settings, there is likely to be more diversity in the way the role is handled and in related job titles.

Traditional product or brand management evolved where a number of products were serving the same (or broadly similar) customer groups and channels. The key was improving the 'market presence', share position and profitability of each individual line.

As already mentioned, this is very much the scenario in many service markets, and they are moving this way at the same time as FMCG is moving in other directions (including multi-brand responsibilities).

Where products are serving a range of different industries or application sectors, often with very different requirements or channels, this introduces considerable complexity (as most industrial product managers are only too aware!).

Ames, Baker, Thomas and others have for some time been advocating the need for a **market manager** role, or a division of the job into product and market specialists who effectively coordinate together. While the CIM survey did not pick this up as a significant development in 1991, the early 1990s have seen a number of larger industrial and service organizations moving in this direction (for example, IBM and British Telecom). It may well gather momentum in other organizations like these through the 1990s.

Category management is likely to become much more widely adopted, particularly in more mature FMCG product areas, as it has already in the USA.

Also in FMCG, the move from 'highly-focused, office-and-agency-based brand manager', to more broadly based 'business manager' or '**business development manager**' is likely to gather pace (driven on at least in part by the increasing incidence of category management, which demands this kind of 'direct' involvement in the 'sharp end' of the business). At the same time, this role also assumes a much fuller role in new product development, as one of the key 'development' routes.

In a sense, this means a move in FMCG to a role much closer to the one an industrial product manager would accept as 'normal'.

STRATEGIC INVOLVEMENT AND PROFIT RESPONSIBILITY

Overall, the strategic involvement of product managers is likely to increase, though this will be made up of separate elements.

In consumer markets, at least some of the strategic responsibility which 'moved upstairs' over the past decade, will be delegated back down. (A high proportion of the upstairs offices are now empty in companies like Procter & Gamble!)

At the same time, the removing of layers below brand management means that much of the detail of the role (low-level analysis and related number-crunching together with promotional detail, for example) will have to be delegated across to agencies or other functions to handle. Even then, this will require excellent time management and prioritizing, to allow the necessary 'thinking time'.

Then there is the international dimension, with product managers from larger or more successful national organizations being asked to participate more in wider strategy issues.

In industrial and service markets, product manager strategy involvement is not being 'regained', but increasingly being expected, demanded or delegated. This is especially true in more technical or specialist fields, where 'general' management cannot be expected to provide this.

Similar patterns apply in **profit responsibility**.

In consumer markets, it is at least partly a case of gradually regaining previous levels of profit responsibility and this is likely to accelerate with the move to more of a business development manager role (i.e. fully plugged back into the business and the trade).

In other sectors, the progress towards greater profit responsibility (and therefore the need for greater financial 'literacy') is likely to continue its onward progress.

In both cases, *profitable* product management will be the key measure of your effectiveness.

SOCIAL AND ORGANIZATIONAL ISSUES AND THEIR IMPACT ON THE ROLE IN THE 1990S

In Europe in particular, growing 'social responsibility' and concern for 'green' issues are likely to come more into play through the 1990s.

Some factors (for example, 'through-life' responsibility for the product, including its disposal and recycling) are already strongly in place in the dominant market, Germany, and are increasingly likely to impact more generally on other markets as European Union policy leans heavily this way.

The organizations product managers work for and within will also be changing. Among the key factors are likely to be further **cost and headcount reductions** which at least in the short term and maybe longer will be the norm among larger marketing organizations. This will almost certainly push more responsibility and even more work pressure onto the product manager level.

More **international links** and new forms of **team-working** will evolve. As more of the role becomes 'business development', this may involve you in acting as team leader to new product or new business area **venture groups**.

Broader models of marketing organizational change

The future of product management is clearly linked to the future of marketing, which in most organizations has developed to connect company thinking and actions back to the marketplace. Some writers, like Morris (1987), are forecasting the general move to '**meta-marketing**', within which the whole organization becomes so marketing-oriented that a marketing department (or specialists, such as product managers) will not be needed.

A situation very close to this has been the case with many major Japanese organizations, where every functional member of a team is expected to think like a marketeer (and an accountant, and an engineer, and a production man etc., etc.). But even here, someone has to be the overall organizational 'champion'. Someone has to give the lead and direction to these product teams. In this context, Clark and Fujimoto (1991) suggest that in some successful Japanese companies, the product management role – far from being subsumed – is in fact being upgraded by the advent of '**heavyweight product managers**', particularly to drive new products quickly and effectively through the organization, and working at quite a high organizational level. A significant point is that *these individuals will not necessarily be from the marketing department*. They could be engineers, for example. The character and qualities required for the role are seen as more important than the department the individuals are from.

Dominguez (1971) predicted in the 1970s that product management could become *a specialist function in its own right*, with its own line structure right up to director level. In this scenario, 'marketing' will be just another of the interfaces to be managed.

One way of looking at the way marketing organizations are evolving is that proposed by Tyebjee *et al.* (see Table 12.1). This suggests that most of you will currently be operating in companies at Stage 3, where product (or a combination of this with market) management is the most appropriate organizational system. You may even be at Stage 2, where product management is being introduced to help direct or support sales growth. But as the more mature organizations some of you are working for move to Stage 4, then not only the *focus* of the job needs to change, but this may well involve changes *in reporting point*.

Table 12.1 Stages of marketing organization

	Stage 1 (Entrepreneurial)	Stage 2 (Opportunistic)	Stage 3 (Responsive)	Stage 4 (Diversified)
Marketing strategy	Market niche development	Market penetration	Product/market development	New business development
Marketing organization	Informal, flexible	Sales management	Product/market management	Corporate and divisional levels
Marketing goals	Credibility in the market	Sales volume and share	Customer satisfaction	PLC and portfolio management
Critical success factors	A little help from your friends	Production efficiency	Functional coordination	Entrepreneurship and innovation

Reprinted by permission of *Harvard Business Review*. An exhibit from 'Growing ventures can expect marketing stages' by T. T. Tyebjee, A. V. Bruno and S. H. McIntyre, January/February, 1983. Copyright © 1983 by the President and Fellows of Harvard College; all rights reserved.

Rather than being a function within the company's marketing department, you may in future be reporting into a 'business management' structure at company, divisional or even international level.

Some final thoughts

One thing is for sure. In spite of the 'doomsayers' predicting the demise of product management (even then, they are only talking about FMCG 'brand' management in its current form), the overall role appears to have a strong and healthy future. It is likely to involve greater responsibility (though not necessarily any more authority!), more variety and many new challenges and lines of career opportunity.

The titles used to describe the function may change, as may the reporting point within the organization, but the vital function provided by the job will go on. At least well beyond the 1990s.

CHAPTER CHECKLIST

Your own future role in product management

Unlike the earlier chapters, which offered a wide range of topics and questions for you to consider, my recommendation here is that you think more generally about how the changes covered in this chapter are likely to affect you and your future career.

Perhaps have a look at some of the further reading which sounds interesting, then go back through the chapter and jot down all the points and likely changes which are most likely to affect your own situation. Do this as a kind of SWOT exercise, to kick off your own personal 'marketing plan'.

From analysis and SWOT, you then need to work out objectives, strategy and necessary actions:

- **Objectives**: where do I want to be in job and career terms over short, medium and longer timeframes?
- **Strategy**: what are my range of options for getting there, and what overall 'game-plan' does this suggest I should be following?
- **Actions**: what do I need to organize in terms of additional training, extensions to current role, additional job rotation experience in other functions or roles, and gaining sufficient 'visibility' and credibility to be thought suitable and 'ready' for next-step and follow-on developments?

Set your milestones, so you can effectively **monitor progress**. Then get on and make it happen!

I wish you every personal success in achieving your future progress in product, marketing or general management, and hope that this book may also help in some small measure to improve your collective success, as a new generation of profitable product managers.

Further reading

Ames, B.C. (1971) Dilemma of product/market management. *Harvard Business Review*, Mar./Apr.

Clark, K.B. and Fujimoto, T. (1991) Heavyweight product managers. *McKinsey Quarterly*, no.1

Collier, R.A. (1991) The changing role of the product manager in industrial marketing. Unpublished University of Bradford MBA dissertation

Dominguez G.S. (1971) *Product Management*, American Marketing Association Inc., ch. 18

Howley M. (1988) Is there a need for a product manager? *Quarterly Review of Marketing*, spring

Mazur, L. (1986) Branded as yesterday's heroes. *Marketing*, 24 July

Morein, J.A. (1975) Shift from brand to product line marketing, *Harvard Business Review*, Sept./Oct.

Morris D.J. (1987) Meta-marketing: unifying focus to achieve marketplace goals. *Journal of Marketing Management*, spring

Prothero A. (n.d.), *Green Consciousness and the Societal Marketing Concept: Marketing Strategies for the 1990s*, Cardiff Business School paper no. 1101

Raper, J.P. (1989) Product management: Has it outlived its usefulness? Unpublished University of Bradford MBA dissertation

Richards, A. (1994) What is holding back today's brand manager? *Marketing*, 3 February

Thomas, M.J. (1982) Product management versus market management. *The Marketing Digest*, Summer

Thomas, M.J. (1991) The future of product/brand management, in *The Marketing Book* (ed. M.J. Baker), Butterworth-Heinemann

Turner, P. (1989) Product management for major accounts: an opportunity to differentiate. *European Journal of Marketing*, July

Tyebjee, T.T., Bruno, A. V. and McIntyre, S. H. (1983) Growing ventures can expect marketing stages, *Harvard Business Review*, Jan./Feb

Appendix

SOME THOUGHTS ON THE RANGE PROFITABILITY EXERCISE FROM CHAPTER 5

Part (a) of Table 5.2 shows the overall profitability of the five product groups. Two groups jump out of the table as loss-makers, with D and E making a combined loss of £6000 per month.

Using traditional financial analysis, only these two should be considered for deletion, but a more thoughtful analysis shows some rather different conclusions.

C and E combined

Firstly, part (b) shows that C and E together (as a system) are delivering the best overall performance within the whole range. E, as a key supporting product to C, must be retained.

In some more financially dominated companies, there would be pressure to adjust price and margins on both C and E so that both were showing a 'profit'. It would be more productive to either:

● Examine the costs and market realities of E. If the market will not pay more, can some costs be reduced?
● Better still, why not remove the 'emotion' by repositioning as the 'C & E System', where price and costs are always shown combined?

D remains as a loss-maker

Product D is showing the highest individual monthly losses and clearly requires some investigation and corrective action, but this may not necessarily be deletion.

It has two main problems: a negative contribution to overheads and very high levels of dependent investment for its current sales level. Why?

Commonly, this combination may be present with a new product which is still being highly subsidized (launch deals and sampling) but where stock has been built up in anticipation of sales. If this is the case, there is no 'problem', it just requires a careful watching brief as the situation develops.

Another scenario is that this line has suffered a sharp drop in business. Heavy price-cutting to restore volume or share may be damaging short-term contribution, and stock levels have not had time to be brought back down to a more appropriate level. If this is the case, again this will be largely self-correcting.

If neither applies, then a more detailed examination of the items which make up the line is needed. Are there late-life loss-makers which do not affect other business, which could be deleted? Are there cost or pricing actions on other D items which could further help the process of bringing this line back into profit?

The drag factor of B

As the largest sales turnover line, improving the miserable performance of B (0.4% profit on sales and only 2% ROI) can potentially have an even greater beneficial effect on total range performance than just tinkering with the fairly small negative performance lines.

Part (c) gives some of the detail required, and shows three of the five items as inadequate performers. B5, as a newly launched product, should only be a temporary drag factor but does need to be watched carefully.

B4 appears to be performing much worse than B1, which is also in growth stage. Gross profitability or contribution clearly needs investigation (only 25% as against B1's 33%). Is the line still being too heavily 'subsidised' or a 'full price' not being achieved?

What to do with B3?

B3, as an end-of-life product, appears to be a prime deletion candidate. With its remaining high level of sales, it probably also accounts for a high share of working capital, so investment could also possibly be reduced by taking it out. But customers clearly still want to buy it.

Before we delete it, have we asked:

- Is it priced too low? Will these customers still be prepared to buy it if we put prices up? (Could this be the full 6.26%, i.e. £5000 over £80,000, we need to at least break even?)
- Can its costs be reduced? Again, only £5000 of cost needs to be saved to stop the loss, so this needs some urgent investigation.

If a combination of both could be used, then B3 could be restored to positive performance, with a 'double-count' benefit for B range overall.

Other lines of thought may need to include:

- Do we have a replacement for B3? When will it be ready? Does this indicate we need to keep B3 going, or face an uphill battle to win those customers back if the gap is too long?

- If there is no obvious replacement, can we sell enough of the other products in B range to take up the slack (difficult, when it accounts for almost half of B range sales)? How long would this process take and what are the sales, profit and cashflow implications?
- Will any overheads really be saved if B3 is deleted? How much? How much more does this mean the other lines will have to carry? What will that do to their profitability?

Don't forget B2!

In most companies, B2 would sail through any investigation like this. Its highest £ profit and second highest percentage profitability would mean it would automatically be placed with the 'good guys' (i.e. ignored for improvement purposes).

However, the only reason it 'looks good' is because of its extremely low overhead allocation of £2000. B4, with only £5000 more sales per month, is carrying £9700. This disguises B2's problem of relatively low contribution (20%) which probably means that as a mature product some cost investigation is required.

Index